FAMILY BLOOD

A child's birthday. A warm reunion of loved ones. A quiet evening at home with the wife and kids. Times when we're at ease, protected from lethal danger of any kind.

But nothing is sacred to the vicious breed of insane killers who prey on unsuspecting families — and brutally murder them! Grandparents and children, babies and teenagers — no one is safe from their sick need to destroy entire families in their homes!

Now, from the authentic files of *True Detective* Magazine, read the shocking true crime accounts of the grisly crimes of the hated murderers who committed FAMILY SLAUGHTERS including: John List, the New Jersey accountant who killed his entire family then disappeared for seventeen years before he was caught; or Sean Sellers, the Oklahoma teen who shot his parents to death in their bed in a weird pact with Satan; or Dr. Jeffrey MacDonald, Green Beret doctor who slaughtered his wife and children in a drug-crazed frenzy!

FAMILY SLAUGHTERS

**PINNACLE BOOKS AND *TRUE DETECTIVE* MAGAZINE
TEAM UP TO BRING YOU THE
MOST HORRIFIC TRUE CRIME STORIES!**

FROM THE FILES OF <u>TRUE DETECTIVE</u> MAGAZINE

FAMILY SLAUGHTERS

Edited by
ROSE G.
MANDELSBERG

PINNACLE BOOKS
WINDSOR PUBLISHING CORP.

The editor expresses her sincerest thanks and appreciation to Karen Pellino whose painstaking efforts made this book possible.

The editor dedicates this book to all the families of the victims.

PINNACLE BOOKS

are published by

Windsor Publishing Corp.
475 Park Avenue South
New York, NY 10016

First Printing: May, 1993

Printed in the United States of America

TABLE OF CONTENTS

"MASS MURDER ON THE MISSISSIPPI COAST"

by Gary C. King

It was hot and muggy in Nicholson, Mississippi, on Saturday, September 15, 1990. The mercury approached a hundred in much of the state, but down south, particularly in Pearl River County next to the Louisiana border, the high humidity of the Gulf Coast made it seem even hotter. By nightfall it began to cool down a bit, but it was still sultry and uncomfortable. It wasn't a good time to begin a major murder investigation; but, then, there really isn't any good time to start a murder probe.

It had been a busy evening so far at the Pearl River County Sheriff's Department, and one of the deputies on duty that night, puffing on one cigarette after another, didn't expect things to slow down much as the evening wore on. It was, after all, a Saturday night, and the department had already been called out to settle more than its share of bar fights, domestic squabbles, and robberies. Things could, in all likelihood, only get worse.

It was only minutes before 9:00 p.m. when the call that would ultimately prove to be the worst of the evening came in. At first this latest call had seemed simple enough. It was from a relative of the local

Frierson family who said she was worried because she hadn't been able to reach them by telephone all day. There was supposed to be a Frierson family reunion for 200 family members the next day, and the relative had last-minute details to discuss. But the Friersons, who lived just off Mississippi Highway 607 in the community of Nicholson, weren't answering their phone. It just wasn't like them. The relative asked the sheriff's department to send someone out to check on them.

A team of deputies arrived a few minutes later at Ray Merle "Smokey" Frierson's small brick home, located on the northwest corner of a NASA buffer zone near the Hancock County line. Ray Frierson had lived there with his wife Mollie since 1973. They liked it there and were well known and well liked throughout the community.

Except for the sounds of crickets and an occasional passing car on Highway 607, everything was quiet — almost too quiet — as the deputies stepped out of their patrol cruisers. The night's stillness was made even more eerie by the incessant insect sounds and by the sight of occasional lightning bugs blinking their tails in the pitch black. Making the deputies feel even more ill at ease, no one came outside the house to find out why they were there. Nothing moved in or around the house.

One of the deputies knocked loudly on the door. Nobody answered. The lights stayed dark inside the house. After several repeated attempts, all futile, the lawmen decided that they had better go inside. Gaining entry through an unlocked door, the deputies began turning on lights as they slowly went from room to room.

When they reached the front bedroom, the deputies reeled back in horror at the atrocity that lay in front of them. An older man, whom the deputies believed to be Ray Frierson, and an older woman, whom they believed to be his wife Mollie, were lying sprawled on the floor, covered in blood. A young boy lay nearby, also covered with blood.

After regaining their composure, the deputies carefully checked the victims for signs of life. They found none. The deputies cautiously retraced their steps out of the bedroom, not wishing to disturb anything of evidentiary value.

Before leaving the house, however, the deputies checked the other rooms. It was possible, they reasoned, that additional victims might be in other areas of the house. Speculating that the perpetrator might also still be inside, they drew their guns as a precaution.

They soon learned that their reasoning about possible other victims had been correct. In the second bedroom, they found the partially clad body of a woman, whom they believed to be in her late 30s or early 40s, spread-eagled on the floor. Noting that the victim's clothing had been ripped or forcibly removed, the investigators strongly suspected that she had been sexually assaulted, either before or after she was killed.

After making certain that there were no other bodies and that the perpetrator was not on the premises, the deputies cleared the house and reported their grim findings to headquarters. Pearl River County Sheriff Lorance Lumpkin was located and notified of the carnage at the Frierson residence. He instructed that the area be sealed off from all unauthorized personnel and identified as a crime scene. Lumpkin arrived a short time later, accompanied by a medical examiner, a deputy district attorney, and a crime scene technician.

Each of the victims, Sheriff Lumpkin observed, had been shot more than once and in different parts of their bodies. The older man appeared to have been shot in the back of the head at close range. Tissue, blood, bone, and possibly brain matter had been dispersed about the room as a result of the force of the blast, some of which had traveled several feet from the body. The older woman had been shot in the face, resulting in severe disfigurement. It also appeared that she had been beaten on the head.

The boy, whom the sheriff believed to be in his teens, had also been shot in the head, but with a small-caliber weapon. He also had other wounds to his body, primarily bruises and abrasions. The female victim in the other bedroom had been shot in the abdomen and head, also with a small-caliber weapon.

During a preliminary examination of the house, Lonnie Arrinder of the Mississippi State Crime Laboratory discovered two bloody footprints in one of the bedrooms. There was so much blood in the bedrooms that Arrinder couldn't help but wonder why there weren't more bloody footprints. He also found a 20-gauge shotgun and a .22-caliber rifle on the premises. The shotgun had blood and possible tissue fragments adhering to its stock and barrel. Arrinder theorized that it might have been used to beat one of the victims, most likely the older woman, in addition to shooting her and others. He also found scattered about articles of bloody clothing, which he carefully placed in paper bags so that the bloodstains could dry.

After the scene was carefully photographed, crime lab technicians collected blood and other bodily fluid samples, which they carefully marked according to source and location. They also vacuumed for trace evidence of hair and clothing fiber, using separate filter bags for each location, and searched for identifiable latent fingerprints.

During the evening, deputies ferreted out important information from several of Ray Frierson's relatives. As a result, they eventually had enough information to positively identify the bodies. The bodies in the front bedroom were identified as 61-year-old Ray Frierson, 56-year-old Mollie Frierson, and 13-year-old Joshua A. Morrell, the Frierson's stepgrandson.

The body in the second bedroom was identified as 38-year-old Pamela Ann Howard. Pamela and Joshua, family members said, were relatives who had lived with the Friersons for some time. Relatives claimed that Pamela and Joshua were both retarded, one of the main reasons that Ray and Mollie had taken them in. Sheriff Lumpkin was also told that yet another relative, 17-year-old John Morrell Frierson, nicknamed "John Boy," lived in the house. No one, however, knew where he could be found. It being a Saturday night and John Boy being a teenager, the lawmen surmised that he was out partying with his friends.

As the lawmen continued questioning family members, they learned that John Boy and Joshua were brothers and that Ray and Mollie Frierson, who had adopted him eight years earlier after his mother was murdered, were John Boy's stepgrandparents. According to police sources, his mother's body had been discovered in the central part of the state, but her murder was never solved. Pamela Howard was John Boy's and Joshua's aunt.

With the help of relatives, a sketchy inventory of the Friersons' possessions was obtained. Afterward, the detectives determined that the only thing of value that was missing was Mollie Frierson's 1988 Ford Escort. Because very little money was found in the victims' clothes or inside the house, the investigators also suspected that cash may have been taken, but they didn't yet know how much, if any.

With the missing car, an obvious lack of cash on hand, and the possible rape of Pamela Howard, Sheriff Lumpkin and his detectives felt that they had established clear motives for the murders. The strongest motive of all, however, appeared to be the elimination of witnesses. All of the aforementioned were aggravating factors that could bring a death sentence for the perpetrator if convicted of the crimes.

According to Sheriff Lumpkin, certain signs indicated that Pamela Howard had been raped and Mollie Frierson sodomized after having been shot. However, the sheriff wouldn't elaborate on the specific reasons leading to this conclusion.

When the criminalists no longer needed the bodies at the crime scene, morgue drivers placed the corpses inside body bags and removed them one at a time to a waiting van. As a small gathering of onlookers watched from behind barriers, the van left for the morgue where definitive autopsies would be conducted.

While sheriff's investigators and crime lab technicians searched for clues and collected evidence at the crime scene over the next several hours, the sheriff and several deputies questioned the victims' acquaintances and relatives in search of clues to the killer's identity. It wasn't long before their efforts paid off. One person in particular provided information that ultimately broke the case wide open.

Two days before, the informant told the investigators, Mollie Frierson had expressed concern for her safety, telling a family member that she was afraid John Boy was "going to kill them all." John Boy, sleuths were told, drank to excess. His drinking sometimes made him violent and abusive, and family members suspected that he also used drugs. Mollie had even told a family member that she planned to take John Boy to a drug and alcohol rehabilitation center following the family reunion—if, she added ominously, she "made it through the weekend."

Investigators in any homicide case always start out looking "close to home" for suspects, and now Sheriff Lumpkin believed he would have to look no further than John Boy Frierson to find the family's mass murderer. John Boy, he believed, had both the motive and the opportunity to carry out the killings. The evidence, he hoped, would rule him in or out as a suspect.

Lumpkin and his deputies worked fervently as they gathered leads from John Boy's friends and acquaintances on where the teenager might be. By the early-morning hours of September 16th, while crime lab technicians continued working at the Frierson house, deputies traced John Boy to a girlfriend's apartment just outside Picayune, a town only a few miles north of Nicholson, Deputies quietly surrounded the apartment complex, then moved in to make the arrest.

Frierson was there, all right, but they didn't have to worry about him putting up a fight. He wasn't in any shape to make a break for it. When the deputies made their presence known, John Boy staggered into their midst, making no effort to flee. He appeared to be heavily under the influence of drugs and alcohol. The deputies arrested him at his girlfriend's apartment without incident. He was taken to the Pearl River County Jail where he was booked on suspicion of murder in connection with the deaths of his family.

Shortly after the suspect's arrival at the jail, Sheriff Lumpkin and Deputy Joe Stuart took Frierson into an interrogation room. The youth looked pale, tired, and weak. He was apparently coming down from his alcohol and drug-induced intoxication. After deciding that he had sobered up enough to be fully aware of what was going on, the probers read the suspect the Miranda rights again, after which Frierson agreed to give them a statement. As Sheriff Lumpkin asked questions, Deputy Stuart took notes.

Surprisingly, according to Lumpkin and Stuart, Frierson admitted that he had shot his relatives. He said he was "mad at the world" because Ray Frierson wouldn't allow him to go raccoon hunting. Frierson said he took $200 from a purse and wallet that was in the house, but he denied raping his grandmother and aunt. Afterward, Deputy Stuart typed up the youth's statement and provided a copy to the district attorney's office.

Meanwhile, Dr. Paul McGarry, a New Orleans pathologist, was brought in to conduct the autopsies. A pathology assistant prepared the corpses for the post-mortem examinations, which included running an ultraviolet light over the bodies of the female victims in search of semen. Semen appears as bright white under the ultraviolet, thus facilitating its collection by the pathologist. Semen was detected on Pamela Howard's body, and vaginal swabs were taken. Additional swabs were obtained from other parts of Pamela's and Mollie's bodies, just in case trace amounts of semen had been overlooked. These would be combined with acid phosphatase, a sensitive enzyme that turns pink when mixed with semen. Following the autopsies, Dr. McGarry reported his findings to Sheriff Lumpkin and Assistant District Attorney Buddy McDonald.

Pamela Howard, said Dr. McGarry, had been shot once in the abdomen and four times in the head with a small-caliber weapon. The presence of semen and signs of violence other than the gunshot wounds led

Dr. McGarry to believe that Pamela had also been raped.

"Was sexual battery inflicted prior to death?" asked the assistant D.A.

"Yes, it was," Dr. McGarry replied.

The pathologist explained that he had collected and preserved from the victim's body semen that could be used for deoxyribonucleic acid (DNA) testing. The seminal fluid samples were air-dried and frozen and sent, along with a sample of John Frierson's blood, to a court-recognized DNA diagnostics lab.

Dr. McGarry found that both Ray and Mollie Frierson had been shot at close range with what he believed to be a 20-gauge shotgun. The pathologist said that Ray had been shot in the head three times with a small-caliber weapon, but it was the shotgun blast to the back of Ray's head that had caused his death. Ray was already dead when the shots with a small-caliber weapon were inflicted, said McGarry.

The pathologist determined that Mollie Frierson had sustained a gunshot wound to her chin and had subsequently been beaten on the head with a weapon consistent with the shotgun found at the crime scene. McGarry said Mollie had received five powerful blows to the head. The approximate time of the victims' death was sometime on the morning of September 15th.

McGarry said that Joshua Morrell had been shot three times in the head with a small-caliber weapon. Also present on his body were several bruises and abrasions, primarily on one of his arms, an elbow, and a shoulder, all of which the pathologist characterized as defensive wounds. He said that the wounds were probably caused when the boy held up his arm as he tried to fend off the attack.

Meanwhile, a DNA diagnostics laboratory in

Maryland began processing John Frierson's blood and the seminal fluid found on and inside Pamela Howard's body. Using conventional serological typing methods, the lab first determined that the blood type of the semen found at the crime scene was of the same blood type as John Frierson's. Had the blood and semen been of different types, Frierson could have been eliminated as the suspect. He was not so lucky.

Next, DNA was extracted from the semen collected from Pamela Howard's body and from Frierson's blood samples. The DNA strands were then "cut" into small fragments by an enzyme and compared. The result, according to the scientist who conducted the DNA typing, provided an autoradiograph, a genetic "print" as unique to each individual as a set of fingerprints. As was expected by the investigators, the DNA extracted from Frierson's blood and from the semen found inside Pamela Howard's vagina matched.

Adding fuel to the case against the suspect, according to Lonnie Arrinder of the Mississippi State Crime Laboratory, the two bloody footprints found at the crime scene matched John Frierson's footprint.

Meanwhile, according to Pearl River County Justice Court Judge Richard Cowart, authorities began receiving a number of threats against Frierson's life. People were outraged over the senseless, brutal murders that had been committed in their community, and some were determined to do something about it. Residents couldn't understand how someone could have so ruthlessly murdered such a nice couple as Ray and Mollie Frierson and their family.

As a result of all the threats, when Frierson made his first court appearance, he was taken to the Justice Court building in an unmarked police car and

16

was required to lie down in the backseat. He was ushered by several armed deputies into the courthouse through a side door.

Despite the apparently irrefutable evidence stacked against him, Frierson pleaded innocent to four counts of capital murder and asked for a jury trial. Defense Attorneys Rex Jones of Hattiesburg and William Ducker of Poplarville were appointed to represent him. The judge set Frierson's trial for the following August, and he continued to be held without bail.

Shortly after Frierson's arrest, the question of his ability to stand trial and assist in his own defense was brought up. At the request of the defense team, Frierson was sent to the state mental hospital at Whitfield where he underwent extensive psychiatric examinations. After subjecting him to a battery of tests and interviews, psychologists and psychiatrists at the hospital determined that he was, in fact, competent to stand trial.

Although Frierson was a juvenile at the time of the slayings, the prosecution sought to have him remanded to adult court over the objections of his defense team. If he was prosecuted through the juvenile system, prosecutors argued, he would be released on his 21st birthday. The severity of the crimes, they argued, demanded a more severe punishment. A judge agreed, and Frierson was ordered to stand trial as an adult.

Because of the publicity and the charged emotions surrounding the murders, Frierson's trial was moved to Natchez, a town several counties west in Adams County. Jury selection began on Monday, August 12, 1991. After a jury was seated, Judge R.I. Pritchard III ordered that the jury members be sequestered throughout the trial because of the extensive publicity.

Dressed in a black, short-sleeved shirt and blue jeans, John Frierson appeared to be in a somber mood as he was led into the Adams County Chancery courtroom. His legs were shackled for added security, and spectators were required to pass through a metal detector before entering the courtroom.

The jury was led step-by-step through the case by Assistant District Attorney Buddy McDonald, from the time the bodies were found, through the evidence gathering and DNA testing, and finally to Frierson's confession to Sheriff Lumpkin and Deputy Joe Stuart.

At one point Dr. Paul McGarry, the New Orleans pathologist who had performed the autopsies on the victims' bodies, explained the details of the deaths and the manner in which all the victims were killed. McGarry used sketches to show jurors the points where bullets and shotgun pellets had entered the victims' bodies. Gruesome color photographs showing how the victims were found were also introduced as evidence. Tearful family members were present in the courtroom. Occasional gasps could be heard from spectators who managed to glimpse the photos as they were passed between attorneys, judge, and jury.

Later, the deputies who found the bodies described the locations and manner in which the bodies were found. Sheriff Lorance Lumpkin and Deputy Jo Stuart also testified that Frierson agreed to make a statement confessing to the murders after his arrest. The two lawmen said they believed Frierson was fully aware of what was going on when they read him his Miranda rights and when he made the incriminating remarks.

One of the most dramatic moments of the trial came when Frierson took the witness stand in his own defense. Because the state's case against Frierson was so strong, the best defense strategy seemed to be to simply put the defendant on the stand and try to gain sympathy from the jury. Defense Attorney Ducker asked Frierson if he had anything to say to the jury.

"I'm sorry," said Frierson as his voice broke. Speaking softly into the microphone between sobs, Frierson said that the day of the murders seemed like a dream to him. He said he didn't remember giving a statement to the lawmen. He said that he had been under the influence of drugs and alcohol before he was arrested and had remained intoxicated for a while after his arrest.

Responding to questions from Defense Attorney Rex Jones, Frierson said he could only remember "bits and pieces" of his arrest. He said he didn't remember telling the officers that he had shot his relatives, took $200 cash, and stole his grandmother's car. He said that he had a long history of alcohol and drug abuse problems, and that he had only been "straight" for the few months after his arrest.

In closing arguments, Jones maintained that Frierson's drug, alcohol, and emotional problems had in effect turned him into a "walking time bomb" that detonated on the morning of the slayings. Jones argued that Frierson never received the drug and alcohol rehabilitation when he needed it most. "He was a ticking time bomb. The Mississippi juvenile system failed.

"There was an explosion," said Jones. "I don't think he intended to rob them, and I don't think he intended to commit sexual battery. After hearing the evidence, I think he killed them, but I don't think he did it while in the commission of other crimes."

Co-counsel Ducker then literally begged the jury to spare Frierson's life, contending that the defendant might be able to turn his life around and do something constructive someday. He suggested that Frierson might be willing to participate in a prison program in which inmates held talks with teenagers warning them about the dangers of drug and alcohol abuse.

In rebuttal, Assistant D.A. McDonald pointed out for the jury that the defense never questioned the DNA testing or other evidence of sexual assault on Pamela Howard, which he said "spoke the loudest."

"I cannot look at the photographs of the four victims here and feel that the system failed John Frierson," said McDonald. "If this is not capital murder, there has never been capital murder in the state of Mississippi, and there will never be capital murder in the state of Mississippi." He urged jurors to sentence Frierson to death.

On Thursday, August 15, 1991, the jurors announced after three and a half hours of deliberations that they had found John Morrell "John Boy" Frierson guilty on four counts of capital murder. They were, however, unable to agree unanimously on whether to sentence Frierson to death by lethal injection or to life in prison. As a result, Fifteenth Judicial Circuit Court Judge R.I. Pritchard III was bound by Mississippi statutes to sentence Frierson to life in prison for each of the four counts.

Frierson, with his chin resting in his hands, remained emotionless and without expression.

"I didn't know what to think," said Defense Attorney Ducker afterward. "I am just very thankful that's the way it came out. The boy did a very terrible thing and he'll be punished for it for a long time, but I don't think we're in the business of killing seventeen-year-olds."

"We're disappointed," said one of several family members of the victims who had been in attendance for the entire trial.

"We wish the jury would have been able to return a death sentence verdict," commented Assistant D.A. McDonald.

John Boy Frierson is now serving his life sentences at the Mississippi State Penitentiary. Unless his convictions are overturned on appeal, Frierson will not be eligible for parole for 40 years, until the year 2031.

"RAMBO-CRAZED KILLER'S FAMILY MASSACRE!"

by Bud Ampolsk

Anybody who has seen combat at first hand can only hate war. Anybody who feels otherwise is a sadist.

This was the expressed opinion of no less an expert on the horrors of warfare than General of the Army Dwight David Eisenhower, as quoted by Merle Miller in his thorough biography of the soldier-statesman, *General Ike*.

The abhorrence of the slaughter and maiming which marks the battle scene is almost universal among all the ranks of combat veterans, from Army War College graduates to the rawest recruit.

Typical of this attitude was the reaction of a group of aging ex-GIs who, during the bloody days of 1944-45, had slogged their way from the killing sands of Omaha Beach to the heartland of Nazi Germany.

Now in their late 60s and 70s, these men had embarked on one last pilgrimage to pay their final tributes to battle comrades who had fallen victim to the hellfire of the attack on "Festung Europa."

Showing the marks of advancing age, the group

made its way by bus across the old battlefields, visited the seemingly endless rows of crosses which marked carefully tended military cemeteries and often wept unashamedly at the terrible memories awakened by the experience.

Their feelings were caringly and reverently recorded by famed commentator, author and former presidential press secretary Bill Moyers for a 90-minute documentary recently shown on the stations of the PBS television network.

At one point, Moyers pointed out that at the end of World War II, he himself had been a wide-eyed 10-year-old growing up in Texas. He told of longing to hear the heroic tales of adventure and gallantry as told by returning servicemen. But there had been no stories of derring-do. Instead, there had been tight-lipped silence.

Those he now accompanied readily understood his point. Even now, almost half a century later, they stood mute, their faces etched in the pain of what they had experienced.

When they did talk, these old men — who had been in their teens when they had come under Nazi fire — made little or no mention of heroism. Many said, "We didn't hate the enemy. We only knew that if we didn't kill him, he would kill us."

One physician, who had been a medical student when commissioned a first lieutenant and sent to a med-evac station in France, told of the terrible secret he had kept over the years. It concerned the sight of an entire French family resembling wax figures in a house of horrors. Most had been seated at the table of their home when they had been killed by the concussion of a Nazi artillery shell, which had smashed away the side of their house.

The children awaited the serving of the food that never came. A woman stood with platter still in hand. Even the family dog remained in the attitude he had held at the instant of concussion.

When Moyers asked why the doctor had remained silent for so long, the medic's answer was that even though he thought he had seen that death tableau, he couldn't be sure. It might have been something he had imagined. Not until he had met an old comrade-in-arms at a reunion four decades later and the man had asked him, "Doc, remember the dead people in the house?" did he know for sure.

And so the stories went. Summed up, they spelled out the lyrics of the World War II battle song "Roger Young": "They have no time for glory in the infantry."

Thus it is that while hobbyists may rush through domestic woods in camouflage dress and fire blanks at imaginary enemies in simulated Sunday campaigns, you'll seldom, if ever, see a combat veteran in their ranks. Those who have been where the real mud-and-blood battles have been waged have no stomach for the fantasy world of make-believe combat.

To them, Hollywood's fictional "Rambo" characters with their rages, need for vengeance and blood-and-guts warfare are just so much garbage. They've seen the real thing and they long to forget its hideous cost.

Had blond, curly-haired, muscular and not unhandsome Brian Thomas Britton had the experience of countless other teenagers at Bastogne and Iwo Jima, of those who had been caught by the Chinese sweep into South Korea or had tasted the stench of rotting bodies in the rice paddies of Vietnam, things might have been quite different in the Dutchess County city of Poughkeepsie on the cold spring morning of Wednesday, March 22, 1989. Shock and revulsion would not have spread through the upstate

24

New York community as word of what had taken place on Van Wagner Road made the rounds.

Brian Thomas Britton might have remained what he had seemed to some—a peculiar, but nonviolent, 16-year-old. His problems might have been typical of countless adolescents. The sense of rebellion he felt at strict parental discipline might have continued within reasonable bounds.

After all, the midteen years are not without stresses. In just about every family, this period is marked by some signs of tension. Glandular and hormonal changes which mark the transition from childhood to adulthood compound the emotional desire to create one's "own space." However, the overwhelming majority of families manage to survive these situations with nothing worse than a variety of mutually bruised feelings.

But the Brittons would not survive intact as a family. They would be cut down because 16-year-old Brian Britton had more than the usual rage at parents who were keeping the reins too tight. He had a fantasy that was to prove a prelude to mass murder.

Referring to what had happened on Van Wagner Road, Poughkeepsie Police Chief Stanley G. Still Jr. would later comment, "I don't want to say Rambo did this, but it surely played an important role here, absolutely."

The police chief was speaking of the call that had sent 10 of his best officers racing to the Van Wagner address in the predawn darkness.

It was 5:22 a.m., March 22nd, when the 911 call came in. A breathless and understandably distraught man told of a shooting that had taken place in the house next to his. The house in question belonged to close relatives of the caller.

Even now, Brian Britton was cluing the caller in

25

on what had occurred on Van Wagner Road. Brian had told his relative that Brian's father, 44-year-old Dennis Britton, was shooting the family. Brian had been the only one able to escape the fusillade, according to the boy's version of what had happened. He had managed to jump out of a second-story window and race across the intervening turf to seek help at his relative's home.

The time of the call, the urgency on the caller's part and the graphic, if bizarre, details given over the phone dispelled any thoughts the police might originally have had that they were being victimized by a hoax.

Veteran officers who were racing to the indicated crime scene knew with a chill of apprehension that they were dealing with a policeman's nightmare—an episode of family violence. They thought they were prepared for the worst. However, the worst was to far exceed anything the officers might have ever imagined.

Entering the Britton home, the cops first stumbled across the body of 42-year-old Marlene Britton, Brian Britton's mother. The woman was still dressed in her nightclothes as she lay on the living room floor—bloody, inert, eyes staring sightlessly in the aspect of sudden and violent death. She had been shot once in the chest and once in the head.

Their bellies churning with what they had already discovered, investigators now made their way further into the house. In the master bedroom on the second floor, they discovered the remains of Dennis Britton. The tree-trimmer appeared to have been attempting to get out of bed; his body was still half under the covers. It appeared that the slug which had killed him had blasted into his skull as he was making the first effort to protect himself from his killer.

As horrifying as the discovery of the two dead

bodies had been, there was still worse to come—the sight of the small form of Jason Britton. The youngster still lived, but barely. Not only had he been shot in the head, but he had been beaten severely around the head and torso.

Time was quickly running out for the eight-year-old. He was rushed to St. Francis Hospital in Poughkeepsie, where he died at 8:00 a.m.

Of the four people who had faced the point-blank aim of the mass murderer, only one would survive. She was Brian Britton's 20-year-old sister. The girl, a nursing student at Dutchess Community College, had been shot in the head and chest as she had tried to escape through the front door of the Britton home. After extensive surgery at Vassar Brothers Hospital in Poughkeepsie, the young woman was in serious but stable condition and expected to live.

After the emergency evacuation of Brian Britton's siblings to nearby hospitals, police and forensic experts stayed at the murder house, going about the grim business of creating a scenario for what had occurred. Among the items of evidence they had uncovered were a number of .20-gauge shotgun shells strewn around the rooms where the killings and woundings had taken place.

From the position in which the dead and wounded had been found, detectives built this chronology:

Dennis Britton had most likely been the first to die, shot as he had tried to get out from under the tangle of blankets and sheets.

Marlene Britton, who had been employed as a teller in a local bank, had risen early. She had been in the kitchen, letting out the family dog, when she heard the first blast of gunfire. Rushing toward the bedroom to find out what was happening, she had come face to face with her slayer. Two shotgun blasts

27

had ripped into her, causing instantaneous death as the slugs entered her head and chest.

The murderer had then made his way to Jason's room. The child had fled at the sight of the shotgun barrel leveled at him at point-blank range. He had bolted from his bed and made it down the stairs to the first floor. His maddened slayer had followed in close pursuit, clubbing at him with the stock of the shotgun.

As Jason had fallen almost beside the body of his dead mother in the living room, the killer had fired once more, catching Jason in the head.

The lone surviving student nurse had been shot twice as she had tried to flee the house. She had gotten as far as the front door before the buckshot had ripped into her.

Now came the search of the premises in hopes that some logical background could be established for the seemingly incomprehensible brutality that had destroyed what was thought to be a typical, closely knit, and law-abiding American family.

The crucial clues were to be uncovered in the bedroom occupied by Brian Britton.

The boy's room was strewn with dozens of movie posters featuring heroic representations of the film series character Rambo. In addition, there were piles of magazines dealing with military and soldier-of-fortune subjects, as well as military paraphernalia such as army packs, smoke grenades and ammunition pouches. Most incriminating of all was a collection of guns, which included a revolver and four shotguns. Pending forensic tests, ballistics experts reasoned that one of the shotguns had been used as the murder weapon.

Having completed their preliminary probe into the lethal gunplay, Poughkeepsie detectives proceeded to the home of the Britton relative where Brian had remained after calling in the alarm. Then, they began intensive questioning of the teenager and his relative.

From the adult male relative, probers learned that Brian had arrived at the relative's home shortly before 5:22 a.m. The relative repeated what Brian had told him: that Dennis Britton had gone berserk and opened fire on his family. The boy, the relative alleged, had told him that in order to survive he had been forced to jump from a second-story window.

To interrogating officers, the yarn spun by Brian Britton appeared too pat. It didn't tie in with the pile of military equipment and posters of *Rambo III,* the latest of the *Rambo* films, which had been recovered from his room.

Following several hours of questioning, Brian Britton was placed under arrest and charged with three counts of second-degree murder and one count of attempted murder. At 2:00 p.m. on March 22nd, he was taken before Justice Paul O. Sullivan in the Poughkeepsie Town Courthouse. Judge Sullivan ordered the youth held without bail for further court action.

Throughout the proceedings, the blond, curly-haired high school student stood, clad in jail clothes, his hands manacled behind his back by handcuffs.

He remained silent, but appeared to be swallowing hard as he was read his rights by the court. In another show of nervousness at his plight and surroundings, Brian Britton kept blinking his eyes.

Other than agreeing to have the Dutchess County public defender as his counsel, the teenager made no comment.

Following the court formalities, Brian was remanded to the Dutchess County Jail in Poughkeepsie without bail for further court action on the charges leveled against him.

For those who had known the family, the sense of

shock at the fate the Brittons had suffered was all-consuming. The rural neighborhood where the Brittons had lived on the edge of Poughkeepsie was abuzz with recollections of the three who had died, the one who had been seriously wounded, and the 16-year-old who was now accused of having carried out the bloody predawn massacre.

Townspeople gathered on the tree-lined streets and in their backyards, talking of nothing but the violence which had transpired on Van Wagner Road.

Said a neighbor who lived directly across the street from the death house, "Nobody wants to believe it. This is a tragedy for our neighborhood. Brian wore camouflage outfits, but he didn't seem much different from other kids."

The principal of Arlington High School, which Brian had attended, contended there was nothing in the boy's earlier behavior that indicated a capacity for such savage violence. He commented, "There were no trends with this kid to indicate a problem of this magnitude." He noted that Brian had attended classes as late as the very day before the multiple murders and had showed no aberrations at that time.

The educator called Brian "academically sound," saying he had maintained a C average in most of his classes.

If there was anything strange in Brian's school career, it was that the boy had not taken part in any of the numerous extracurricular activities offered by the high school. However, the school principal did not regard this as important.

Said the school official, "He was an average-type kid who didn't stand out in the crowd. He seemed to be well liked by his peers, as well as the teachers, and he did academically sound work with grades in the seventies and eighties."

Despite this seemingly innocuous evaluation of the

youth, certain oddities had become apparent in the hours following the slayings of his father, mother and brother and the wounding of his sister.

For example, Police Chief Still recalled that when Brian had been asked his nickname, he had replied, "Rambo." The lawman felt that the suspect had been emulating his fantasy hero when he shot his family.

Neighbors gave weight to this theory as they talked of how Brian had constantly worn fatigues, had been obsessed with the idea of joining the United States Marines as soon as he reached his 18th birthday, and how he had frequently spent long hours playing military-type games with his eight-year-old brother and the neighbors' sons.

One element of the violence that might have lain close to the surface was the recollection that Brian had fired his rifle in the yard on occasion and had previously shot his own sister and brother with a BB gun.

Despite his wounding by his older brother, the eight-year-old Jason was said by these sources to have "idolized" Brian and to have wanted to be just like him.

If Brian Britton had presented a facade that had caused adults to consider him quite typical for a boy his age, a number of young people who had known him offered a completely different perspective. Several schoolmates said they were not the least bit surprised that he had become a killer.

They called Brian "an obnoxious loner" who displayed an uncontrollable temper and was obsessed with his Rambo fantasy. They reported that his peculiar and antisocial ways had caused them to give him a wide berth.

Commented one Arlington High School student who had been informed of Brian's homicide arrest, "If anyone was going to do that, he's the type. None

31

of us liked him. He always called himself 'Rambo.' He always read those magazines and would pretend to be shooting at people in class. . . .

"He'd point his fingers like a gun and go, 'Got you!' or 'You're dead, you creep!' I don't know if he was trying to incite a fight or if he was just weird."

School officials reported that Brian's attendance at school had been erratic enough for them to feel impelled to call his parents and notify them of his unexplained absences.

Other students recalled that Brian had continually read gun magazines in the school's gym locker room. They said, "All he wanted to talk about was guns."

One adult who had been somewhat upset by Brian Britton's behavior noted that the teenager had carried "a knife with him at all times. A Rambo knife."

The man continued, "He (Brian Britton) used to play GI Joe with the kids. He used to take them to the woods to a hole. He would put them in the hole. . . . He sometimes tied them up. We just kept our kids away from him after they told us about this. He was an Army person, that was his dream — to go to the Marines."

The neighbor's daughter recalled that Brian Britton's younger brother Jason had told her how "Brian cut himself and watched the blood run."

Noted one classmate, "For as long as I can remember, he liked to wear camouflage and talk about guns."

Added a sophomore who was also a member of the tennis team, "Boy, was he obnoxious. That's why he didn't have many, or should I say, any friends. He was basically a loner because he couldn't get along with anybody."

The question of whether or not Brian Britton had maintained any friendships with youngsters of his own age was somewhat clouded. Although a number of sources reported that he hadn't, some said he had had a girlfriend.

Within a few days of his arrest, the confusion over the "girlfriend" issue was resolved when a teenager who claimed to have been his friend went public with an open letter addressed "To All Newspapers and Newspeople."

The missive, which was backed not only by her own signature, but by those of eight other teenagers, read as follows:

> We don't think what you're doing to Brian Britton is right. He is not a bad kid at all. He is just seeking for help which his parents did not give him. They left him out of everything, grounded him for every little thing he did wrong. All he wanted was someone to love him. We also want this Rambo stuff *stopped*. We don't want everyone thinking that Brian is just killing everyone for the fun of it. He is not Rambo. He is a very sweet and kind person. Again he is not Rambo. He's just seeking for help. This was the only way out for the poor kid. He is not Rambo. Please stop calling him Rambo.
>
> THANK YOU VERY MUCH

A girl who claimed to be Brian Britton's girlfriend placed the blame for his troubles at the feet of his dead parents. She, too, cited what she called the harsh discipline exacted by his family. Said the girl, "He was disciplined by his parents for every little thing, but he craved their love and approval."

She maintained that the accused killer had had no overpowering interest in guns or military life, but had wanted to please his father.

Noting that Dennis Britton had been a Vietnam

veteran, she charged he had been responsible for Brian's preoccupation with weapons.

"He had guns to please his father," the girl claimed. "To get love from him."

Of Brian's relationship with his mother, Marlene, the girl argued, "His mother did not approve of every little thing."

The source also denied assertions by other students that Brian Britton had been gripped by a Rambo mania.

Her feelings received support from an adult whose children were friends of the teen killer. The man called the Britton household "a pressure cooker that overheated and the lid blew."

He commented, "Dennis and Marlene (Britton) thought their son was a 'problem child' and sent him to a psychiatrist two years ago.

"Brian was calling out for help. He just wanted someone to give him a little understanding and a pat on the back."

Of the rumors bandied about concerning Brian's volatile temper and the report that he had brought an unloaded 9mm handgun to school following an altercation with a fellow student, his girlfriend claimed that her boyfriend of five months had wanted to be a policeman and "all he wanted to do was break up violence. All he wanted was love, but his parents did not give him love."

Of the events immediately surrounding the pre-dawn slayings of three of his family members and the serious wounding of a fourth, the girlfriend told of Brian's visit to her home on the evening of Tuesday, March 21st, the eve of the shootings. She said the visit had been cut short after 20 minutes when Marlene Britton called and ordered Brian to return to his own home immediately.

Turning to the depth of her relationship with the

embattled youth, the girlfriend said that it had been serious enough for the two of them to discuss the possibility of their becoming engaged in January 1990, when she reached her 16th birthday.

"We love each other a lot," she stated in a halting voice.

After receiving a call from Brian (placed from the Dutchess County Jail), the girl, her eyes red and swollen from weeping, stated, "He's okay. I love him very much. What the police are saying about him is not true. He's not the way they describe him. He's a nonviolent kid. He really didn't like guns."

She also revealed that Brian had planned to move in with her and her parents because his own parents had been contemplating a divorce.

However, the girl's one-sided portrayal of the killer's familial relationships was at odds with what other Britton acquaintances had to say.

For example, a co-worker of the slain Dennis Britton revealed how the elder Britton had been so worried about Brian that "he used to go home at noon just to make sure that nothing was wrong with the kid."

Then there was the strange essay that Brian had written for an assignment on what he had done during summer vacation. A classmate revealed that a portion of the composition dealt with how Brian had shot a bird out of a tree and had ridden his bicycle over a cat.

Despite the rage that had caused the eruption of deadly gunfire in the Britton household, Brian, through public defender John Garrity Jr., sought the privilege of attending the wake for his mother, father and younger brother. The plea was supported by surviving Britton family members, who agreed that Brian should attend the wake. Under an arrangement worked out with Dutchess County Sheriff Fred

Scorolick, Brian was taken to the funeral home where the bodies of the murdered trio lay in their coffins. Escorted by a detail of Dutchess County sheriff's deputies, he arrived at the funeral home on Friday evening, March 24th, after other mourners had left the premises.

The teenager remained for less than half an hour and was back in his cell at the Dutchess County Jail by 9:20 p.m. He was not given permission to attend the actual funerals for Dennis, Marlene and Jason Britton.

Throughout the long days and nights to come, Brian would remain behind bars, awaiting further court action.

Dutchess County Assistant Prosecutor Thomas Dolan went about the business of preparing the people's case against the accused teenager. Included in the dossier were the confession the young man had given concerning the killing itself, the ballistics tests, the medical examiner's reports (which showed that Dennis and Marlene Britton had died of gunshot wounds and little Jason had succumbed to the beating he had received from his older brother) and the overwhelming circumstantial corroboration from statements made by those who knew of the family's troubles.

On January 3, 1990, as Prosecutor Dolan was about to bring the Britton case to trial, Brian Britton entered court once more. This time he pleaded guilty to three counts of murder in the second degree and was sentenced to 25 years to life.

At the time of this writing, the young man who lived a fantasy of war-like derring-do without ever having been near a battlefield and who snuffed out the lives of three close family members in their own home in the predawn hours of March 22, 1989, has begun serving the sentence meted out to him.

36

"GREEN BERET CHARGED WITH FAMILY SLAUGHTER!"

by Joseph Terrell

The country still reeled from the awful shock of the Charles Manson "Family" murders, in which the pregnant actress Sharon Tate and members of her party were ritualistically butchered. People throughout the United States and much of the civilized world were emotionally staggered by the senseless California carnage.

Then, a few months later and 3,000 miles away in Fort Bragg, North Carolina, a doctor's wife, also pregnant, and her two small children were stabbed and beaten to death in their home under similarly bizarre circumstances, including the blood-scrawled word "Pigs."

At 3:30 in the morning of Tuesday, February 17, 1970, a telephone operator in the city of Fayetteville, North Carolina, which surrounds and is almost a part of the huge military complex of Fort Bragg, answered a call to hear a man gasp out identification of himself and his address and plead for an ambulance. The words, "I've been stabbed," were uttered.

Quickly, a rescue unit was dispatched. What the medics, who were joined by military police, found has haunted witnesses for years, and proved to be the beginning of a decade-long investigation and legal battle.

The caller was Green Beret Captain Jeffrey MacDonald, a 26-year-old Army doctor. He lived with his wife and two children in one of the many red brick row-apartments on the base. The layout of the residential section was identical, with front and rear entrances to the six-room, red brick apartments. When authorities arrived at the MacDonald residence, the front door was locked but one of the two back doors was not. There was no sign of a forced entry.

The handsome Green Beret medical captain lay sprawled on the floor near the bloody, half-nude lifeless body of his wife, Colette. He was semiconscious, with what appeared to be a stab wound in his chest. He also looked as though he had received a blow to the head, and there were some lesser stab wounds or cuts around his abdomen.

His beautiful, light-haired wife, who was pregnant with a third child, had been bludgeoned and stabbed to death. She had stab and puncture wounds in her neck and chest; her skull had been fractured and so had her forearms, as if she had been desperately and vainly trying to ward off the blows of the clubbing.

On the headboard of the bed, in eight-inch letters of blood, the word "pig" had been scrawled.

The scene of gore and sickening brutality did not stop there. Two small children also lay murdered.

In a different bedroom, authorities found the couple's six-year-old daughter, Kimberly, stabbed 10 times in the neck and repeatedly clubbed around the head.

The second child, two-year-old Kristen, was found in her bed; she had been knifed 12 times in the back and four times in the chest, and then stabbed 12 times with what turned out to be an ice pick.

Medical examination of Colette MacDonald, the wife, revealed she was five months pregnant; the 26-year-old woman had been smashed in the head six times with a club, her chest was punctured 21 times with an ice pick and her neck and chest were stabbed 16 times with two different knives.

Officers from the Army's Criminal Investigation Division began a search of the apartment for the murder weapons, and also attempted to question MacDonald as he was rushed to an Army base hospital. Inside the apartment, in the master bedroom, officers found a paring knife that obviously had been used in the slaying. Outside, in the grass near the rear entrance, they found another paring knife, an ice pick and an 18-inch slab of wood that had been used as a club.

These were gathered as evidence, the area was roped off and roadblocks were immediately set up. The military installation is not fenced off. Highway 87 runs right through the fort and there is easy access to—and from—the area.

While authorities were busy with the grim task inside the apartment, such as photographing the bodies, making note of the toy-cluttered children's rooms and the way the apartment appeared to have been the scene of a terrific struggle (furniture and lamps were strewn about in the living room), officers quizzed MacDonald as to what happened.

The Green Beret captain told a story gruesomely similar to the Sharon Tate murders. (In that butchery in California, which had occurred in August, Charles Manson and his drug-crazed followers ritualistically stabbed the pregnant actress and three of her party to death and scrawled the words "Pigs" and "Death to the pigs" in blood.)

The wounded doctor, still shaky and weak from the ordeal, said he had been in the bed with his wife when the oldest child, Kimberly, got in the bed with them. Apparently she wet the bed and MacDonald went into the living room, stretched out on the couch and went to sleep. He said he was awakened by a scream and then his wife screaming, "Help, Jeff!" The captain said he tried to get up to aid his wife but was attacked himself. He said he did see, in the semi-darkness, three men and a woman stabbing repeatedly at his wife. He was hit with a club and stabbed himself, he told authorities.

Describing the assailants, he said two of the men were white and the third was black and wearing an Army fatigue jacket with sergeant's stripes. The woman was blonde, he said, wearing a floppy-brim hat, with long, stringy hair flowing beneath it. She wore knee-length boots that were muddy from the all-night drizzle that had occurred. The woman carried a candle and chanted, "Acid is great! Kill the pig! Hit 'em again!" Officers found a candle behind the apartment where they also found the other knife, ice pick and club.

Despite almost immediate roadblocks and checking out of known "hippie" hangouts, officers found no trace of the mysterious quartet. Fort Bragg and Fayetteville were centers of a growing drug culture. Many of the returning Vietnam veterans were hooked on the use of drugs of various sorts. Narcotics treatment was one of Capt. MacDonald's specialties. Officers would use that as a lead to try to track down various patients he had treated to see whether any of these might have held a grudge against him or his family.

At least one business place frequented by hippies posted a sign in the window urging its customers to come forth with information that might lead to the solution of the bizarre killings if they knew anything. No leads developed.

Literally hundreds of hippies and known drug users were questioned. No substantial evidence developed concerning the foursome MacDonald had described.

Jeffrey MacDonald and his wife, Colette, were such all-American types, complete with the success story and former high school sweethearts bit, it seemed impossible something like this could have happened. They were both from Patchogue, Long Island, in New York. After his graduation from high school there, he was accepted at Princeton for his pre-medical work. Because of his high grades, he was accepted at Northwestern University Medical School, and was graduated in 1967. In addition to his studies, he helped earn his way through college working on the side.

He was described by colleagues as self-assured, confident, handsome and personable.

He did not seem at all like the type who would be involved in a brutal slaying. Yet, there were some things that bothered officers investigating the triple-murder.

MacDonald told officers the four people who attacked him and killed his wife and two children appeared to be "completely out of it" on LSD, a hallucinogenic drug often referred to on the street as "acid," a word he said the woman in the foursome chanted. Officers asked themselves, "Aside from his work in drugs, why had the four decided on MacDonald's residence?" Apparently, robbery was not the motive; the only motive seemed to be to kill, senselessly. This had been accomplished extremely quickly according to the Fort Bragg provost marshal, Col. Robert Kriwanek. At the time, this cryptic statement was issued by investigating Army officers: "It appears that whoever did this may have been familiar with the interior of the house."

It was true, investigators agreed, that a struggle appeared to have taken place in the apartment, in so much as furniture was knocked about or turned over. Some of the furnishings appeared to have been thrown about. The scene bothered Col. Kriwanek and his investigators. The disordered furniture and furnishings looked too much as though they had been arranged in disorder. It lacked the authentic appearance of a struggle, and in short, made investigators suspicious that it was more staged than spontaneous.

Officers went back over the scene, noting exactly where everything had been found. One item of clothing they had carefully lifted from the body of Mrs. MacDonald was the captain's pajama top. He said he had placed it over her face and upper body after he had realized she was dead, apparently as a gesture of modesty and respect for his slain wife.

MacDonald told investigators he had been wearing the pajama shirt, that it had been pulled over his head when the attack on him occurred. He said he had struggled with the attackers with the shirt up over his head and kept taut by his raised, outstretched arms. The pajama top would figure further in the puzzling case.

Among other things that bothered investigators was the physical condition of MacDonald. Why had he been spared?

Apparently, according to his story, he was left for dead. But there was no question the wife and two small children were slain. Whoever did this brutal thing made sure. Colette MacDonald's head had been smashed six times with a club; her chest was punctured 21 times with an ice pick, and her neck and chest were stabbed 16 times with two different knives.

The viciousness of the attacks on the two girls was

just as complete: six-year-old Kimberly, found in her bed in a different room, had been knifed 10 times in the neck and repeatedly clubbed on the head. The utterly defenseless two-year-old Kristen was stabbed 12 times in the back and four times in the chest with a knife, and in addition had been stabbed 12 times with the ice pick.

By contrast, the wounds the Army doctor received were relatively minor, thorough medical examination revealed. Doctors believed he was more conscious than semi-conscious, as he appeared, when authorities arrived at the scene. The only wound he received that required stitches was the stab wound on his right side that went one-quarter of an inch deep in his right lung, causing a 20 percent collapse, temporarily, of that lung. The cuts about his abdomen and chest — about a half a dozen — were essentially superficial, medical authorities reported.

Subsequent investigation of his condition, when compared with his story, further aroused investigators' suspicion. Although he was supposed to have tried to fight off the intruders with his arms raised over his head, curiously there were no cuts at all on his arms.

In the meantime, investigators were losing no time carrying out a search for people MacDonald described as the assailants who attacked him and slaughtered his wife and two children. Known hippie hangouts were visited by officers. Literally hundreds of people in the sub-culture of the military installation were questioned; drug users and suspected drug users were quizzed. At least one favorite spot of hippies posted a sign asking anyone knowing anything about the slayings to volunteer information. All of these efforts drew a blank.

However, suspicion grew concerning MacDonald himself. Officers felt there were too many unanswered questions about the alleged attack, too many inconsistencies, little facts that didn't add up to presenting a whole, logical picture.

Because of sedation and a semi-state of shock, questioning of MacDonald the first 24 hours or so was somewhat hampered. But following that period, investigators grilled MacDonald thoroughly. Since they knew MacDonald had been involved in the treatment of people suffering with problems from narcotics, officers attempted to find someone who might have had a motive for killing him and his family because of this. They drew blanks.

Then an interesting item came up. A friend and colleague of MacDonald's, another Green Beret, told officers he had been at the MacDonalds' apartment on Saturday and MacDonald showed him an issue of Esquire magazine that carried an article about the Sharon Tate murder, with all of its similarities to this slaying. MacDonald had read the account thoroughly, apparently, and was able to discuss it in some detail.

Officers close to the case began to feel more and more that MacDonald had actually staged the entire killing, that he alone was responsible for the deaths and that he had then wounded himself precisely as he wanted to as a cover-up.

Although all details of the investigation were not revealed at that time, and there were some items that would be more thoroughly analyzed at a later date, a number of things added to the investigators' suspicion. There were reports of a growing marital strain between Jeffrey MacDonald and his wife prior to the slaying with strong hints of infidelity. The pattern of blood in the apartment bothered investigators; it was not completely consistent with MacDonald's account of what had happened. There were other things, too, that were to come out a long time later.

Nevertheless, officers began closing their investigation in on MacDonald, himself, the "nice kid from Patchogue, Long Island."

Shortly after the murders in 1970, a detective major with an adjoining law enforcement agency told this writer he was convinced MacDonald had actually committed the murders himself. Although not directly involved in the investigation, the detective had firsthand knowledge of the initial interrogations of MacDonald. He said it appeared at that time that MacDonald was definitely about to "break"—to confess. Then the quizzing was stopped for a period of time, and when it resumed, MacDonald was "cool and collected." His story did not budge from that point on.

Then on April 6th, about a month and a half after the slayings, the Army official told Capt. Jeffrey R. MacDonald he was a suspect in the grisly murders. Although not formally charged at that time, he was placed under restriction and confined to his quarters. He was allowed to attend mess and other necessary facilities only under escort. He was relieved of his duties as a doctor.

A hearing was set for that summer at which time it would be determined whether there was sufficient evidence against the former Green Beret doctor to bring him to trial on charges of murdering his wife and two children. The hearing was set after MacDonald was charged with the crime May 1st.

The hearing was closed to the press and public. Evidence was heard by Colonel Warren Rock, who presented a 2,000-page report to MacDonald's commanding officer, Major General Edwin M. Flanagan. The commanding officer in October ruled that the case, as presented by Army investigators, was not sufficient to justify bringing a court-martial, or general trial.

Following this ruling the Army's only comment was, "The investigation is continuing."

Captain MacDonald, who asked for an immediate discharge from the Army, was quoted in the New York Times as saying, "It has been a long, arduous nine months and it's finally over—or at least officially."

He was to be proved wrong. It was far from being over, even though the end would be a long time in coming.

One of those determined that the case was a long way from being over was Jeffrey MacDonald's father-in-law, Alfred Kassab. Following the outcome of the hearing, Mr. Kassab said he wanted the investigation continued to find out who really killed his daughter and two grandchildren. When the tragedy first occurred, Mr. and Mrs. Kassab were reported as stout defenders of their son-in-law. As time wore on and bits and pieces of evidence were considered, however, the parents of the slain woman began to sour on MacDonald; in time they became convinced that, instead of being the ideal son-in-law, it was he who had committed the vicious murders.

MacDonald was discharged from the Army and went to California to go into private practice.

The Army immediately reopened its investigation into the bloody slaughter.

But as far as the general public was concerned, the case was more or less closed and the publicity surrounding it subsided. This silence was shattered in the spring of 1973, three years after the slayings.

Following a 15 month investigation by the Army's Criminal Investigation Division, the U.S. Justice Department began to take another look at the evidence, and the new analysis of this evidence. It was learned at the time that the evidence might warrant sending the material to a special federal grand jury. And that was what happened.

46

After a thorough review of the material, the case was turned over to a federal grand jury, convened in the federal court district at Raleigh, North Carolina, some 50 miles from the slayings. MacDonald, now in private practice at Long Beach, California, was summoned to appear at the August 1974 grand jury. As in all cases before grand juries, the official proceedings were kept confidential. But once again the spotlight was on the handsome ex-Green Beret as he came to the North Carolina capital to testify. Following his appearance, MacDonald returned to California while the evidence was considered.

Then in January, 1975, federal agents went to MacDonald's fashionable home in Huntington Beach, California, and arrested him on charges of murder in the death of his wife and two children five years earlier.

Much of the investigative work that went on to bring MacDonald to an official trial was not made public until the actual court case got under way, which because of several attempts by the defense to have the charges dismissed was delayed four long years. The appeals for dismissal went all the way to the U.S. Supreme Court. Finally, in July, 1979, MacDonald was set for trial.

Prosecuting the government's case against Jeffrey MacDonald were Justice Department Prosecutor Brian Murtagh and Assistant U.S. Attorney James Blackburn. The long defense battle was handled by cagey and able Bernard L. Segal. Presiding was Federal Judge Franklin T. Dupree Jr.

Counselor Segal based the thrust of the defense effort on MacDonald's contention that the butchery was performed by four drug-crazed hippies—three men and a woman, who carried candles and shouted acid is groovy, kill the pigs.

The painstaking, evidence-upon-evidence case of

the prosecution was signaled by this opening statement to the jury by U.S. Assistant Attorney Blackburn: "Listen for evidence of where the blood is — and where it isn't."

One witness produced by the defense said he had been a neighbor of MacDonald's almost 10 years earlier and on the night of the killings he had been working on a model plane in his apartment. He said he opened the window to get some ventilation from the glue he was using on the model and noticed three figures in long white robes carrying candles. One of those was a woman, he said, with long, light-colored hair. They cupped their hands in front of the candles, he said, and walked in the general direction of the MacDonalds' apartment.

The prosecution questioned why he had never come forth with this information before. He said he had never been asked. The number of people he said he saw differed from the number MacDonald said attacked him. Also, the witness said these were seen a couple of hours before the slayings.

The prosecution did not spend much time trying to disprove this testimony. In fact, the federal attorneys indicated that even had there been some people wandering around outside, this could have fed MacDonald's imagination for his version of what happened.

The defense also produced a woman who admitted being a drug addict in the Fort Bragg area 10 years earlier, who had made statements to friends after the slayings that tended to show a confusion in her mind as to whether she might have, in a drug-induced state, been a party to the killings without realizing it. At the trial she said she did not participate, but she did not know where she was that night.

But the prosecution kept going back to the evidence that was found inside the house, hammering

48

away, piece by piece, at what it indicated.

To build their case, the prosecution brought in Army chemist Janice Glisson, who at the time of the trial was chief of blood analysis section at the Fort Gordon, Georgia, lab. At the time of the killings she had made blood tests at the scene. Her testimony turned out to be among the most damaging for the defendant.

Mrs. Glisson stated that all four members of the family had different blood types. Starting with this, her testimony began to weave a pattern that indicated events may not have occurred as Jeffrey MacDonald had described them.

He had maintained he was attacked in the living room, where he had been asleep on the couch. He said his pajama shirt was pulled partially over his head and entangled in his arms while he was beaten and stabbed. Earlier, it was determined that he had no cuts or stabs on his arms. The blood expert testified that blood was found in the living room, where MacDonald alleged he was attacked, in only two spots—on the Esquire magazine that contained the article about the Manson killings, and on MacDonald's glasses. But neither of these spots of blood were the same type as MacDonald's.

Mrs. Glisson cautioned the court that she could not tell whose blood these samples belonged to—only whether the types matched a member of the family.

She further testified that only one spot of blood on the pajama top worn by MacDonald matched his. Most of the blood on the top, and on a pocket ripped from it, matched his wife Colette's blood type. One spot of blood on the pajama top was the same type as that of his daughter, Kimberly.

Another Army chemist, Terry Lee Laber, testified the blood stains on the pajama pocket appeared to have been made before the pocket was ripped off, damaging MacDonald's position still further. This tended to bear out the prosecution's contention that MacDonald was wearing the pajama shirt when, enraged over an argument with his wife, he attacked her with the wooden slab, splattering her blood on his pajama top; then, in the struggle, she reached out and grabbed his pocket, ripped it off after her blood was already on it. After she was killed or dying, the prosecution charged, MacDonald folded the pajama shirt over her and stabbed her repeatedly.

MacDonald, to the contrary, claimed he was wearing the pajama shirt when attacked and only later placed it over his wife's body.

But then the prosecution lashed out with more testimony that tightened a loop of guilt around MacDonald. Prosecutor Murtagh brought a former FBI fabrics expert, Paul Stombaugh, to the stand. The fabrics authority told the jury that not only did the pajama shirt have 48 puncture holes in it — 12 times the number of wounds MacDonald had received — but the holes definitely appeared to have been made while the shirt was folded over Mrs. MacDonald's body, and not in a struggle, as the former Green Beret contended.

To demonstrate this point dramatically to the jury, Murtagh donned a similar shirt, pulled it over his head and taut between his arms, which was how MacDonald claimed his shirt ended up pinning his arms.

While Murtagh moved his arms back and forth, his fellow prosecutor picked up an ice pick and stabbed at the shirt. Accidentally, the knife-wielding attorney stabbed Murtagh slightly in the arm and some first-aid had to be administered in the courtroom. But the two attorneys graphically proved their point — the holes made in the demonstration shirt were jagged instead of circular.

Pros. Murtagh said later he felt his demonstration was the "clincher" for the jury.

There were other findings presented in court that shattered MacDonald's defense.

A Dr. George Gammel of Lincoln, Nebraska, a former Army pathologist, said the mass of stab and puncture wounds in Colette's body appeared to have been made while she was not moving. MacDonald kept his eyes averted while the slides and photos of the body were shown.

Testimony revealed that Mrs. MacDonald's blood type was found in all three rooms and her blood type and Kimberly's blood types were found in the hallway by the master bedroom, where Mrs. MacDonald's body was found.

Too, there was a large bloodstain on the floor of the master bedroom that matched little Kimberly's—but she was found dead in her bed, as was the younger child.

The blood found in the bathroom and kitchen was type B, the same as MacDonald's—yet none of his blood was found in the living room, where he said he was attacked.

All of these findings obviously stuck in the jurors' minds, and they couldn't help but remember the prosecutor's opening statement: "Listen for evidence of where the blood is—and where it isn't."

Also, a bedsheet with bloodstains on it was found. The prosecution maintained that MacDonald beat his wife in a rage in Kimberly's room, then wrapped her bleeding body in the sheet and carried her into the bedroom they shared. Kimberly, the prosecution stated, was drawn into the argument because of the noise and was clubbed and then taken to her bed. To cover the whole grisly scene, the government's attorneys said, MacDonald then cold-bloodedly went to

51

the bedside of his youngest child and stabbed her repeatedly. Next he arranged the living room as if there had been a struggle with him there, stabbed himself slightly about the abdomen and, very precisely—as a doctor might—in the right side.

On Wednesday, August 29, 1979—nine and a half years after the slaying—a federal jury, after deliberating six hours and 35 minutes at the end of the seven and a half week trial, brought back a verdict of guilty against Jeffrey MacDonald . . . guilty of first degree murder in the death of his youngest child, who lay in her crib, and guilty of second-degree murder in the deaths of his pregnant wife and his other daughter.

The former Green Beret captain was sentenced to three life terms.

After the trial, Murtagh and Blackburn agreed the verdict came because of the "tremendous amount of re-investigation"—eespecially concerning the pajama top and blood analysis.

One witness to the long summer trial said, "I went to the trial thinking perhaps MacDonald was innocent. But day after day the evidence was piled up against him. I left the trial with no questions. He is guilty."

"DID A BURIED TREASURE TRIGGER A BLOODBATH?"

by Kathleen Chandler

Sometime after one p.m. January 3, 1980, the words Mars Hill and Massacre became synonymous, fused forever in a fusillade of gunfire. Ripped by buckshot and bullets, four brothers and sisters fell that bright, cool winter's afternoon. Three died on the spot in their ancestral home, another a few days later in a hospital. All belonged to the close-knit Roberts clan of rural Cleburne County in far north-eastern Alabama. Four years later after the biggest unsolved crime in modern Alabama history, mystery still shrouds the case.

Salt of the earth. Deeply religious. Self-sufficient. Frugal. When folks talked about the Roberts, the words naturally came to mind. Country life in the foothills of the Appalachians — even three days into the eighth decade of the 20th Century — was a matter of basics. There simply wasn't time for non-essentials; 179 acres of gentle farm and timberland nourished the five relatives who lived upon it, body and soul. The family raised hogs, a few cattle, chickens, turnip greens and corn. What they couldn't use themselves, they sold in nearby Tallapoosa, Georgia, just across the state line. In an age of pre-packaged, ready-to-serve consumerism, the Roberts were proudly self-sufficient. Nobody *told* them what they needed. A neighbor remembers that they "didn't bother anybody. They stayed here and minded their own business. I never knew them to fool with anybody."

The family's frugality helped give birth to a rumor in sparsely-inhabited Cleburne County, a rumor about an old brown trunk, 22-by-22-by-40 inches in dimension. Inside the unassuming foot-locker—so folks whispered—was money, lots of money. No one could be sure just how much. That was the tantalizing part.

Columbus Roberts was the eldest family member. By the time he was 79, his once strong body was wracked with cancer. Before his health had betrayed him, he was physical master of the land. From it he helped wrest what was—by country standards—a tidy sum. While in the prime of life, the Great Depression hit and banks folded like houses of cards. Like many of his generation, he believed that there were safer places for hard-earned money than banks. A neighbor says, "About 25 or 30 years ago, Lum passed up banks and put his money in the trunk. He may have had $25,000 in there at one time. But that was a long time ago. He started using banks after a while." Still, the legend persisted of a fortune stored in a footlocker.

Instead of bringing the rain that was forecast, the morning of Thursday, January 3rd broke crisp and clear. That meant a family member would be able to safely negotiate the narrow, twisting backroads to Cedartown, Georgia to deposit the check Columbus had just received. The money came from the sale of cattle. In the old days, before cancer cells began their rapacious march through Lum's system, he would drive the animals to market in nearby Carrollton, Georgia himself. This time, the family had to hire outsiders to do the job.

At 10:30 a.m., the relative pulled out of the yard in front of the Roberts' homestead and headed the quarter-mile up the rutted blacktop to the highway. She then turned left, passed the Mars Hill Cemetery and drove north to intersect with the Cedartown highway. While in town, she would deposit the money and do some shopping. She was a punctual woman. The entire trip should take no more than three hours. She didn't want to stay away long. Her relatives took turns caring for Columbus and she wanted to return in time to do her share.

After completing her business, the relative stopped off on the way home to telephone Columbus' doctor in Rome, Georgia. The call from the Cedartown area was local; from the Roberts' it was long distance. Frugal.

Lum was almost out of medicine. She would telephone to find out if the doctor needed to see him before ordering refills for the vital prescriptions. She called the physician's office at 1:00 p.m. On this Thursday, the doctor wasn't due at the office for a half hour. She'd have to delay her return to Mars Hill. A little over 30 minutes later, she called again. Columbus' doctor told her that he wanted to see Lum the following Monday, but that first she should go ahead and refill the prescriptions. The phone call took five minutes. If lives can be measured in such short intervals, hers was almost certainly among them.

At precisely 2:00 p.m., the relative drove up in front of her well-kept but weathered wood frame home. She remembers, "When I drove up in the yard, I always looked at my watch to see how long I'd been gone." Three and a half hours had passed since she left.

No one was outside when she arrived. She went to the car trunk, removed her groceries and walked toward the porch. Orderliness, along with a host of other country virtues, was woven into the Roberts' way of life. Now, something was out of sync. As she stepped upon the wide, sheltered veranda, the relative noticed that the kitchen screen door was ajar. A throw rug protruded from the crack. She shudders in remembrance, "I thought, *Lord, something's happened!* I trembled so bad that I couldn't hardly go in that house to save my life."

She put down the groceries, leaned over and removed the rug which was preventing her from opening the screen door. An inner door of solid wood was "wide open." Once in the kitchen, she saw that cabinet drawers had been yanked from their fittings and scattered on the floor. Her terrified mind raced and she stumbled to the living room. It was hell on earth.

Seventy-seven-year-old Mae Bell and 64-year-old Floy lay sprawled in pools of blood on the once immaculately clean parlor floor. The relative knelt down and called their names. There was no response. Seventy-two year-old Mack Roberts lay on a nearby bed in blood-soaked pajamas. It was his habit to take a short nap after lunch. The relative rushed over to him: "He was trying to get off the bed; but he couldn't make it. I got down over him and called his name. He couldn't speak, but I could hear him breathing."

Her thoughts flashed to Columbus, confined to a hospital bed, in the next room. Hooked to a catheter, the elder Roberts was propped up in bed, his head turned to one side: "I could see he had been hit in the head and a hole shot through his neck." Through the horror of it all, the relative maintained control: "I never touched a *thing.* I thought maybe they could get fingerprints."

She picked up the phone to cry for help. It was dead. At the time, she figured the wires were cut. Not knowing if she could manage to drive or not, the relative herself was driven by the primal conviction that she had to do *something*. She ran from the death house, got into her car and sped for help. It took three stops before she was able to summon "any men" for assistance. When she finally found them, she told them to "call the law and the undertaker."

Like his father before him, Jack Norton is a lawman. A deep, gentle drawl and relaxed manner mask a methodical mind and vise-like persistence. When he gets hold of a case, he doesn't let go. Mars Hill would test the veteran Cleburne County Sheriff's mettle like nothing before.

Sometime just before 2:30, Norton's secretary received a strange phone call. The caller's tone of voice was casual. The person said only that the sheriff was needed in the Mars Hill area. No reason was given. Norton was out at the time. A few minutes later, the phone rang again. This time the dispatcher radioed Sheriff Norton and provided details. Lights flashing, he covered the 18 miles from the county seat in Heflin to Mars Hill in 20 minutes. He arrived on the scene at 2:55 p.m. Norton was the first lawman there, but not the first person. A crowd had already gathered in the Roberts' yard. Norton bounded up the short steps leading to the porch—a place where he had often sat and talked with the Roberts—and entered the house.

Norton first saw Mae Bell and Floy. Although certainly no stranger to death, what he saw that day was particularly grisly. Recalls Norton, "Very few times do you see women who have been killed like that unless you see it in a wreck." Following the path taken by the relative less than an hour earlier, the sheriff pulled back a curtain separating the parlor from Co-

57

lumbus' bedroom. "He was looking at me," shuddered Norton. The sheriff said nothing, his mind recoiling in abject horror. "Good God! What took place?" In his six years as sheriff of Cleburne County, Jack Norton had never seen anything like it. Indeed, he had "never heard" of such carnage. "You go and search the history of the county and you'll find sometimes where a man shoots his wife or a wife shoots her husband. Maybe the man turns the gun and shoots himself and then shoots the kid. "But," he sighs, "we've *never* had anything like this."

Later that day, the motive for the murder was clear. The family trunk was missing, the one with the purported fortune. The throw rug which had become lodged in the back door had apparently been used to drag the trunk outside.

Mack Roberts — still breathing but unable to speak — was rushed to a hospital in Cedartown. From there, he was taken to a larger medical center in nearby Rome. Doctors operated on the 72-year-old man three hours. He had been riddled by bullets, hit five times in all: twice in the neck and once each in the chest, left hand and right leg. Whoever attacked the Roberts' home clearly meant to leave no witnesses. Yet one man still lived. Now he lay in intensive care, protected by a security guard.

Medical science was doing all it could to save the surviving brother. Now, it was up to the law to find who had killed his kin.

On arrival at the Roberts', Norton called for backup. Within hours, investigators from the crack Alabama Bureau of Investigation, the Polk and Haralson County Police Departments (both in Georgia) and the Heflin, Alabama Police Department were either on the scene, setting up impromptu road blocks to question residents or processing the scene itself for the scant forensic evidence which was available. No fingerprints were found in the house. Spent shell casings and recovered bullets offered the only clues.

Autopsy reports on Mae Bell, Floy and Mack indicated that at least 11 shots were fired from three different weapons. John Case, a criminologist at the state forensic lab in Jacksonville, Alabama, said that a shotgun and two handguns were used. Because of the number of weapons fired, it seemed certain the massacre was the work of more than one person.

Cleburne County Coroner Hollis Estes determined that two of the victims had been hit by bullets, the other by buckshot. Columbus Roberts was sprayed by pellets from what amounted to a cannon. Twelve-gauge shotguns were not the most precise of weapons, but when they hit the mark it is with devastating ferocity. Lum was shot twice, once in the rib cage and once in the neck.

Floy had been hit three or four times, according to autopsy reports. Bullets slammed into her right shoulder, right rib cage and right side. Mae Bell was shot one time — at close range — between her neck and left shoulder. Her sister and brothers were shot at room range according to reports. Coroner Estes said that the bodies bore no bruises, scratches or other signs to indicate that they had resisted their assailants. The weapons the family kept inside the house for protection were never fired.

Estes speculated that the killers first shot Floy, then Mae Bell, then Mack before finally moving to the bedroom to level the 12-gauge at helpless Columbus Roberts. Estes placed the time of death at between 1:45 and 2:00 p.m., within 15 minutes of the arrival of the relative who returned from Cedartown. Had she not been delayed in making the phone call to Lum's doctor and then spent five minutes in conversations, the conscientiously prompt woman would have been — in all probability — the fifth victim.

Friday the fourth, the day after the killings, investigators remained baffled. Whoever had struck, did so quickly. In and out. While the trunk was the obvious target, the killers had overlooked three pocketbooks containing $800 in cash.

Norton said on Friday that there was a "good possibility" the Roberts knew their assailants. There was no evidence that anyone tried to break into the house. "Apparently they just walked right in," said the sheriff. Later, he termed the family "suspicious of things. They kept the doors locked. You didn't get into their house until they let you in their house."

What *had* gone through the Roberts' minds during those telescoped last few seconds of life? Momentary recognition, the opening of the kitchen door, shocked disbelief and then . . . Norton believes once inside, the robbers found their elderly victims easy targets: "If you or I wanted to rob this family, we could have taken a stick in one hand and done whatever we wanted."

If the killers had free reign inside, why the bloodbath? Single shots, like the one which felled Floy, would have silenced any witnesses. Heflin, Alabama Police Sergeant Nyron Bently said shortly after the attack, "It looks like somebody just went in and started shooting. The house was shot to pieces." And so were the people who had called it home.

Sheriff Norton feels that the wild burst of gunfire supports his belief that the Roberts knew the robbers. Professionals would have been surgical, more precise in their killing. And they probably would have used — at least in one instance — a different weapon.

Ballistics tests and spent shell casings indicated that a 380-automatic pistol had been used. The lethal weapon fires a slug just a bit larger than a .25-

caliber bullet. Norton calls the 380 "a very unique pistol. I hadn't even heard of it." Not only is the bullet relatively small, but its unusual caliber could make the handgun — were it ever found — easier to trace.

The other pistol was far more common: a .38.

Norton believes that three or four people participated in the murders. "It's my feeling that you got three weapons, you got three people that actually were in the house. Maybe one person could have been in the car."

A mid-day raid in broad daylight. Even in the country, people see and hear things. It was up to the police to find them. Investigators were bereft of any substantial physical evidence, much less suspects. The weekend following the shootings, Sergeant Ed Traylor of the Alabama Bureau of Investigation said, "We're pretty much in the dark on that score right now. We've got almost nothing to go on."

The prober concentrated on taking statements. One investigator personally interviewed 30 people living along the Alabama-Georgia line. He said that folks were hesitant to talk: "I don't know if it's because they don't know anything or what."

A friend of the Roberts' said that residents feared that they might endanger themselves if they stepped forward.

A hundred yards or so behind the Roberts' house — on the same blacktop lane which leads to the highway — was the home of a neighbor. The family was home that afternoon. One person was in the yard enjoying the mild weather and listening to the radio. He heard the shots. Sheriff Norton remembers that the person told him they sounded "like beating on tin." The roofs of some of the out buildings on the Roberts' spread are made of tin. Anyway, gunshots in the country aren't all that uncommon.

Hunting is still a way of life in parts of the rural south.

Investigators checked out the neighbor's story. Says Norton, "We actually went into the house and took some shots." Officers were stationed down the road in the same place the neighbor heard the noise. Norton says it sounded as if "you could have been beating on tin."

The last people to see the Roberts alive—save for their slayers—were a couple of men who delivered a load of firewood to the Roberts' place about 12:45 p.m. When the men pulled into the yard, the family's two German Shepherd guard dogs began to bark, boldly staking out their territory. A hand-lettered sign on a big oak tree read "BEWARE OF DOG." The firewood merchants took it seriously. One of them recalled, "The older lady (Mae Bell) came out to put the dogs in a shed by the house. The younger lady (Floy) came out and told us where to put the wood. Then she paid us." They were gone by one p.m. When asked what else they remembered, one said, "We didn't see anything suspicious. We didn't even meet a car on that main blacktop road."

The relative who discovered the bodies believes that had the guard dogs been roaming the property that afternoon as they normally did, they would have sounded a warning. She says they never barked when locked up. She is convinced the 12-gauge was meant for the canine protectors the killers expected to encounter. Instead, it was used on an emaciated old man already dying of cancer.

Although the wood haulers saw nothing suspicious, someone else apparently did. According to Norton, one man said he remembered a car with three young men drive down the quarter-mile road leading to the Roberts' sometime *after* one p.m. 15 minutes later, he said the car returned with something protruding from the trunk. Under hypnosis and Pentothal, the man could recollect neither the make of the automobile nor its license number.

The local church in Mars Hill had never held such a gathering. On a sun-chilled Sunday afternoon, January 7, 1980, three of the congregation's most beloved members were buried beneath the sandy soil which had given them life. The simple country church couldn't contain all those who wanted to attend services for Mae Bell, Floy and Columbus Roberts. Although none of the three murder victims were married, they had more than their share of friends and loved ones.

Standing behind a four-foot-high pulpit, surveying three metal caskets topped with red roses, the cleric intoned, "It is indeed a sad occasion when people go into somebody's home and murder as easily as they swat a fly." Beginning a sing-song cadence, the preacher told the swollen congregation, "Precious people, remember that the first boy born upon this earth slew his brother Abel." Then he recalled the lessons of the Bible, especially those promising life after death. As the pastor spoke, bright white sunlight filtered through 14 windows to illuminate two rows of wreaths, one just behind the pastor and the other along the wall to his right.

Near the conclusion of his homily, the preacher recalled that he "visited the Roberts' home many times and got a hearty welcome. I could see that they loved each other very much. It was the kind of love that Jesus taught us. If that kind of love prevailed throughout the nation, we wouldn't be grieving today."

Yet, grieve they did. Especially the person who had discovered the bodies four days earlier. That relative sat in the front row, stoically courageous, staring at the caskets which held her loved ones.

Outside the packed church, others huddled near the door to hear the pastor's sermon. In the crowd was an elderly man, wearing a broad-brimmed hat. He approached Jack Norton:

"Got any clues?" the old man asked.

"Not yet," the lawman replied.

"It's a bad thing, a real bad thing," said the elderly gentleman turning toward the 33-year-old frame church.

"You don't go to many triple funerals," said Norton. "But we've got a lot of good people on this case. And I just don't think the Almighty will let this thing go unpunished. I think we'll get a break soon."

Inside, with a farewell to the Lord, the country preacher motioned for the pallbearers to open the three caskets. A second entrance to the church was opened and mourners slowly filed inside. Floy lay in the first casket. The boy of the younger sister was dressed in a blue gown. Next was Lum, the agonizing pain of cancer now beyond memory. In the next coffin, Mae Bell lay, bedecked in a gown. She had been sewing when she was shot, the thimble still on her finger when she was pronounced dead.

Death for the three had not come as the Bible literally promised "like a thief in the night," but in the middle of a halcyon Alabama afternoon. Still, the meaning of the verse held. Lives had been extinguished without warning and with frightening ferocity.

When time came for the family to pass the gray metal coffins, the control of the relative who discovered the butchery broke. She sobbed, "Oh, Lord, Lord, Lord. How am I ever going to live without you? Am I ever going to miss you."

It was a short drive from the church to the old Mars Hill Cemetery. The caskets were temporarily laid under two green canopies at the family plot. Before the earthly remains of Floy, Mae Bell and Columbus Roberts were lowered into their native soil, the pastor supplicated, "Bless this family, Lord, as only Thou art able to bless them." He then offered condolences to the relative who had been delayed returning home that terrible day. She said simply, "It hurts bad and it hurts deep."

Before the second week of the new year was over, there was another funeral. Mack Roberts died January 9th and was pronounced dead at 10 p.m. He had remained in a coma for the better part of the preceding six days. On one occasion after his condition was stabilized, a relative said that the 72-year-old victim "opened his eyes once and moved his hand once." That was all. The only apparent known eyewitness never gave a hint as to his assailants' identities.

A siege of frustration set in for those still working the mysterious murders. The death toll now stood at four, and the law was no closer to solving the case than they were the day it began.

The Alabama media became fixated on the inherently dramatic mass murder. Norton, usually a genial person willing to talk about what had been learned, one day was asked by a reporter if an arrest was near. He responded, "There's no way of knowing. But even if I did know, I wouldn't tell you."

In October, 1980, authorities named an Oxford, Alabama man as the "prime suspect" in the case. He had been lodged in a Florida jail and had been charged with grisly killings in Arkansas and Georgia. Norton and ABI Investigator Sergeant Ed Traylor flew to Florida to interview the man in his jail cell. He denied any involvement in Marsh Hill. Since no fingerprints were lifted from the Roberts' home, sophisticated ballistics tests were done to determine whether weapons confiscated from the suspect in

Florida matched with the bullets found during the Roberts' autopsies. The results were negative.

In late 1980, the veteran district attorney for Calhoun and Cleburne Counties, Bob Field, dropped plans to employ a New Jersey-based psychic to aid in the murder investigation.

Meanwhile, the relative—who had moved from the Roberts' 100-year-old ancestral homestead—grew increasingly frustrated. Although she regularly heard from Sheriff Norton, she said that he rarely had anything to report: "I just wish they could come up with something. It would help me a lot if I knew who did this to my family."

Christmas, 1979, had been a joyous occasion for the Roberts. A year later, the relative returned to the cemetery and past the once warm home where so much of her life had been spent. Still, she could not bring herself to enter the place: "I just see them all lying there like I found them," she said. She called Yuletide, 1980, "the lonesomest Christmas ever."

Two years and three days later, the case almost broke wide open.

Tuesday, December 28, 1981, two hunters were walking through some woods near Cleburne County Highway 40, some three miles from the Roberts' place. There, lying in the forest, was a rotting trunk. It was the same one which had been dragged from the Roberts' farmhouse almost three years earlier. Investigators hoped the trunk and whatever was left of its contents would provide the forensic touchstone which would lead to the killers. Criminologist John Case said it was possible that fingerprints could be lifted from the papers remaining in the 50-year-old footlocker "if they haven't gotten too wet." Case added that hairs or fibers might be found in the trunk, but he doubted the value of fiber evidence that had been exposed to the elements for such a long time.

In the trunk—as the relative remembered it—were insurance papers and birth certificates. When the hunters located it, they were still there. What was missing was the money, the fabled "Fortune of Mars Hill." The small tin box which contained the cash was gone. No one knows how much. Remembers the relative, "What money was in there, I couldn't tell you to save my life." One of the billfolds in the metal box belonged to her. It contained about $100. Another one held some silver coins—"about $8 in quarters and half dollars," she remembers. The killers had been right about one thing: the scarred old family trunk *was* a treasure chest. But the treasure was beyond their comprehension. The Roberts' trunk held sacred memories of home and family and love. The frail tin box and its contents were incidental.

As it turned out, almost 36 months of constant exposure to the elements had scoured away any forensic evidence the old footlocker might have picked up. Investigators were back to square one with a handful of empty tokens to show for their efforts.

In November, 1983, Sheriff Norton suffered a heart attack. He dismisses the notion that the strain of living with Mars Hill had anything to do with the coronary. Still, he says, "I'm a sensitive man. I knew the Roberts." There's more to Sheriff Norton's frustration. Much more: "You feel like that anytime there's more than one person involved in a crime, you stand a real good chance of at least getting knowledge of it. You may not be able to *solve* the crime, but at least you have knowledge of it. To me, if you have knowledge, knowing that someone could commit a crime and not being able to solve it, that's bad."

Norton pauses, "If you could go back to the way they used to investigate some 30 to 40 years ago, we'd have solved this case. It's not worth 15 cents to solve the case if you can't take it to court."

What Jack Norton has is information. In a criminal justice system governed by stringent rules concerning the protection of suspects' rights, information does not necessarily equate with evidence.

After the murders, a person contacted Det. Norton and gave him some information concerning the killings. Norton says that the informant was approached by "a boy" who told the informant about the Roberts' case *before it happened!* "Ya see," said the sheriff with increasing fervor, "We don't just have *one* instance (like this), we've got about *four* of them!" Norton says that the people who have talked with him concerning the Roberts' murders have "dreamed about it. They're definitely upset." The demeanor of the gentle spoken lawman was transformed during the final few moments of our conversation. Leaning forward in his chair, he fixed me in the eye and said, "It's the damndest thing you've ever been involved in." Norton's record has been exemplary. He's respected and admired by fellow law officers. Still, he said, "You're not supposed to say what I say in law enforcement. This person — or persons — that I'm talking about, if you could take them out behind the woodhouse or over the knob somewhere and have a heart-to-heart talk with them, you'd do a lot more good than what we're allowed to by law."

Does the sheriff have any *specific* individuals in mind? He leaned back in his chair and said deliberately, "Oh, yeah, sure have."

A total of $15,000 in reward money has already been posted for information leading to the arrest and conviction of the killers. Norton feels more is needed, that an appeal to greed might prompt someone to provide the crucial legal link. In mid-1982,

Norton appealed to Governor George Wallace to raise the ante. He says he's received no reply. Norton wants $10,000 or $20,000 added to the $10,000 the state has already put up. A relative has $5,000 of her own offered. Says the sheriff, "A person will do a lot of talking for $30,000 or $40,000." Currently the reward stands at $45,000 for information leading to the arrest and conviction of those responsible for the mass murders.

The Roberts' house is empty now. The word "home" ceased to apply four years ago. The relative moved out after the slayings. So did the neighbors just down the road. On a cool, sunny afternoon in early 1984 — much like the one that terrible day — the century-old house seemed to sulk in shadow. Perhaps it was just the weathered wood, or the dark, spine-like patterns cast by the boughs of ageless oaks. The only sound was that of wind in the leafless limbs, softened by the gentle rustle of tall grass whispering from untended fields. Were Hitchcock alive, he would be hard-pressed to conjure a more serenely chilling scene.

Down the rutted, unused road leading to the highway and a bit to the northeast lies Mars Hill Cemetery. The Roberts plot is among the largest and most lovingly cared for. To the casual visitor — someone unfamiliar with the horror of the place — the dates on four of the headstones might spark visions of a car wreck, or perhaps a fire. But what happened the third day of this decade was no accident. For certain it wasn't.

To this day, a sort of gothic fear still shrouds Mars Hill, like the fog which gathers around the base of the nearby Appalachians. Except *this* veil doesn't blow away, and the bright light of day makes it even more impenetrable. Even in the refuge of her home in another state, the relative is scared. She believes whoever killed her kin may someday come for her. "I'd just give anything to know who did it," she says. "That would take the fear out of me some, if I knew who did it."

"WEIRD TWIST IN THE MARSHFIELD MASSACRE!"

by Bruce Gibney

To the local officials, the farm crisis experts and a good many farmers, the killing frenzy that took place outside Marshfield, Missouri, on September 25, 1987, made a tragic sense.

The suspect was a 14-year-old Marshfield Junior High student named Kirk Buckner who, seemingly pushed to the breaking point by searing poverty and a relentless workload, apparently loaded his gun and killed as many people as he could before he, too, was gunned down.

Residents felt sadness for the boy as well as his victims. "Kirk was a fine young man," said a farmer over a coffee at a Marshfield coffee shop the day after the killings. "We can't condone what he did, but we can understand it. These are tough times and that could have been any one of us pulling the trigger."

But the killings didn't make sense to students at Marshfield Junior High. "Kirk just couldn't have done it," said a classmate, who knew the boy about as well as anyone. "He didn't have a mean bone in his body."

No one seemed to be listening to just a bunch of

kids—except for police. Initially, they went along with the theory that Kirk had just snapped. But when the evidence didn't add up they started agreeing with what the kids had said all along—that Kirk just couldn't have done it.

At 6:45 in the morning of September 25, 1987, the Webster County Sheriff's Office received a call for help from a man who said he and his wife had been shot.

Deputies raced to a farmhouse near Elkland and about 10 miles east of Marshfield. Pulling into the gravel driveway, they saw a man curled up in the doorway, holding his side. He was moaning in pain and his fingers were pressed against his bloodstained shirt.

As a medic attended the moaning man, deputies ran into the house. They found a teenage boy in front of the bedroom door, a pistol clutched in his right hand. He had been stabbed and shot and lay dead in a huge blood pool.

In the master bedroom, they found a woman sprawled across the bed. She was dressed in a white nightie that was stained with blood.

In another bedroom, they found two kids. They were dressed in nightclothes and were huddled together terrified, but otherwise unhurt.

The deputies returned to the front porch where the medic worked on the wounded man.

"What happened here?" asked one deputy.

"The boy just went crazy," the wounded man said. "He shot me, he shot my wife. He would have killed us all if I hadn't killed him first."

The wounded man was James Schnick, 36. He said he had been the one who made the call for help. The woman in the master bedroom was his wife, Julie, 30, and the boy lying dead in the hallway was his nephew, Kirk Buckner, 14.

"The boy just went crazy," the shocked farmer said. "He started spraying bullets everywhere. Damn, I am lucky to be alive."

Schnick was bandaged and loaded into the back of a waiting ambulance. A deputy accompanied him on the short trip to the hospital to take down any statements Schnick cared to make.

Investigators under Sheriff Eugene Fraker arrived at the farmhouse. After locating a relative to take care of the children, the sheriff dispatched an investigator to the Buckner home to notify the family that Kirk had been shot to death.

Several minutes later, the excited deputy reported back that there had been a shooting at the Buckner place—"I count three dead children."

Investigators raced to that farm, seven miles from the Schnick place. Inside the farmhouse, they found 2-year-old Michael Buckner lying in his playpen, and his brothers Dennis, 8, and Timothy, 7, in an adjoining bed. All had been shot to death.

The sight of the murdered children sent a chill up the investigators' spines. "Where are the parents?" asked a deputy.

The shocking answer came after deputies searched the barn directly behind the front house. In one of the stalls that housed the milking cows, they discovered the body of 36-year-old Jeannette Buckner. She lay face-down in the straw, shot in the back of the head. Near her was an overturned pail. She was apparently getting ready to milk the cows when a bullet dispatched her to an early grave.

Deputies frantically searched for 36-year-old Steve Buckner. He was not in the barn or anywhere on the property. Investigators hoped that the man had gone to town and escaped the slaughter.

Then a deputy reported that he had found the body of a man lying off a road near the local cemetery a half mile from the Buckner farmhouse. Steve Buckner, dressed in bib overalls and work shoes lay face-down in the earth. Like the others, he had been shot to death.

Sheriff Fraker set up a command post at the Buckner home and ordered every available detective to assist in the investigation. He also made a request to the Missouri Highway Patrol office in Marshfield to send lab technicians to the Buckner and Schnick farms.

Reporters and photographers swarmed over the rural farmhouses. They were joined by farmers and townfolk who knew the Schnicks and the Buckners and could not believe what had happened.

The murder of seven persons—including the wholesale slaughter of a family of five—was overwhelming, even for the case-hardened deputies.

"They were slaughtered like cattle," one deputy told a reporter. "Them little kids look like they were shot while they slept."

Autopsies on the seven victims were conducted that evening. The preliminary results showed that Jeannette Buckner and her sons—Dennis, Timothy and Michael—had been shot once each in the head, while Julie Schnick and her brother, Steve Buckner, had been shot twice in the head.

Kirk Buckner had been shot twice and stabbed four times with a steak knife found protruding from his chest.

Ballistics confirmed that the seven victims had been shot with the revolver found clutched in Kirk's right hand.

Investigators reasoned that Kirk shot his parents and three brothers, then hauled his father's body to the graveyard before driving to his uncle's home and murdering his aunt.

Late that evening, detectives received word from

the hospital that James Schnick felt better and wanted to make a statement.

Sheriff Fraker found him propped up in bed, a thick bandage around his middle, but otherwise okay.

"I still can't believe it," the 36-year-old farmer said. "Kirk was like my own flesh and blood. Why did he want to kill me or my family?"

Schnick said he rose early that morning as he always did and staggered from his home in the darkness to repair a broken stretch of fence.

When he returned to the house for breakfast his brother-in-law's pickup was in the driveway. Suddenly, he saw muzzle blasts come from the house. "I ran into the house and saw Kirk," Schnick said. "He looked kinda' crazy and wild and I asked him what happened and he pulled out this gun and pointed it at me."

Schnick said he grabbed a steak knife from the table and lunged at the boy as he fired. The slugs ripped into his gut, but he managed to wrestle the boy to the ground.

The struggle continued into the hallway, where Schnick said he overpowered the boy and killed him with the knife.

He said he ran into his bedroom and saw his wife lying on the bed with blood on her nightie. He checked the kids before stumbling to the telephone.

"You have any idea why he did it?" the sheriff asked.

"I can't think of none," Schnick said. "We have been close for years. Kirk was just the nicest kid you can imagine. We would have him over here anytime."

"How did he get along at home?"

"As far as I know, okay," Schnick replied. "Life might have been kinda' tough on him. My brother was having hard times—but we all were. I don't have

75

to tell you these are tough times for the little farmer."

Even in good years, farmers in Webster County had it tough. And these weren't good years. Investigators learned that Steve and Jeannette Buckner were two years behind on payments to the FHA and Federal Land Bank and were in hock up to their necks.

Their house was run down, the farm machinery was old and always breaking down, and there was no money to fix anything, even if they had the time, which they didn't.

"I'd see Jeannette and Steve, ten times a day and they were always working," a neighbor told investigators. "They never complained, not even the kids, but I think it had to get to them after a while."

As the oldest, Kirk spent every spare minute working. He rose two hours before school to milk the cow, then did a full day's work after school.

On weekends, he worked on the farm or hit up neighbors for part-time jobs. "The boy did the work of ten men," one neighbor remarked. "I would hire him to slop the pigs and feed the cows and he would finish what I gave him and ask for more."

Kevin worked as hard at school as he did on the farm. While he was no "brain," he did his homework every night and eked out a "B" average.

But exhaustion was starting to show. Instructors said that Kevin showed up at school with big bags under his eyes and sometimes fell asleep during class.

"I guess he was just worn to a nub," said one instructor.

Funeral services were held on September 28th at the First Baptist Church in Elkland. Mourners jammed the modest church and filed past the caskets that held Julie Schnick and the six members of the Buckner family.

Jim Schnick was brought to the funeral by his wife's parents. He wore a white shirt and dark jacket and hobbled on crutches. He was visibly moved by the emotional eulogy and, toward the end of the service, appeared to slump.

Afterward, he stood by the door and thanked mourners as they filed out the door.

Several hours later, Sheriff Fraker contacted the Missouri Highway Patrol office in Springfield and talked to his hunting buddy, Sergeant Tom Martin.

"Tom, I need your help," the sheriff said. The MHP is the largest law enforcement agency in Webster County and lends out investigators and lab technicians when requested.

"Sure thing," the sergeant said. "We've been following that mass murder case like everyone else. I guess the kid just snapped."

"Maybe," the sheriff said. "But we got a lot of things here that don't add up."

"How is that?" Martin asked.

Fraker said that initially he was ready to accept the story that Schnick had murdered his nephew after Kevin had turned a gun on him. He was also ready to believe that Kevin had wiped out his family before driving to the Schnick farm. It was a wild, crazy story, but it did make sense. A few years earlier, a deranged man had walked into a McDonald's in San Diego, California, and wiped out 25 women and children before he was finally cut down. If that could happen, then it was logical that a kid stretched to the breaking point could turn on his own family.

"I bought it for a while," the sheriff said. "And it still might be true. Except a lot of things just don't add up."

The sheriff explained that he first suspected something wasn't right when the search of the two farmhouses did not turn up a single cartridge casing.

"There were eighteen shots fired in the rampage," the sheriff said. "If Kirk had gone crazy, why did he

-77

have the presence of mind to pick up the casings. And what did he do with them?"

There was also the question of body weight. Fraker said his investigators had discovered blood in the back of the Buckner pickup, indicating that it had been used to haul Jim Buckner's body to the graveyard.

"But how did Kirk get his dad's body in and out of the truck?" the sheriff asked. "Kirk didn't weigh more than 130 pounds, while his dad weighed almost twice that. There was no way he could have moved him."

Another clue that cast a shadow of doubt on Schnick's story surfaced after a deputy returned from conducting interviews at Marshfield Junior High School.

The deputy told the sheriff that none of the students who knew Kevin believed he could have committed the murder.

While questioning a teacher, the deputy happened to glance at some of Kirk's recent schoolwork and noticed how the handwriting slanted to the left.

The deputy told the sheriff that he showed the schoolwork to the teacher, who told him that Kirk wrote that way because he was left-handed.

"If Kevin was left-handed," the sheriff asked Martin, "what was he doing clutching the murder weapon in his right hand?"

Martin agreed. The gun should have been in Kevin's left hand.

"What kind of guy is your suspect?" he asked.

"That's the strange part," Fraker replied. "Everybody we've talked to likes him."

James Schnick was from near Billings, Missouri, which was southwest of Springfield in Christian County. He'd moved to Elkland eight years earlier,

78

where he married Julie Buckner and raised his two children.

He tended a small herd of 30 dairy cows on his 95-acre farm and also worked part-time at a feed company.

Quiet and easygoing, Schnick had few outside interests. Unlike his neighbors, he didn't like to hunt or fish and showed little interest in firearms.

"Jimmy kept guns in the house like we all do," one farmer told investigators. "But he never used them, not even at target practice. They just didn't hold his interest."

Most of Schnick's energies, investigators learned, were directed towards work. He labored sunup to sundown, rarely with a break, and worked on weekends.

About his only outside interest was the Elkland Volunteer Fire Department. Schnick attended the meetings on the first Monday of every month and was on call if needed.

Firefighters said Schnick loved hanging around the fire station and had applied for a full-time position with the Springfield Fire Department. He passed the physical and written requirements and was expected to be hired within the month.

Not exactly the portrait of a mass murderer, Sergeant Martin agreed. But why was he lying?

The detective reached that conclusion after more inconsistencies in his story emerged.

Paramedics said Schnick held his sides and screamed in agony on the way to the hospital. Yet a doctor who examined him said the wounds were superficial and barely cut the skin.

When asked if the wounds could have been self-inflicted the doctor nodded. "It is possible," he admitted.

Schnick also told detectives that during the struggle in the house he stabbed Kirk with a steak knife, then shot him by turning Kirk's hand that held the gun around so the barrel pointed at his nephew's chest.

But, according to the coroner's preliminary report, the angle of the bullet wound through the boy's heart wasn't consistent with the struggle Jim had described.

Perhaps the most damning evidence came after investigators discovered that Schnick was the beneficiary of a $100,000 life insurance policy on his wife. Schnick had also co-signed a bank note that in the event of Steve Buckner's death, would have given him debt-free title to his brother-in-law's farm. Moreover, Schnick was a possible beneficiary of his father-in-law's large holdings and a 24-acre farm which had been willed to the Buckner children and grandchildren.

"By killing those people, he eliminated seven heirs," Sheriff Fraker cursed between tight lips.

"I can't believe someone would be that cold-blooded, but I guess it is possible," Sergeant Martin agreed.

Schnick also had someone to spend it on. Police discovered that the hardworking farmer had a mistress whom he had been seeing for the past two years.

They learned that the mistress had learned Schnick was married and had threatened to go to his wife. The ultimatum was given shortly before the murders.

"Money and sex," Sergeant Mason said. "Two powerful motives."

On October 5th, police contacted Schnick and asked him if he was up to coming to the station and answering a few more questions. Schnick said that was okay with him and hobbled into the station.

The 36-year-old farmer told investigators the same story he had a week earlier. Sergeant Martin watched him closely; he didn't believe a word of it.

Martin then asked Schnick if he was willing to take a lie-detector test. He said it would involve sitting in a chair and having electrodes attached to his nipples and other parts of his body. The test would take about an hour.

"Why do you need that?" Schnick asked.

"Because I think you are lying and this machine will tell us if you are or are not," the sergeant snapped.

"I didn't hurt anyone," Schnick shot back. "That boy was trying to kill me."

"Then you won't mind taking the lie box," the sergeant said.

"No," the farmer said. "Let's do it."

Schnick rose from his seat then appeared to slump. He grabbed his side and sat back in the chair. He remained silent for several moments before saying, "I guess you would find out sooner or later."

Schnick was advised of his constitutional rights. He was asked if he wanted a cigarette or something to eat before he made his statement.

Schnick shook his head. "No, I'm fine just as I am."

The worst mass murder in Missouri history began when Schnick went to Buckner's home on September 25th to help him with some chores. He said he arrived early as always, then waited for his brother-in-law to meet him outside before he shot him in the back of the head. He then shot Jeannette and turned the gun on Kirk and the other kids.

Schnick said he dumped Buckner's body in the graveyard, then drove seven miles to his house and shot his wife while she slept. He dragged Kirk's body into the house and shot himself superficially before calling for help.

"Once I started I couldn't stop," Schnick told detectives.

"Why did you do it in the first place?" Sergeant Martin asked. He already knew about the money, but the answer surprised him.

Schnick said that Jim Buckner had raped his wife Julie when they were children. He said the incest had scarred Julie and was a reason for the deterioration of his marriage over the past two years.

Schnick said he had confronted his brother-in-law about the alleged rape. That had resulted in a series of arguments.

Schnick said he did not expect trouble when he went to Buckner's house the morning of the murders. However, he had another shouting match with his brother-in-law which led to the shooting.

Schnick was arraigned on seven counts of murder on October 6th. Wearing bib overalls and a white tee-shirt, he told the judge he understood the charges against him and that he believed he had the money to hire an attorney. Judge Max Knust then ordered him to appear in court and to be held without bond in the county jail in Marshfield.

County Prosecutor Donald Cheever said it was likely that his office would seek the death penalty. "If there were ever a death penalty case, this one is it," he remarked.

Schnick went on trial in April 1988 in Webster County Circuit Court before Judge John Parrish, with Donald Cheever as prosecutor. Schnick had been charged with seven murder counts but would stand trial only for the murders of his wife and nephews Kirk and Michael. The other counts were severed in case Schnick was found not guilty and it was necessary to try him again.

Eighty spectators and two dozen reporters packèd the small courtroom to hear testimony and see in person "Missouri's Worst Mass Murderer."

Schnick was not much to look at. Bushy-haired and overweight, he was dressed in a jacket and slacks and slumped next to his attorney for much of the proceedings.

Prosecutor Cheever told the eight-woman, four-man jury that the defendant had carefully plotted the seven murders, then attempted to blame his nephew Kirk in order to collect on the insurance policy and to inherit property.

He said that Schnick had been cheating on his wife for two years and that Julie Schnick had learned about the mistress just before the killings.

Cheever speculated that Schnick had killed his wife because she threatened to divorce him because of the affair.

Jurors watched the lengthy video-taped confession Schnick had given in the police station. On tape, the defendant wiped sweat from his forehead, fidgeted with his fingers and occasionally broke into tears as he described in grisly detail how he'd committed the murders.

The jury then listened to Schnick's attorney, who asked them to forget what they had heard and seen on the tape and not to make any conclusions until they had heard all the witnesses.

He said that his client did not know what he was doing when he made the video-taped confession, and that he had been coached by police into making the statement.

Thirteen witnesses took the stand to testify that Schnick was a hardworking, much-liked person in the community who always went out of his way to help others.

A teenager also testified that he had been a friend

of Kirk Buckner's and had gone hunting and fishing with him many times. On these occasions, the witness said, Kirk used his right hand as often as his left when he shot and fished. The testimony was apparently to cast doubt on the theory that Schnick had planted the gun on the body to make it look as if Kirk were the killer.

The defense also put on the stand two friends of the defendant's who testified that they had helped Schnick put his financial affairs in order after his wife's death and suggested he apply for the $1000,000 benefit from the life insurance policy on Julie Schnick's life.

Courtroom observers later said that they thought the purpose of the testimony was to cast doubt that Schnick committed the murders for the money.

The jurors were not swayed. They found Schnick guilty of three counts of first-degree murder on April 14th after just one hour and 45 minutes of deliberations.

"It was overwhelming," a juror said later.

The same jury was then asked to determine in the penalty phase of the trial if Schnick should be sentenced to death or to prison the rest of his natural life.

A psychologist testified for the defense that Schnick's violent behavior on the morning of September 25th had been completely contrary to a life of compassion and caring for others. He said it was likely that the defendant had simply "exploded" because he had difficulty expressing anger and sought acceptance through hard work.

"Most people have outlets for anger, fear and hurt," the psychologist said. "His outlet was to work harder. He had nowhere to go if you pushed him into a corner or up against a wall."

Friends testified that Schnick was a hardworking, loving father, while members of the Elkland Volunteer

Fire Department said that "he was one of the best."

One man who had known him for 30 years said, "Jim never lost his temper and was the type of guy who would stop a truck from moving across a field so he could remove nests of baby rabbits rather than run over them."

Prosecutor Cheever reminded jurors that there was ample evidence to vote for the death sentence. "Think about Julie Schnick and the two children," he told jurors. "The defendant showed them no mercy."

He then described 2-year-old Michael lying dead in the crib. "It's difficult to imagine anything more defenseless and helpless than a two-year-old asleep in his bed."

The jurors returned to chambers on April 16th. This time they spent two hours and 30 minutes before returning to the packed courtroom.

"Have you reached a verdict?" the judge asked.

"We have," the jury forewoman said.

A slip of paper was passed to the judge, who quickly read it and passed it to the court clerk.

"We, the jury, find that James E. Schnick should die in the gas chamber," the clerk read aloud.

James Schnick wept as the jury sealed his fate. Bailiffs removed him from the courtroom.

Schnick became the 57th person on Death Row at the Missouri State Penitentiary. It is unlikely that his sentence will be carried out in the near future. His case is on appeal to the state supreme court and it could be years before a ruling is made.

Missouri is also slow to act on capital cases. No one has been executed in Missouri since 1965.

Schnick is currently on Death Row waiting the outcome of his appeal.

"OHIO FAMILY MASSACRED AS THEY SLEPT!"

by George Stimson

When winter comes to the Midwest, there isn't much to do but stay inside and wait it out. The frequent combination of low temperatures and high precipitation means that most outdoors activity, besides snow-related sports such as sledding or skiing, comes to a virtual halt. Home supply stores put away their displays of barbecue grills and charcoal briquets. Backyard swimming pools are either drained or covered over for the season. And motorcycles are stored inside garages until spring arrives.

And so, on Wednesday, January 16, 1991, there wasn't much happening at a motorcycle shop located at the end of Commerce Drive in rural Warren County in southwestern Ohio. The owner of the shop, John Macy, was killing the downtime by staring out the shop's front window.

Macy focused on the one-story building, about a hundred yards in front of his establishment, that housed offices and a small Greyhound bus station.

As Macy looked down the road, he saw two people come out of the bus station, which was really little more than a ticket counter and several chairs, and walk toward a dumpster on a gravel apron on the side of the street. Macy watched with interest as the pair, a man and a woman, opened the dumpster and threw several items inside. It was early evening, and the winter darkness was descending quickly, so Macy could not quite make out what the couple was disposing of. Some of the items, however, appeared to be papers of some kind. When they had finished disposing of the refuse, the man and woman returned to the bus station and stayed inside.

The motorcycle shop owner was puzzled. Why, Macy wondered, would two people walk out into the cold to throw something away in the dumpster when there were plenty of garbage cans inside the warmth of the bus station. The more he pondered the pair's actions, the more Macy thought they might have something to hide.

Thoroughly suspicious now, John Macy went to the phone and called a friend to tell him about the couple's strange behavior. The friend happened to be a detective in the police department of nearby Middletown.

Middletown, located in Butler County, is just west of Interstate 75 about midway between Cincinnati and Dayton (hence the town's name). Forty-six thousand souls live in Middletown, making it the second largest populated area in the county.

The police department sent officers to the scene near the bike shop to have a look inside the dumpster. What they found was disturbing. Loosely distributed among the plastic bags of business-related trash were papers and other items that were clearly the personal effects of several people. One of the items was a woman's purse that contained identification with an address on Middletown's west side.

The officers went into the Greyhound bus station to question the couple inside about the suspicious circumstances. There they found 18-year-old Jose Trinidad Loza and his 16-year-old girlfriend. The police separated the couple and began interrogating them.

When asked why they were disposing of other people's personal effects, Loza and the girl gave conflicting stories. More ominously, a search of Loza's belongings turned up a .25-caliber semiautomatic pistol. Convinced that something illegal was going on, the police decided to hold the couple until further notice, and they arrested Loza on a charge of contributing to the unruliness of a minor.

With Loza and his girlfriend safely in custody, the police began sifting through items from the dumpster, looking for any clue to the reason for the couple's furtive behavior.

The recovered purse contained identification for one Georgia Davis, age 46. The I.D. showed an address in the 1400 block of Fairmont Avenue in Middletown. This dovetailed with information a computer query gleaned about a pickup truck Loza and his girlfriend had driven into the lot in front of the bus station. The vehicle was registered to 20-year-old Gary Mullins of the same Fairmont Avenue address. With this evidence and with the couple's suspicious activity near the bus station as grounds, police were able to obtain a search warrant for the Fairmont Avenue address. At about 8:50 p.m., officers arrived at the house.

Knocking on the front door but getting no answer, the officers were finally able to enter the house through a door in the rear. What they found inside was a horrible confirmation of their worst suspicions.

In the upstairs bedrooms, the officers found the bodies of three people. All had been shot one time in the head, apparently with a small-caliber weapon. A fourth person had also been shot in the head but was not dead. This survivor, identified as 17-year-old Jerri Jackson, was immediately taken by ambulance to the University Hospital in Cincinnati to be treated for her wound.

The dead were identified as 46-year-old Georgia Davis, 25-year-old Cheryl Senteno, and 20-year-old Gary Mullins. The women had been shot just above the left ear. Gary Mullins had been shot between the eyes. All of the victims were found in their beds. It appeared to the officers as though the victims had all been shot in their sleep. Butler County Coroner Richard Burkhardt would later comment, "It appears they were all shot at the same time, sometime on Wednesday; but they didn't die at the same time."

The shooting victims were all members of the same family. Georgia Davis was the mother of the younger victims. Police learned from neighbors that she was also mother of the juvenile girl who had been with Jose Trinidad Loza when he was arrested at the bus station in Warren County.

While police tried to piece together the story of the shootings, Jerri Jackson fought for her life in the neuro-intensive care unit at University Hospital. A hospital spokeswoman described the victim as unconscious and in critical condition. The spokeswoman also revealed that the wounded teenager was about six months pregnant.

With the crime scene secured and a likely suspect in custody, police tried to determine the circumstances surrounding the multiple shootings. Why, they wanted to know, would a young man coldbloodedly enter his girlfriend's family's house and shoot the sleeping occupants in the head? Police set out to answer this question by interrogating the suspect, the girlfriend, and neighbors of the victims.

From neighbors, police learned that the Fairmont Avenue house had been a center of turmoil for several months, ever since Georgia Davis and her children had moved in the previous September. Before then, the family had lived in Los Angeles, California, where the youngest daughter had become acquainted with Jose Trinidad Loza. Apparently, tensions in the house arose when Mrs. Davis allowed Loza to accompany the family to Middletown. According to both neighbors and the LAPD, Loza was a member of a Los Angeles street gang.

Complicating matters in the household, Loza wanted to return to Los Angeles with his 16-year-old girlfriend, who was pregnant with Loza's child.

The family's Fairmont Avenue neighbors had been put off by the sometimes raucous goings-on at the house, and several times, the police were called to deal with conflicts between family members.

According to police, the problems in the Davis household just kept getting worse until they exploded into the massacre that occurred on January 16th. Of the shootings, an officer commented, "Right now it looks like it was more domestic-related than drug-related."

Another officer added, "He shot them and killed them execution-style. It shows the brutality of the crime."

Loza was arraigned in the Middletown Municipal Court where he was charged with three counts of aggravated murder and one count of attempted murder. His young girlfriend was held in custody as a potential witness.

On January 31, 1991, Jerri Jackson succumbed to her gunshot wound, bringing the number of murder counts in the indictment up to four. Miraculously her baby was born before her death and was adopted by a family member.

Loza was transferred to the Butler County Jail in Hamilton, Ohio, to await his trial. He stayed there for months until the court dockets cleared and it was his turn to face justice. The trial was scheduled to begin on August 5, 1991.

Although Loza had entered an innocent plea at his arraignment, his lawyer announced that he would change his plea to no contest and would request a trial in front of a panel of three judges instead of a jury. The court-appointed attorney, Michael Shanks, said that Loza was making his own decisions against the attorney's advice. "He intends to plead no contest, which will result in his electrocution," the lawyer said.

But when Loza appeared in court that Monday, presiding Judge George Elliot refused to accept the no contest plea. Loza then entered a plea of not guilty by reason of insanity. The trial was then ordered to begin before the three-judge panel of Judge Elliot, Judge John Moser, and Judge Matthew Crehan. These events have been sorted out, the trial began the same day.

In his opening statement, the prosecutor referred to the mass murder as "a cold, calculated act, the act of a coward, committed while the family lay sleeping in bed."

Defense lawyers declined to make an opening statement until the beginning of the defense phase of the trial.

The first witness to testify was the only surviving member of Georgia Davis' family, the 16-year-old girl who was carrying the defendant's child. The girl claimed that she was a constant target of abuse from her other family members because of her relationship with the defendant. She said her relatives beat her continually and that her mother, angered by her pregnancy, had threatened to kill her baby.

Another witness, a neighbor of the slain family, testified that she had purchased the murder weapon, a .25-caliber Raven semiautomatic pistol, at a Middletown department store. The witness said she purchased the weapon at the request of Loza's girlfriend who had told the neighbor that they would need the gun for protection when they moved back to gang-ridden Los Angeles.

Then the prosecution presented their key piece of evidence, a videotape made the day after Loza's arrest.

On the tape, Loza at first denied any knowledge of the massacre. But after over an hour of denials, when the interrogating detectives appealed to his impending fatherhood, he finally began to change his story.

"What you're trying to do," Detective Roger Knabel told Loza on the tape, "is put yourself in the electric chair, along with [your girlfriend]. This child's going to go off into never-never land and won't be seen again."

Apparently, this appeal to Loza's familial instincts worked. He began telling detectives his side of the terrible story. "I had to do it," Loza said on the tape, "because that was the only way I was gonna be able to live with [my girlfriend], have a life, and have my kid."

Loza went on to describe an atmosphere of constant harassment in the house on Fairmont Avenue, saying that Georgia Davis and her children continually beat and threatened his girlfriend. In one instance, Loza claimed, Gary Mullins said he would "beat the baby outta her." These threats had occurred every day for at least two weeks prior to the murders. On the very morning of the murders, Loza said, Gary Mullins told Loza he would have him arrested if he and the girl attempted to leave Middletown together.

Referring to the murders themselves, Loza said, "I didn't think about it until it occurred. If I hadn't had the gun, it would not have crossed my mind." He said that he initially shot Georgia Davis and then the others, "or they would have known it was me. If I shot all of them, no one would ever find out."

Loza stated repeatedly that his girlfriend was not present during the shootings and knew nothing about them until he told her en route to the bus station. "I did it, and I'm wholly responsible for it," Loza said.

After playing the taped confession, Middletown police officers testified on the circumstances at the dumpster that led to Loza's arrest and the discovery of the bodies. Court then adjourned for the day.

The next day, August 6th, the prosecution showed a videotape of the crime scene as it appeared on the evening of January 16th when the crime was discovered. As the judges viewed the 20-minute tape, they saw the bodies of the three slain family members lying in their beds. They saw the paramedics working to save the life of the mortally wounded Jerri Jackson. When the paramedics asked the girl her name, she wailed, "My baby, my baby!" Loza sat expressionless as the tape was played.

Butler County Coroner Richard Burkhardt took the stand and said that while Gary Mullins, who had been shot in the forehead, probably died instantly, the other victims apparently survived several hours after being shot. Georgia Davis and Cheryl Senteno had each been shot in the side of the head.

Middletown Police Detective Robert Walton testified that spent cartridges from the crime scene and the clothes Loza had been wearing when arrested had been analyzed at the Ohio Bureau of Criminal Investigation (OBCI).

Detective Gary Gingerich testified that the telephone lines into the Fairmont Avenue home had been disconnected in an outside junction box.

Two other detectives testified regarding items from the house that were recovered from the dumpster near the bus station where the defendant had been arrested. And the ticket agent at the Greyhound station testified that he sold Loza two one-way tickets to Los Angeles.

But one of the most significant aspects of the case occurred outside the courtroom that day. On that Tuesday morning, Jose Loza's girlfriend delivered the baby that had been at the center of the conflicts on Fairmont Avenue.

Loza's reaction to events was expressed through his lawyer, who told the press, "He's ready to face the ultimate sanction, as long as [his girlfriend] stays out of prison and his child . . . is born free."

On Wednesday, August 7th, defense attorneys surprised everyone by asking for a mistrial, claiming that the prosecution had been too slow in furnishing the defense with results of the tests done on the defendant's clothing. These tests, which had been revealed in court the previous day, had showed that there was no blood present on Loza's clothing.

The prosecution said that they had just received the test results the previous day and called their failure to give the results to the defense an "oversight."

"It is not our intent to hide anything," Assistant County Prosecutor Noah Powers said.

But the defense didn't buy that. "As far as I'm concerned, this exculpates Mr. Loza, [and] creates a reasonable degree of doubt," Shanks said. If the defense had had this information before the trial, he continued, they would have asked for a trial before a jury instead of the three-judge panel.

The judges called for a recess in order to consider the defense's motion.

On Thursady, August 8th, the three-judge panel voted two to one in the defense's favor and granted the mistrial. Speaking for the majority Judge Elliot said, "Here, the issue is not whether the result of the trial would probably have been different . . . but whether there would have been a bench trial at all, had that [clothing] evidence been available to the defendant. Failure to disclose the evidence in question denied the defendant his due-process right under the Fourteenth Amendment to a fair trial. There is no question that the results of such tests were exculpatory in nature."

County Prosecutor John Holcomb responded to the judges' ruling saying, "The reason for a mistrial is to correct a problem. We'll start all over and we'll do it right."

Loza was returned to the Butler County Jail, to await a new trial date.

On October 10, 1991, Judge Elliot overruled a defense motion that sought to dismiss the charges against Loza on the grounds that a new trial would violate Constitutional provisions against double jeopardy. The new trial was scheduled to begin, this time before a jury, on October 21st.

On Monday, October 21st, jury selection began in the retrial of Jose Trinidad Loza. Seventy-five prospective jurors were called that day and both sides were quickly able to agree on a 12-member panel composed of eight women and four men. Four alternate jurors were chosen the next day and the retrial got under way.

The first step was a visit by the jury to both the murder scene and the bus station where Loza had been apprehended.

Trial resumed back at the courthouse where the prosecution and defense made their opening statements. Assistant County Prosecutor Noah Powers called the defendant "a coward. He shot them while they were sleeping . . . coldly and methodically went to [their] rooms, put the gun at their heads, and shot them."

Defense Attorney Michael Shanks countered that the evidence "exculpates Jose, and we believe Jose is covering for his girlfriend. He confessed only when told [by police] they would execute his girlfriend and send his baby off to never-never land." The attorney added that the girlfriend's family would "beat her and threaten to kill her. The whole family was cruel. Mr. Loza sometimes tried to help by taking the blows himself."

Jose Loza's girlfriend then took the stand and testified that she met Loza the previous year in Los Angeles and that he accompanied her and her family when they returned to Ohio. She described a household constantly in turmoil over her relationship with the reputed gang member. After having a neighbor purchase a gun and ammunition, she said, she turned them over to Loza. The girl said that the day before the shootings, Loza had expressed a desire to murder her family, "but I didn't think he would do it." Even when Loza admitted the slayings on the way to the bus station, she did not quite believe him.

The girl said Loza claimed to have used a house slipper as a makeshift silencer when he shot her mother, brother, and sisters. She said she later saw Loza dispose of the slipper by throwing it onto the roof of the bus station where they were later arrested.

The next day, Loza's videotaped confession was introduced as evidence and played for the jury. In the two-hour tape, Loza initially denied the shootings before finally confessing. He completely exonerated his girlfriend and expressed his desire to see her before he paid the price for his crimes. "I did it [the murders], and I'm taking full responsibility for it. She didn't do anything. I might spend my life in jail, or get the gas chamber, but all I want is to see her one more time. Not for a whole day, just for five minutes."

Loza's girlfriend was back on the stand that same day. She told the court that she did not see the murder weapon after obtaining it and giving it to Loza the day before the murders. She said that she obtained the gun at Loza's urging. She denied shooting her family members herself. She claimed that on the morning of the murders, she left her home and did not return. When Loza later picked her up in her dead brother's truck, he told her about the murders, but she did not take him seriously.

The following day, the prosecution played the videotape of the police's arrival at the death house on January 16th. The defendant doodled in a notebook and showed no interest as the 20-minute tape was played. Jurors saw close-up views of the three dead family members lying in their beds. They also saw paramedics working to save the life of Jerri Jackson.

Also that day a ballistics expert from the OBCI testified that the bullets recovered from the victims' bodies were fired from the pistol that was taken from Loza when he was arrested.

On Friday, October 25th, the defense called their witnesses, including a technician from the OBCI. He testified that there was no blood on the defendant's clothing after the murders. After that brief presentation, the defense rested. The defendant did not take the stand. Closing arguments were scheduled for the following Tuesday.

Tuesday came and both sides had their final words. The defense continued with their strategy of implying that Loza's girlfriend may have been the actual killer. "She was the one who was there to purchase the gun," Defense Attorney Greg Howard told the panel. "She was the one who had the problems with her family. She has all the answers. [She] knows too many details of what happened on January sixteenth that [Loza] doesn't know. This can only mean that she was there, that she was inside the house, and that she did [the shooting]."

The prosecution mocked the defense's insinuations. They said that Loza should be convicted on the evidence of his videotaped confession alone. "They are trying to blame this whole thing on [Loza's girlfriend], and they didn't even question her for ten minutes," Prosecutor Holcomb argued. "They are playing a legal shell game. But there is one thing the defense never explained—where was Loza? He was where he told police he was. He was killing four people."

The jury began their deliberations at about 3:00 p.m. on Tuesday, October 29th. After deliberating the rest of the afternoon, they were sequestered at a Middletown hotel at 7:30 p.m. At 8:30 the next morning, they continued with their task. They worked throughout the day before again adjourning without reaching a verdict.

Finally on Friday, October 31st, the jury returned to the courtroom with their decision. Jose Loza showed no emotion as the verdict was announced. He was found guilty on all four counts of aggravated murder. The jury further decided that the killings had been committed during the course of an aggravated robbery. Fourteen other specifications in the verdicts meant that the convicted man would be eligible for Ohio's death penalty.

Prosecutor John Holcomb expressed satisfaction with the jury's decision. Calling the verdict "fully warranted," he added, "I'm happy. He's a bad dude, and I'm glad that the judicial process took care of him."

Judge Elliot expressed his thanks to the jury. "There is no more agonizing duty than sitting in judgment of your fellow man," he said. "I appreciate the agony you've gone through. It shows in your face."

Loza's attorneys said, "[We] are disappointed with the verdict, but we accept it and we are proceeding to work on the mitigation."

The jury returned to the courtroom the following Wednesday to determine the fate of the convicted man.

Judge Elliot advised the jury to consider such factors as Loza's age, his lack of a criminal past, any reasonable doubts as to his guilt, and the possibility that the victims may have provoked the killings. The jury had the choice of recommending death, life with the possibility of parole after 20 years, or life with the possibility of parole after 30 years.

A female relative of the convicted man, speaking through an interpreter, described to the jury Loza's childhood, after being abandoned by his father. She described the family's meager existence in a small apartment in Los Angeles after they immigrated illegally from Guadalajara, Mexico.

Defense Attorney Shanks asked the jury, "What will be gained if he dies in the electric chair? Will society be better off for it? You don't have to kill Jose Loza. You don't have to think about it the rest of your life."

Prosecutor Holcomb countered by demanding the ultimate penalty. "No one forced this guy to do this thing," he said. "It was cold-blooded and it was horrible. It was the worst kind of crime."

On Tuesday, November 7th, after 10 and a half hours of deliberation, the jury handed down their recommendation as to the fate of Jose Trinidad Loza. As usual, the defendant was expressionless as the somber members of the panel recommended he be sentenced to death for the murders of Gary Mullins, Cheryl Senteno, and Jerri Jackson, and that he be sentenced to life without the possibility of parole for 30 years in the murder of Georgia Davis.

Prosecutor Holcomb commented on the jury's recommendation, "I take no pleasure in it, but considering all the facts and circumstances, Loza earned it. He deserved it and the jury put the whammy on him. He had it coming."

Formal sentencing was set for the following Tuesday at 9:30 a.m. When court reconvened that day, Judge Elliot asked Loza if he had anything to say before formal sentence was passed. The young man answered, "No."

The judge then concurred with the jury's recommendation and sentenced Loza to death for three murders and life without chance of parole for 30 years on the fourth. He also sentenced the convicted man to three additional years for using a firearm during the crimes.

After sentencing, Loza was taken to the county jail to await transfer to Ohio's death row, where he would join three other men who had been sentenced from Butler County.

Defense Attorney Michael Shanks recalled the testimony of a psychiatrist who said during the trial that Loza would do anything, including sacrificing his own life, to protect his girlfriend and child.

"[Loza] says he doesn't fear death," Shanks said. "I think his feeling right now is, 'Let's get it over with.'"

EDITOR'S NOTE:
  John Macy is not the real name of the person so named in the foregoing story. A fictitious name has been used because there is no reason for public interest in the identity of this person.

"DESSERT DISHED OUT
FIVE SERVINGS OF DEATH!"

by Richard Walton

Dinners at the home of retired publishing tycoon Joseph Cleaver and his family were enriching experiences for their guests, who included friends, old business acquaintances, and, on occasion, members of the royal family.

The Cleavers' home was a spacious six-bedroom mansion, built in the 1930s on the banks of England's River Avon in the southern county of Hampshire. With the river and the historic New Forest nearby, the Cleavers had made their estate into their own version of paradise.

Known as Burgate House, the mansion, with its attendant servants' quarters and swimming pool, is situated at the end of a leafy driveway.

The nearest village, Fordingbridge, is roughly equidistant, on the A338 highway, from the medieval cathedral city of Salisbury to the north and the popular coastal resort of Bournemouth to the south.

The Cleavers had bought the mansion in 1948 to use as a weekend retreat while Joseph was still working in London. He had been well known and respected, not only as a publisher of educational materials, but also as the owner of a chain of cinemas and as a sports promoter. The Cleavers moved into the manor permanently when Joseph retired in 1970.

Though out of public life, Joseph maintained a rigorous schedule of entertaining guests with his sumptuous dinner parties. He was a generous and popular host and was proud of both the excellent table he kept and his extensive cellar of fine wines.

At the Cleavers' gourmet dinners, tuxedos and black ties were the preferred attire for the men, elegant evening wear and jewelry for the women. Chilled cocktails were served promptly at 7:30 p.m., followed by a masterfully prepared dinner at 8:00.

Such was the agenda on the night of Monday, September 1, 1986, when 82-year-old Joseph held a small gathering of family and friends. In a wheelchair sat Joseph's 82-year-old wife, Hilda, who had been left disabled and without speech after a serious stroke 15 years earlier. Sitting beside Joseph was one of his sons, 47-year-old Thomas, who had been fitted with an artificial leg following a car accident some years before. Completing the dinner party were Thomas' 46-year-old wife Wendy and Hilda Cleaver's old friend and live-in nurse, 70-year-old Margaret Murphy, who was an American by birth.

Light from an ornate, six-branch candelabra overhead and from elegant fixtures on the walls cast a gentle, pastel-pink glow over the dining room. The centerpiece of the room was a large, antique dining table, which could be extended to seat up to 32 people. The family's silver glistened at their settings, and the soft light was reflected from the crystal cruet set and slender-stemmed glasses standing on the snow-white linen tablecloth.

In back of the mansion, beyond the well-manicured croquet lawns of the 14-acre estate, the placid Avon meandered through on its way to the

English Channel, and swans glided with austere regality in and out of the rushes as the autumn twilight fell.

Wendy, having donned a pretty, frilly apron over her evening wear, was in charge of the dinner. The meal, after hors d'oeuvres, consisted of lasagna with side-salads, broccoli, carrots, zucchini, and sweet peppers, all brought fresh to the mansion door earlier that day by a local gardener friend. For dessert, Wendy planned cool, sweet melons steeped in chilled champagne.

To Joseph Cleaver at that moment, life in the bosom of his family was surpassingly sweet.

By nature a trusting man with no known enemy in the world, Joseph Cleaver always left the front door key in the outside lock until nine o'clock each night, in case any passing friends should stop by.

That, events would prove, was a terrible, expensive mistake.

At a few minutes before the hour when Joseph would normally have locked the front door, the Cleavers' well-ordered world fell apart. Death came to dinner with the dessert, transforming the happy home into a house of horror.

Life has a pleasant and somnolent pace in Fordingbridge. On the morning of September 2nd, the news agent's man arrived to push the morning papers through the mail slot of the door at 8:15, as usual.

The deliveryman found the front door wide open. He could see nothing to arouse his suspicions in the entrance hall beyond or at the front of the building. Assuming that one of the family was taking an early stroll around the gardens, he tossed the newspapers inside.

It was then that the deliveryman noticed the remote-control unit of a video recorder lying on the floor. Thinking someone in the house had accidentally dropped it, he left the unit where it was and returned to Fordingbridge to continue his morning routine.

The news agent's man had not looked up at the first-floor windows of the mansion, which was partly obscured by trees, creepers, and rambling vines. Had he done so, he might have seen what 70-year-old Una Hubbs saw when she arrived about 10:00 a.m. with 80-year-old gardener Frank Darrow.

Both of the longtime servants of the Cleavers were alarmed to discover smoke billowing from an upstairs window. Adding to their alarm, Wendy Cleaver's two dachshunds were barking frantically from somewhere on the upper floor.

Frank and Una looked at each other and cautiously entered the open front doorway.

In the hallway behind the open door lay another of the Cleaver dogs, a poodle named Tina. The dog was whimpering in agony. One of its eyes dangled from its socket and blood was pouring from the animal's mouth.

Shuddering, the servants passed quickly on, noticing as they walked along the hallway that the glass door to the gun cabinet was open. The cabinet was empty.

Inside the dining room, the remains of a partly-eaten meal still lay on the table beside half-empty wine glasses. The chairs had been pushed or pulled back from the table, apparently in a hurry.

The shocked servants backed out of the room and anxiously climbed the stairway to the upper floor. The flinty smell of smoke was heavy in the air, and the staircase wall was blackened. As they reached the landing on the second floor, Frank and Una stared in horror.

A fire, still smouldering, had gutted the master

bedroom. An emptied jewel case held the door ajar, and a heavy pall of thick smoke obscured what lay inside. Small fires were still glowing cherry-red here and there in the gloom, and there was an ominous stink of burning flesh in the air.

Hurrying on to the sound of the barking dogs, the two servants entered another bedroom along the hall and were met with a sickening sight.

Spread-eagled on one of the twin beds, her hands lashed behind her back and her mouth gagged, lay Wendy Cleaver. A black silk ribbon was knotted tightly around her throat. Her clothes had been torn from her body—she was naked except for the frilly apron. There was a look of indescribable horror on her battered features.

Frank gently touched the victim's arm, but she was long dead, her flesh cold as marble.

The two servants hurried downstairs to call the police, but they found that the telephone wires had been ripped from the wall. Frank and Una sped by car to the village police station, three miles away. With remarkable calm—which he later put down to shock—Frank told Constable Roger Carter that he wished to report one murder and possibly more.

After giving the stoic old man an appraising look, Carter picked up Policewoman Jan Bulfield and sped to the mansion in their own patrol car, with the servants close behind, to investigate.

Following a quick glance into Wendy Cleaver's bedroom, the officers soon found three more bodies in the smoke-filled master bedroom and a fourth in a bathroom adjoining.

One victim was sitting in a wheelchair near the bedroom door. At first the investigators took that victim to be male because of the trousers on the body. But the appalling burns to the head made determination of gender impossible.

Lying amid the charred remains of a bed that had collapsed to the floor and was still burning were two other bodies.

Then came the gut-churner. A trail of sticky, burned human flesh led to the bath of the master bedroom's, where the last body lay huddled below the window.

Constable Carter remained with the bodies while Policewoman Bulfield left to ask the servants to take care of the frightened dachshunds still in Wendy's room and then to secure the mansion for investigators.

Detectives and other constables soon arrived. Among them was Detective-Constable Malcolm Slaughter, who was known affectionately to colleagues in the Hampshire County Force as "Sherlock." Slaughter wasted no time in undertaking his investigation. He began with the room Wendy Cleaver was found in.

Detective-Constable Slaughter found that a strip of torn bedding had been used to gag Wendy Cleaver. He also found a cigarette end smelling of gasoline under the bed on which Wendy Cleaver lay and tiny fragments of inflammable fire-lighters scattered on the ground floor. Other fragments lay on the staircase along the hallway and into the master bedroom. The odor of gasoline was pervasive upstairs and downstairs.

Initially, because they were so badly burned, the other corpses were unidentifiable and simply marked A, B, C, and D until they were positively tagged through the help of jewelry, dentures, and other distinguishing features unmarred by the flames.

Body C, sitting in the wheelchair, was later identified as Hilda Cleaver from a caliper fitted to one leg. Body A, lying on the floor, turned out to be nurse Murphy, who was identified by wires on the corsets she was known to wear. Joseph Cleaver was determined to be the body among the charred ashes of the bed, and the body in the bathroom was that of his son, Thomas.

Dr. Roger Ainsworth, a consultant pathologist, was called in. He soon confirmed that Wendy Cleaver had been gruesomely raped and had bled heavily from a large tear caused by the insertion of an object like a hand or fist, or perhaps some similar-shaped blunt object, into her vagina. She had been strangled after the rape—which had been committed by more than one person, as vaginal evidence proved—and it had taken her at least half a minute to die.

Then gasoline had been poured on Wendy's back, legs, and buttocks. Though it had not been ignited, the chemicals in the fuel had badly burned her skin tissue.

As for the other victims, all had been cold-bloodedly burned while they were still alive.

Joseph Cleaver, with arms tied behind the back above his elbows, had been so badly burned that one arm was completely missing. His wife had also burned to death, but probably more quickly. There was not much left of Nurse Murphy's body, apart from her legs. The fire in her case was so severe that the heat had started to turn her skull into a chalklike substance.

Thomas Cleaver, although also seriously burned, apparently died from the searing effect of fire and fumes on his lungs. His wrists had been tied behind his back, and his legs were also bound. He had apparently broken free by dragging off his artificial lower right limb and was able to crawl from the master bedroom into the bathroom to try and raise the alarm. Ghastly proof of this was a trail of burned flesh he'd left behind him. He had apparently tried

108

to butt his head through the bathroom window but had mercifully succumbed to the fumes in the process.

Police wondered why, with a fire so intense in the master bedroom, the flames had not engulfed the whole mansion. No doubt this question was in the minds of the killers at the time. The answer came from a forensic scientist, Dr. Rodney May.

The fire in that room was of an explosive force sufficient enough to blast ornaments out the window into the garden below, billowing out the curtains like the sails of a ship with a whoosh of sound. But, the initial blast burned so fiercely that it rapidly used up the oxygen in the room, even with the windows open. Afterwards, it just died away, leaving smouldering fires where the gasoline had been scattered, and then feeding itself on the fats of the burning bodies.

The building had been extensively rebuilt after World War II, and, because timber had been in short supply, reinforced concrete was used throughout, even on the floors. The killers were apparently unaware of this fact and had probably counted on the fire consuming the entire house and destroying all evidence of their crime.

Wood and furnishing fabrics might burn, but not the main structure, which is why the contents of the master bedroom did not crash through to the ground floor below, nor did the fire spread extensively to other rooms along the hallway.

As news of the horrific discovery was released to the press, residents of Fordingbridge were stunned with shock and anger. They were preparing to celebrate the 900th anniversary of the Norman Domesday Book in the area, but plans were switched instead to forming vigilante posses to protect family and home from murderous maniacs.

Meantime, police took evidence from the mansion, particularly from the bedroom where Wendy Cleaver had endured multiple rape before being slain. Included were items for saliva- and semen-testing, and samples of carpeting from the bedrooms, the landing, the stairs, and the other areas of Burgate House.

From clear signs of disturbance on the ground floor and from the obvious ransacking of Joseph Cleaver's study desk, the sleuths deduced that the killers had been searching for money and other valuables, although rare paintings and valuable silver had been left intact. Wall paintings were hanging awry, an indication that the perps had been looking for a hidden safe. They did not find it. It lay behind a simple window-wall curtain in an alcove, its contents secure.

The perps had also missed another secret cache in a most unusual hiding place. Seven hundred pounds in U.S. dollars and other currency remained hidden in Thomas Cleaver's artificial leg!

At that stage, with no survivor to talk to, police had no idea what was missing beyond three shotguns, a small-caliber rifle, and a quantity of ammunition and hunting equipment stolen from the gun cabinet on the first floor. But interviews with the temporary domestic staff and with other relatives of the Cleavers, supported by documents in Joseph's meticulously-kept study files, soon revealed that some family jewelry, about $200 in cash, a video recorder, and a TV console were missing.

Those interviews also revealed that a tragic telephone call had taken place on the night of the massacre.

One relative told police that he had telephoned Burgate House shortly after dinner and got no reply. He'd wanted to tell Thomas to watch a particularly interesting TV program that night, so he called again later.

A male voice the relative could not recognize answered. The stranger told him that Joseph and Thomas "were upstairs." The relative left a message and hung up, but, feeling uneasy about the stranger who'd answered the phone, he rang the mansion a third time to ask that Joseph call him back.

This time, Thomas himself came on the phone. He told the relative that all was well in the mansion, except that Wendy could not come to the phone because she was upstairs in bed, ill with influenza.

It was not difficult to deduce that the intruder had forced Thomas Cleaver at gunpoint or knifepoint to fabricate that information. He had probably agreed to do so hoping that his cooperation would convince the intruders to commit nothing more drastic than robbery.

Meanwhile, a classic example of national cooperation between local police forces was about to bear fruit in what had initially seemed to be a motiveless massacre short on clues.

By six o'clock on the night of September 2nd, the Hampshire force had at their disposal the highly sophisticated HOLMES computer, which can cross-check all relevant information in its immense databank at the touch of a switch. The manufacturers had installed the machine with the Bedfordshire County force to the north of Hampshire, and Bedfordshire swiftly sent down three of its men, specially trained in the use of the machine, to help their colleagues.

Coincidental with this cooperative approach to crosss-county crime detection came one result from the painstaking perusal of documents found in the mansion.

A ledger contained the names of two people in the

111

town of Bournemouth who had been given as character references by a former handyman employed by the Cleavers—one 36-year-old George Stephenson.

Stephenson had answered an advertisement Joseph Cleaver had placed in the *Bournemouth Evening Echo* in July seeking "a homely couple" for a "happy home."

Stephenson and his wife got the job. They were appointed on July 19th as joint housekeepers and were given the adjoining servants' quarters. But his wife walked out after Stephenson beat her in a drunken brawl and, on August 7th, the Cleavers somewhat reluctantly asked Stephenson himself to leave, too. He did so, after stealing a TV console from the quarters and 16 bottles of vintage wine from the cellar.

Thus it was that Wendy Cleaver and her husband Thomas were standing in for their parents as housekeepers until permanent domestic help could be found.

Bournemouth police, part of the Dorset County force cooperating with their Hampshire colleagues, interviewed the couple who had given the Cleavers references for George Stephenson and learned some interesting facts.

Stephenson had left the Bournemouth area after his dismissal from Burgate House to stay with 25-year-old George Daly and his 21-year-old brother John in the industrial Midlands city of Coventry. Stephenson, who had a long list of previous criminal convictions, including illegal firearms possession, had met George Daly in jail.

On Monday, September 1st, before the mansion massacre began, Stephenson had arrived at the home of the couple in Bournemouth. He offered to find them a video recorder and TV console as partial payment for their looking after the wine he had stolen when dismissed from Burgate House. The next morning, September 2nd, the witnesses told police, they found the equipment on their doorstep.

Later that day, Stephenson telephoned the couple from the Midlands, asking if they liked the gifts and saying he would return soon to Bournemouth to collect some money from them. The couple also described for police a car Stephenson had been driving, a red Rover with a license plate number beginning with the letter C. The TV and video set were soon identified from sale slips as the items stolen from Burgate House on the night of the massacre.

After initial reports of the massacre appeared in newspapers all over Britain, Stephenson's estranged wife came forward to talk with Scotland Yard detectives in London.

While confirming that she and her husband had worked in the Cleaver household, she gave the detectives some insight into Stephenson's violent behavior and handed them photographs from their wedding album and other documents to help police identify and trace him.

On the heels of this development, a Coventry car-hire firm contacted their own West Midlands police force to confirm that Stephenson had hired a red Rover with registration number C-352-YRW in his own name. They added that George Daly paid the bill by check. The car had been returned to the firm on Tuesday, the rental agent said, with a mileage consistent with a trip to the southern coast and back.

Inexorably now, the evidence was being pieced together.

Having seen, to his surprise and consternation, his photograph flashed on TV, George Stephenson telephoned the Hampshire County police, saying he intended to return to give himself up. Nevertheless, he denied all knowledge of the rape and murder.

113

Stephenson took a train south, but instead of going to the police immediately, he spent that Wednesday night at a campsite on the edge of the New Forest, drinking and talking to two nurses he'd met at a tavern.

They all returned to the women's tent, where, for a joke, one of them read Stephenson's palm in gypsy fashion. She foretold "big trouble" ahead for him. Stephenson had a copy of the *Coventry Evening Telegraph* with him, and the women saw his photograph in it. He admitted to being the man the police were looking for. The women either were not alarmed or were playing it remarkably cool, because after a few more minutes of conversation, Stephenson autographed the newspaper and left it with them "as a souvenir."

Then, borrowing a lighted candle from the two nurses, Stephenson walked off into the night to telephone the police from the campsite callbox.

Two officers picked up George Stephenson at the camp a few minutes later.

Stephenson was to say, initially, that he'd waited outside Burgate House in the hired car while the Dalys went in. This was just one of many accounts he gave of the massacre.

Later that Thursday morning, the Daly brothers were picked up by armed detectives in Coventry, and escorted south, too. All three suspects were subsequently charged with the murders, rape, and robbery at Burgate House.

There had been no sign of the stolen guns and jewelry at the Daly home, but police later recovered the weapons from a hiding place, and other property from the murky waters of Grand Union Canal in the Midlands.

When their 18-day trial began in Winchester Crown Court in October 1987, attended by press representatives from all over Europe, all three suspects denied having murdered the five victims. Stephenson denied raping Wendy Cleaver or aiding and abetting George Daly to rape her. George also denied the rape, and he and Stephenson denied robbing the Cleaver family.

John Daly, however, pleaded guilty to robbery and rape. Later, he admitted to the murder of Wendy Cleaver.

Crown Prosecutor David Elfer told the jury that the total profit from the mansion massacre had been those paltry few dollars — worth about £90 sterling — aptly described by one of the Daly boys as "blood money."

But their obvious plan to gut the mansion with fire and destroy all the evidence, Elfer said, failed because of the building construction. Elfer described to a visibly shaken jury the horrifying details of the victims burning alive, particularly Thomas Cleaver's agonizing crawl, and Wendy Cleaver's rape ordeal by two or three men.

While awaiting trial, Stephenson concocted one story that he had picked up two Hells Angels on the night of the murder and that *they* had committed the crime at Burgate House, not he or the Dalys. But, times have changed for the better in British police investigation. No longer is it necessary to rely on written statements alone to back up evidence. Videos made of all interviews with the accused men were played back to the jury. These brought out the true and terrible story.

The trio had hired the Rover in Coventry, loaded it with pickax handles and fire-lighters, and bought cans of gasoline at a filling station near their target. Rubber gloves, garden twine to bind the victims, and nylon stockings for face masks were bought in Bournemouth department stores. All of the lethal merchandise was later traced by police.

Stephenson, knowing the domestic routine, picked the moment for the assault. As the dessert was about to be served, the trio burst into the Cleaver dining room, masked and brandishing ax handles.

In disguised voices, they demanded the diners' jewelry and money, then herded their victims up into the master bedroom.

As the others were being bound, Wendy Cleaver was dragged away into the other room by Stephenson, who was by then holding a stolen shotgun. He pinioned and then raped her. Then it was George Daly's turn, and, finally, his brother John's.

While John Daly was raping Wendy, Stephenson entered the room again and put a knife beside the bed. The message, John Daly said later, appeared obvious. Stephenson wanted John to kill Wendy. But instead of stabbing her, he rolled his victim onto her stomach and strangled her with a black silk ribbon torn from her ripped clothing. Her face turned blue, and she fell off the bed in her final convulsion, but he dragged her back on it and left her corpse on the gore-stained sheets.

George Daly was the man who threw lighted fire-lights inside the master bedroom where the rest of the family were helplessly tied up. But he claimed that Stephenson had told him the occupants were already dead, doused by gasoline, and ready for cremation.

"I didn't know they were still alive!" he screamed hoarsely on the courtroom video playback. "I didn't want to kill anyone!"

"He [Stephenson] told me we would just go in and out the mansion, and that would be it . . ."

George Daly insisted it was Stephenson's idea that they all three rape Wendy Cleaver. George did not intend arguing with a man carrying a loaded shotgun,

116

he claimed, so he went along with the rape. But, Wendy was alive when he was finished with her, George said.

Stephenson, George added, had earlier shown them a luxury house in the Bournemouth area which he'd allegedly robbed some time before, to give them confidence in the attack planned on Burgate House.

When George threw the fire-lighters into the master bedroom, there was a tremendous explosion and a flare-up of scorching, rolling flame. He fled from the room to the car parked outside with the stolen loot, which included bottles of wine and spirits stolen from the Cleavers' cocktail cabinet.

While driving through Fordingbridge, Stephenson stopped once to see if the mansion fire was illuminating the night sky. It was not, but, satisfied that all was going well, he drove on toward Bournemouth to deliver the stolen video and television set to his friends.

A few miles from the mansion there was nearly another massacre. Police were blocking the highway because of a traffic accident, and Stephenson ordered the Dalys to get the guns ready for a shootout. But a smiling policewoman waved their car on through the roadblock, and the guns were hastily hidden again.

Whether or not what Stephenson alleged about the earlier Bournemouth robbery was true, one certainly occurred there on May 25, 1983. That victim, Horace Makin, who lived in a prestigious area of the town, told the court all about it.

Makin said he and his wife were attacked that night by three armed raiders carrying shotguns and a Rambo-style knife. The marauders robbed them of £43,000 in cash and jewelry. No one, to Makin's knowledge, had been arrested for the crime.

On the day of the Burgate House massacre, it was a dwelling in Makin's road that Stephenson had showed to the Daly brothers.

John Daly did not give evidence in court, but had earlier said in statements that Stephenson planned the raid on Burgate House to steal money and guns for future robberies. Burgate House had to be burned down so Stephenson could not be identified as a former Cleaver employee, and Stephenson had assured the Dalys that all trace of the crimes would be razed by the fire.

But Stephenson claimed in court to have been an innocent bystander who sat in the car while the Dalys went in to steal guns and whatever else they could find. He denied setting fire to the house or going inside it, but forensic evidence from tests confirmed that semen found on the bed where Wendy Cleaver was raped could have come from him.

Dr. Robert Ainsworth, who was present at the crime scene on the initial day of the investigation, described to the jury how Wendy Cleaver had died. Examining his watch in total silence for 15 long, drawn-out seconds, Dr. Ainsworth solemnly told the jurors it had taken twice that long as the ligature tightened around her throat. It was a dramatic display, perhaps, but one glance at the jurors' taut faces proved he had made his point.

Wendy Cleaver had been doused by gasoline for a torching, too, the pathologist added, but the fire never spread to the bedroom she was in; and, therefore, evidence against the accused was preserved within.

Mr. Malcolm Boots of the Home Office Forensic Laboratory described how he examined over 30 items from the house of horrors, many from the room where Wendy died. Saliva on a cigarette end could have come from either of the Daly brothers, Dr. Boots averred, but not from Stephenson or Wendy Cleaver. But, another cigarette in the corridor outside the bedrooms held a saliva sample belonging to Stephenson or Wendy. It was not a type of cigarette normally found in the Cleaver home or used by Wendy.

A pink carpet fiber caught up in the laces of one of Stephenson's shoes matched carpeting on the landing stairs, Dr. Boots said. Similar fibers were found in the hired car.

George Daly's common-law wife told the jury that all three of the accused returned from the Bournemouth trip about 3:00 a.m. They had been drinking heavily, she said.

The woman asked George what had happened earlier. He turned away, muttering in a whisper, "If only you knew what I've been doing!"

The woman told the court that the trio brought guns and ammunition into the house. She later identified the arms — all weapons stolen from Burgate House — for police, who were able to trace their ownership from firearm certificates held on file.

Stephenson's girlfriend also gave evidence for the Crown. She told the court that she had asked Stephenson if he was responsible for the mansion massacre, but he said that other men had done it. Yet, soon after the news was released, she found him shaving off a beard and moustache and John Daly changing his hair style.

One witness who never got to see the end of the trial was the old gardener, Frank Darrow. The tragedy at Burgate House had preyed constantly on his mind, and he was found dead in his chair at home on October 23rd, as the trial neared its conclusion.

Three days later, the jury came back with the verdicts.

Stephenson received concurrent life sentences with a minimum of 25 years each for the murders of Joseph, Hilda, and Thomas Cleaver, Mrs. Margaret

119

Murphy, for the rape of Wendy Cleaver, and for robbery. Judge Hobhouse told him he had shown no mercy—and deserved none. Then Stephenson, smiling sardonically, was taken to the cells below.

George Daly received 22-year concurrent sentences on four counts of manslaughter—not murder—together with 16-year concurrent sentences for rape and robbery. John Daly, who had admitted to raping and murdering Wendy Cleaver and to robbery, received seven concurrent life sentences, three for the admitted crimes, and four for the other murders.

For 18 days, survivors of that victims' families sat through the trial listening to every harrowing detail. In statements given later they said it was their duty to sit through it and show respect not only for the dead, but for justice, and to know what truly happened that terrible night to their dear ones.

It was a grisly crime that shook wealthy old people living in isolation in rural Britain, and not without reason. In July 1985, a wealthy, 76-year-old widow was wounded twice by gunmen who raided her lonely manor house near Maidstone in the county of Kent. They took jewelry, cash, and silver, and then killed her gardener, William Austin, and her dog. The killers were armed with a shotgun and crossbows. Austin was shot in the chest, and the widow, in the face and near her heart. She miraculously survived.

Then, in December of that year in a lonely part of South Wales, 56-year-old Richard Thomas, a millionaire bachelor, and his 55-year-old sister Helen were shot in their ancient manor at Scoveston Hall, near the port of Milford Haven. The house burned down in a fire and it was assumed that the couple had died accidentally—until forensic experts discovered they had been shot. It was classed at the time as a "near perfect" crime.

The "house of horror" massacre at Burgate Manor was almost perfect, too—except for that reinforced concrete used in its rebuilding.

EDITOR'S NOTE:

Una Hubbs, Frank Darrow, and Horace Makin are not the real names of the persons so named in the foregoing story. Fictitious names have been used because there is no reason for public interest in the true identities of these persons.

"LET SLEEPING VICTIMS LIE IN POOLS OF BLOOD!"

by Gary C. King

Friday evening, October 23, 1987, was typically quiet within the city limits of Rickreall, Oregon, a small farming town in Polk County about 11 miles west of Salem, the state's capital. It was equally quiet on the Farmer family's farm a few miles out of town. Only a gentle breeze swept through the filbert orchard on their property, occasionally rustling the parched autumn leaves of the tall oak trees surrounding the farm, left brittle and yellow from the long, dry summer, and kicking up an occasional whirlwind of dust. The silence was broken only by the infrequent passing of a car or pickup traveling along the gravel road that runs by the farm.

About 8:30 the next morning, a close relative walked the few acres from his house to the Farmer mobile home, planning to ask for advice about planting wheat. When he reached a shed on their property, he felt that something was amiss, "out of order." He ran the last several yards to their front door.

He knocked loudly, but Robert Farmer, 70, and Barbara, 69, didn't answer. The lack of response brought on a more dreadful feeling inside him, but the relative nonetheless peered through a window. He immediately saw that his relatives' home was in disarray, apparently ransacked. In a near panic, he ran to another relative's home, also located nearby and called the authorities.

Minutes later, deputies from the Polk County Sheriff's Department arrived at the rural location on Greenwood Road, five minutes off Oregon 22. They were met by the relative who called them and they could see he was greatly distressed. After gaining entry to the residence, the relative called out for Robert and Barbara. The deathly silence confirmed his gut feelings that they weren't going to respond — ever.

Anxious and afraid, he told the deputies that Robert and Barbara usually slept in separate bedrooms. When they checked those areas of the home they found, much to their horror, each of the Farmers, dead of gunshot wounds to their heads. Seeing the grisly sight, the anguished relative ran out of the home. The deputies soon followed and notified their headquarters of the grim discovery.

A short time later, Sheriff Ray Steele, who had lived most of his life only two and a half miles from the Farmer residence, arrived, accompanied by Detective Richard Manning. Each investigator had been enjoying a quiet day off when they received the call from headquarters, located in nearby Dallas. When they saw the grisly condition of the bodies and the ransacked state of the home, each lawman knew they could forget about their time off. It was going to be a long weekend.

Steele and Manning quietly surveyed the site, both inside and out, to determine the boundaries of the crime scene, making detailed notes of their observations. It was obvious that they were dealing with a double homicide as opposed to a homicide-suicide; there was no weapon at the scene. The motive, they noted, looked like burglary and robbery. Because of the delicate nature of the crime scene, and as a matter of routine in such a case, they called in a traceman from the Oregon State Police (OSP) crime laboratory, as well as the county medical examiner. They then sealed the dwelling pending the arrival of the additional personnel.

The case was a difficult one for the lawmen because they *knew* the victims personally. The sheriff and the detective knew firsthand that Robert and Barbara Farmer were good people, decent, hardworking folks who never bothered anyone and thought only the best of others. Having lived their lives virtually unexposed to the darker elements of human nature, these innocent victims had observed the golden rule and had trusted nearly everyone. Highly respected, the Farmers were regarded as honest, charitable people of outstanding character. They were, in other words, like most of the other residents of Rickreall. Until the Farmers' murders, reflected the sheriff, crime had been virtually nonexistent in this community, except for an occasional burglary. No one could remember the last time a murder had been committed there, and it seemed likely that no one would quickly forget the Farmers' deaths. Sheriff Ray Steele was sure he wouldn't.

Steele already knew much of the family's history. The Farmers had lived long, productive lives in the house built on the land originally purchased by Robert's grandfather. Their land had been recently designated a "Century Farm" by the state of Oregon because it had been in the family for more than 100 years, and a road that runs adjacent to the property was, at one point, aptly named after them. Because it was their intention to keep the property in the family, Robert and Barbara Farmer had moved out of the house and bought the mobile home they were killed in, and subsequently transferred the land to their three children. At the time of their deaths, they had close relatives living in houses on either side of them, including the original farmhouse.

While they waited for additional personnel to arrive, the relative who reported the suspicious circumstances tearfully told Detective Manning and Sheriff Steele that the victims' car was missing. He described it as a dark gray 1984 Datsun 300SX, Oregon license plate number HSM 398. He said the car was in very good condition and had blinds on the rear window. Manning promptly issued an APB for the car, and instructed his department's public affairs unit to issue a news release that requested anyone who spotted the car to contact him immediately. Manning also told the grieving relative that he would need his help at some point to determine what else was missing from the home. But first the crime scene had to be properly processed.

When the county medical examiner arrived, he promptly observed the victims' bodies and told Steele and Manning that the couple had been shot as they lay sleeping, just as the lawmen had originally presumed. He obtained the victims' body temperatures, and collected blood and other bodily fluid samples. Because their bodies were cool to the touch, and because there were signs that rigor mortis was beginning to set in, the medical examiner estimated the time of the Farmers' deaths to have been within the previous 12 hours. Detective Manning reasoned that he might be able to narrow down the time of death after he conducted interviews with neighbors and relatives who, he hoped, could tell him when the victims had last been seen. He said he wanted the state medical examiner to perform the autopsies because of the type of death they were dealing with.

The victims' bodies were carefully photographed,

as was virtually every area of the home, after which the scene was turned over to the OSP trace-man. As his title suggests, he was responsible for gathering trace evidence from the crime scene—bullet fragments, hair, fibers, glass, or anything else that could prove relevant to the case.

The criminalist first surveyed the scene and made a mental map, a grid, of his search pattern. Moving delicately through the home, the trace-man and his assistants made every possible effort to walk in the same spots as each other to avoid destroying any unseen evidence. The expert knew that the criminal always leaves something of himself at the crime scene, no matter how minute, and that most everything at a crime scene says something about the crime and the person who committed it. The trick for the crime experts was, therefore, to unravel the mess and decide what was relevant and what was not.

The criminalists spent many hours inside the victims' home. They vacuumed with machines equipped with special filter bags, took blood samples from the victims' bodies, bagged bloodstained bedding and collected fragments of items that had been broken when the dwelling was ransacked. In short, they collected everything of a comparative nature, whether it was obviously important or not-so-obvious, knowing that many times it's the not-so-obvious items that nail a suspect. Results would not be quick in coming, however, since everything gathered at the crime scene would first have to be carefully analyzed at the crime laboratory in Portland to determine what would be useful to the probers.

After additional sets of photographs had been taken, as well as sketches of the scene drawn, the bodies of Robert and Barbara Farmer were zipped inside opaque body bags and taken to a storage location until an autopsy could be performed by Dr.

Larry Lewman, the state medical examiner.

Latent fingerprints were also obtained from all locations of the home but most, the investigators knew, would likely belong to the victims and others who had access to their home, including the investigators. When they finished, they decided to start interviewing relatives and neighbors.

Although he had not done any actual farming for years, everyone, including the lawmen, knew that Robert had actively sold farm and ranch real estate in the area. He had also spent a good deal of his time teaching and advising a relative about the techniques of farming. Barbara, his wife of 46 years, was active in an Oak Grove gardening group when she wasn't reading the latest books, the investigators were told during the long series of interviews.

"There are two thousand volumes in that house," said a relative. "There's a book on every flat surface." Manning, as delicately as possible, turned the conversation toward the murders and the last time anyone had seen the victims alive.

"We all fell apart," said another close relative, recalling feelings of when he learned of the murders. "I just don't know why anyone would do it." He said he saw the elderly couple almost daily, but the last time he'd seen them was at lunchtime on Friday, when they were still alive and well.

Another relative who lived nearby said she had stopped by Friday night to borrow the newspaper and to say hello. She told investigators that she and her husband had driven by the victims' home again later that night, on their way home from dining out. She said she hadn't noticed anything out of the ordinary at the time.

Before she and her husband went to bed that night, the relative continued, they looked out their corner bedroom window at the Farmers' mobile home, situated across Farmer Road about 300 yards away. They never saw or heard anything during the night, she said, and they had certainly not heard any gunshots.

"They never wanted to lock their house," said another relative. It was a carefree, trusting attitude held by many in the area, she said, at least until the murders. "We were trying to get them to get a dog," she continued, wiping her swollen, reddened eyes. She added that Robert and Barbara didn't want a dog, though, because they liked to travel, and they didn't want to be saddled with the responsibility of taking a pet with them or of finding someone to take care of it in their absence.

Relatives also told the investigators that Robert and Barbara had recently returned from a vacation in Reno, Nevada, and that the entire family, including children and grandchildren, had gone to Hawaii in the spring. The relatives said they recorded portions of the vacation on videotape.

"We still have the memories," remarked one family member. "They can't take the memories away from us, can they?"

When asked if the victims had had any enemies, relatives and friends alike told investigators that no one hated the Farmers. They were among the most-liked families in the community, and all of the family members got along well together. Robert and Barbara always exercised good judgement and common sense, police were told, especially when dealing with those outside the family. Prior to their murders, the only times the elderly couple had been victimized was when their home had been burglarized, once in March 1987, when they were on vacation and again in September, a month before they were killed. One other time, police learned, someone had stolen approximately $800 cash from their home in 1986. In that incident, however, burglary didn't appear to be involved. Robert and Barbara had suspected that a temporary employee had stolen the money.

When the killer ransacked the house, noted Detective Manning, they virtually turned the place upside down. In their search for things to steal, they looked in closets, cupboards, chests and nightstands. They even went through a refrigerator and a freezer, both in the kitchen. Had they been looking for cash? he wondered. At this point, Manning had not been able to pin down whether or not it was the victims' practice to keep large amounts of cash in the home. But it was a thought he kept somewhere in the back of his mind.

When an inventory of their belongings was conducted with the help of relatives, Manning noted that, in addition to the victims' car, the killer had taken portable television sets, rare collector-type shotguns, a clock, silverware and Elks-lodge lapel pins. But nothing was sacred to this killer-thief, observed the detective. He had even taken the victims' wedding rings!

This was a troubling case for the investigators, not only because two of the community's most-respected citizens were brutally murdered but because there were some serious questions raised, the answers of which were not readily apparent.

For example, were the crimes committed by a person who acted alone? Or did the killer have an accomplice? Did the killer drive all the way up to the farm? If so, why didn't someone hear a car approach as it traveled up the gravel road? Or did the killer park down the road a bit and walk up to the Farmers' mobile home to avoid being heard?

Unless the killer had arrived on foot, which seemed unlikely considering this was a rural area, it was reasonable to presume that a second person must have been involved, if for no other reason than to drive one of the cars. After all, the Farmers' Datsun had been stolen, and it would be impossible for one person to drive two cars. Unless, of course, he towed one of them. That didn't seem likely to Detective Manning, though. For one, a car in tow would be too conspicuous and someone might pay more attention to it. For another, Manning doubted that the perpetrator of such a heinous crime would take the time to hitch up one of the cars. After carefully considering all the possibilities, Manning felt certain the murders had been committed by at least two persons.

Another thing that bothered the detective was the fact that the killer had ransacked a refrigerator-freezer and another freezer, but apparently hadn't taken any food items. Why? Manning wondered. What had the killer been searching for?

No sooner had Manning pondered the question when one of the criminalists reported finding approximately $1,500 in the freezer and another $1,000 in the refrigerator-freezer. So that had been the motive! Someone *must* have known that the Farmers kept cash in the house and they had come to steal it. But who? Manning made a note to learn the identity of the employee suspected of stealing the $800 the year before.

Manning soon learned that the employee's name was Sally Lynch and that she had worked for the Farmers, briefly performing some kind of nursing care. However, there was no real proof that she had stolen the $800 and there was nothing, at this point, to connect her with the Farmers' murders. Unless he could come up with something substantial, Manning knew he would have to tread lightly with Lynch.

The investigators didn't talk publicly about the significance of the evidence obtained during the early stages of the probe, and they made no public statements about the money they had found. Sheriff Steele would only say that investigators who combed the crime scene "came up with some things, but I can't talk about it . . . . the surprise is what makes it scary . . . you just wouldn't have sat down and speculated that that area would have been involved . . . our feeling is that it's not a random type crime." He said, however, that there were no firm suspects to focus on at that point.

"It has been a very difficult case because it isn't one that points in any direction or at anybody," said Steele. "We just have to dig in and start working." Steele added that he nor anyone else could remember when the last murder was committed in Rickreall, and said there had only been six murders in the entire county during the past five years. He said his department was usually busy investigating burglaries and thefts, but a recent outbreak of forest fires had kept them especially busy. "I wish we were back fighting fires," he said.

Shortly after the victims' bodies were brought to the state medical examiner's office in Portland, Dr. Larry Lewman carefully surveyed the corpses while circling the stainless steel autopsy tables, recording his thoughts and observations by talking into a microphone that hangs overhead. The autopsies were relatively simple: Lewman confirmed that the Farmers had each been shot once in the head, at close range.

By studying the victims' stomach contents and the breakdown of organic compounds in their bodies, Lewman fixed their time of death sometime between 7:00 p.m. Friday and 7:00 a.m. Saturday. That was, at least, consistent with Detective Manning's theory that the couple was killed sometime during the night. Manning just wished the time frame could be narrowed down further, but since it couldn't he resigned himself to live with it for the time being. There was little in the way of trace evidence from the victims' bodies or the sleeping clothes they had been wearing to aid the detective in his probe.

Meanwhile, fear and anger prompted Rickreall residents to begin asking themselves how something so dreadful, so tragic, could strike within their community. They wondered if the killer was one of their own, or if he had come from outside the community. They, like the police and the victims' relatives, wondered if the killer knew the victims or if the Farmers were merely selected at random. Unable to answer their own questions, residents began locking their doors and loading their guns. If the killer planned to strike again, the residents of this community weren't going to make it easy for him.

"I'm an orchardist and I find myself kind of looking over my shoulder," said one resident. "There are people who are now locking doors at night who have never done so before . . . (We're) angry that this kind of thing can happen in this community . . . (but) I think the tragedy has kind of brought people together." He said people were no longer leaving keys in their vehicles and were locking their cars.

"It's just not the idyllic atmosphere out here it once was," said another neighbor. "We're having an electronic intruder detection system installed in the house."

Another neighbor said he had loaded his pistol for the first time in nearly 20 years and kept it near his bed. He said he also kept his bedroom locked at night and his house locked during the day.

"You don't feel safe," he said. "You sit there and think about it at night. Am I gonna be next?"

By Monday, October 26th, the Farmers' car was still missing and investigators had no new leads.

Tuesday wasn't much different either. However, on Wednesday, significant progress was made when the Farmers' Datsun was discovered in the parking lot of a Holiday Inn in Wilsonville, located in Clackamas County just south of Portland. With the assistance of Clackamas County authorities, the car was towed to a site where it was carefully combed for clues. However, no further information was released about the vehicle.

In a display of support and respect for the victims' families, and out of deep respect for the victims, the Independence, Oregon Elks Lodge, of which the Farmers had been members, donated $1,000 to initiate a reward fund to be paid to anyone who could provide information leading to the arrest and conviction of the person responsible for the double slaying. Within days, the reward fund more than doubled to $2,050.

Meanwhile, according to Sheriff Steele, the FBI began constructing a profile in an attempt to characterize the type of person who might be responsible for such a senseless, violent crime, based on everything they believed to have occurred at the crime scene. The Polk County investigators also continued their tedious search of records in the hope they would find a suspect to focus in on.

"We're just checking out every lead that we have," said Sheriff Steele, expressing his anxiety over not having much to work with. His department kept coming up with blanks and they desperately needed a break. The break they were looking for eventually did surface, but it was not until nearly two months after the Farmers' murders. And even then it initially seemed unconnected with the Rickreall slayings.

As it turned out, police in Tualatin, Oregon, a small community just off I-15 in Washington County, was paid a visit from an angry, near-frantic woman on Wednesday, December 2, 1987. The woman, 22-year-old Darlene Davis, told police that her boyfriend, 32-year-old Michael Robert Tucker, had pointed a gun at her and her daughter. She said he had made threatening remarks to them and she was afraid of him. To the officers' astonishment, she also told them she had information about the Rickreall killings, according to Sergeant Gary Billbe of the Tualatin Police Department.

Billbe said that upon checking into Tucker's background, his office did not find any outstanding warrants against Tucker who, he said, had been working at a construction site near Woodburn. But they did learn, said Billbe, that Tucker was an ex-convict who had been paroled from the Washington State Department of Corrections on July 23, 1985. He had served two years and eight months of a five-year sentence on convictions for second-degree manslaughter and attempted burglary. According to Veltry Johnson, spokesman for the Washington State Department of Corrections, Tucker had pleaded guilty to the March 17, 1982, beating death of Jean Haggerty, 48, of Vancouver.

The police wasted no time. They cordoned off all the main routes leading away from Tucker's apartment, located in the 6600 block of Southwest Sagert Street. They made every effort to stay out of view. Plainclothes officers were strategically positioned where they could move in quickly when Tucker left his apartment.

It didn't take long. Michael Tucker soon came out of his apartment and the plainclothes officers arrested him without incident. However, they found a .22-caliber semi-automatic rifle in his belongings. He was initially accused of menacing and of being an ex-convict in possession of a firearm. He was booked into the Washington County Jail, but was later turned over to Polk County authorities.

Tucker's girlfriend, meanwhile, told Polk County authorities that Tucker was angry when he had returned home on the night of October 23rd. Darlene Davis said Tucker arrived at the apartment they shared after 11:00 p.m., and angrily said he'd "wasted" two elderly people. According to Davis, Tucker said the victims were supposed to have had thousands of dollars hidden in boxes behind a television. What had made him angry was that he'd only found $70, but he had taken numerous other items of value, she said. Davis said Tucker told her he would have taken a "nice" china cabinet if it hadn't been so large.

"I did it for us," she quoted Tucker as having said.

Tucker did not act alone, police soon learned, confirming their suspicions that an accomplice had to have been involved. Another man, Bryan Lee Mikesell, 23, was also involved. His companion was Sally Lynch, who had worked at the Farmers' home in 1986. Lynch, police were told, was the source from whom Tucker and Mikesell had learned that the Farmers' kept cash in their home. Manning instantly knew he had hit the jackpot this time.

After obtaining a search warrant, Bryan Mikesell was taken into custody in the early morning hours of Friday, December 4th. He was held at the Marion County Sheriff's Office while Polk County authorities searched his trailer home. Although investigators would not release information on what was found inside Mikesell's trailer, they did, however, formally arrest him following the search, at 5:00 a.m. Both suspects were held without bail in separate jails, Tucker in Polk County and Mikesell in Marion County.

A few days later Tucker and Mikesell were indicted by a Polk County grand jury on charges of aggra-

135

vated murder, burglary, and robbery. Polk County District Attorney Fred Avera said his office would seek the death penalty against both defendants who pleaded innocent to the charges.

In their efforts to obtain additional background information on Michael Tucker, the investigators contacted Detectives Jim Pillsbury and Randy O'Toole at the Clark County Sheriff's Department in Vancouver, Washington. Pillsbury and O'Toole were responsible for clearing the case involving the beating death of Jean Haggerty. Clark County deputy Prosecutor Curt Shelton had convinced a jury to send Tucker to prison in that state, even if it was only for a short while.

"Tucker has a history of woman beating," said Detective Pillsbury. "He's a typical assaultive person who, when drunk or drinking extensively, assaults females. You see (those types) all the time."

"Whether or not Mrs. Haggerty said something to set him off," interjected Detective O'Toole, "or he was just upset with her, or perhaps she just woke him up, the fact remains that he slugged her or hit her, knocked her down hard enough to cause an aneurysm which resulted in her death." Both detectives believed that Tucker kicked Mrs. Haggerty repeatedly after she was down and, after death, dragged her nude body from her own apartment some 60 yards to another apartment, in full view of freeway traffic.

The investigators learned that Haggerty sustained multiple injuries from the beating that resulted in her death, including bruised lips, a black eye, hemorrhaging of the chest muscle, and a cerebral hemorrhage. Because Clark County authorities had been unable to prove that Tucker intentionally caused Haggerty's death and the fact that he and Haggerty had been drinking excessively together the day Haggerty was killed, Tucker got off easy.

At his sentencing in the Haggerty case, Polk County authorities learned, Tucker blamed drugs and alcohol for his problems and claimed that a prison term would only slow his rehabilitation. What rehabilitation? they wondered.

After reviewing the Haggerty case, Polk County authorities could clearly see that Michael Tucker's propensity for violence had increased dramatically. He also appeared to be more gutsy now. Seeing that he was a liar and a manipulative person as well, and that it appeared he would likely commit future violent acts if released from prison, authorities decided to push hard for the death penalty if a jury found Tucker guilty of the Farmer murders.

After numerous delays over several months, Tucker's murder trial finally got underway in October 1988 before Polk County Circuit Judge Charles Luukinen. Much of the trial involved testimony from the deputies who had found the victims' bodies, the investigators and criminalists and the state medical examiner. But one of the most dramatic moments came when the other defendant, Bryan Mikesell, testified against Tucker.

Mikesell told the jurors that he had waited outside the victims' mobile home while Tucker went inside. He said he heard the first shot, the one that killed Barbara Farmer, then watched through a glass door as Tucker shot Robert Farmer in the head from less than two feet away.

Mikesell also testified that his companion, Sally Lynch, robbed the elderly couple of $800 when she worked for them in 1986. Mikesell also said that he and Lynch had burglarized the Farmers when they were on vacation in 1987, and that he and a friend returned later in the year to burglarize their home again.

Mikesell said he had no intention of killing the

Farmers, but said Tucker had told him he killed the couple so they wouldn't catch him stealing from them.

At one point, Tucker took the stand, however, and said that Mikesell was inside the Farmers' home at the time of the shootings. He insisted that it was Mikesell who had suggested shooting the elderly couple.

On Friday, October 21, 1988, after about one and a half hours of deliberations, the jury convicted Michael Tucker on all counts stemming from the double slaying.

During the penalty phase of his trial the following month, District Attorney Fred Avera told jurors that Tucker's "extensive" past violent behavior, as well as the murders of the Farmers, warranted the death penalty. He presented information about the Haggerty case from Washington State and said that Tucker had frequently struck other girlfriends.

"I just do things without thinking; I just react," responded Tucker. In an attempt to gain sympathy, he echoed statements heard previously at the Haggerty trial. He said he had abused drugs and alcohol since he was a youth in Los Angeles and said that he began stealing cigarettes and alcohol at age nine. He said by age 10 or 11 he began experimenting with drugs and developed an anger problem. Although he had completed seventh grade, he said he skipped school regularly. "I was partying a lot."

His statements just didn't wash with the jury, and no one on the panel appeared very sympathetic toward this repeat offender's personal problems. On Wednesday, November 10, 1988, after deliberating about three and a half hours and deciding that he posed a continuing threat to society, the jury returned a verdict that required Tucker be put to death by lethal injection.

On Tuesday, November 29, 1988, Bryan L. Mikesell pleaded guilty to aggravated murder in a plea-bargain arrangement that removed the possibility of the death penalty in his case.

"I did not feel that we could prove that he set out with the deliberate intention of causing the murders and he had absolutely no prior criminal record," said District Attorney Avera of the plea agreement. "I didn't feel a jury would ever impose a death penalty in this case."

A relative of the victims asked to read a statement to Mikesell in court before the sentence was imposed. Judge Luukinen gave his permission to do so.

"May his first thought every day for the rest of his life be that he is responsible for this tragedy. Does he have any idea of how many people he hurt and the depth of that pain? . . . What can we say to express the terror, fear and anguish we felt, the need to all sleep in the same room, not able to feel secure in our home? When will we get over our rage? . . . Bryan Mikesell destroyed the trust and security that people spent one hundred and forty years painstakingly building in this neighborhood. He has hurt our family and our community too deeply for us to ever recover."

Bryan Mikesell showed no reaction to the statement, after which Judge Luukinen sentenced him to life in prison and set a minimum of 30 years before he is to be considered eligible for parole. However, he could be released in 20 years if the state Parole Board unanimously decides to do so.

On Wednesday, February 23, 1989, 33-year-old Michael Tucker pleaded guilty in Washington County Circuit Court to being an ex-convict in possession of a firearm. The state subsequently dropped misdemeanor counts of unlawful possession of a weapon and menacing, stemming from the December 3,

1987, incident against his girlfriend, Darlene Davis, that resulted in his arrest.

"I'm convinced you should never be set free," said presiding Judge Alan C. Bonebrake. In an effort to make certain that he is never released in the event his death sentence is overturned, Bonebrake gave Tucker an additional penalty of five years. Tucker is currently awaiting his execution on Oregon's Death Row, pending automatic appeals.

EDITOR'S NOTE:

Sally Lynch and Darlene Davis are not the real names of the persons so named in the foregoing story. Fictitious names have been used because there is no reason for public interest in the identities of these persons.

" 'DEVIL CHILD' SACRIFICED HIS PARENTS TO SATAN!"

by Charles W. Sasser

Each day of a homicide detective's life, he witnesses evil. It is evil he associates, not with the supernatural, but with the human will, the human psyche, the human condition. During the late summer of 1985, however, when the winds blew Hadeshot up from Texas, Satan seemed to be alive and afoot in Oklahoma.

At 2:16 a.m. on Sunday, September 8, 1985, the telephone shrilled on the communications console at the Oklahoma City Police Station. The dispatcher answered it in time to hear a man at the other end of the line shouting at someone: "Mary, go get in the car. Just get in the car! We're leaving."

"Sir?" said the dispatcher.

"Listen, I'm at the Circle K at Council Road and 122nd. We came here to use the bathroom. And there's a man that's been stabbed. He's dead . . . Do you want me to stay here or not?"

"Yes. I want you to stay right where you are," the dispatcher instructed.

Minutes later, Patrolman Bill Walls sped onto the lighted parking lot of the convenience store to find a nervous young man and two young women waiting for him. They said that they had been partying at a nearby nightclub and were on their way home when the women had to stop to use the restroom.

At first, they said, the Circle K appeared abandoned. But then they detected the warm, fresh, coppery odor of blood. One of the women screamed.

Officer Walls quickly cordoned off the area to preserve it for a homicide team led by Detective Bill Cook and his partner Eric Mullenix. As the slogan on the wall of the homicide room at the Oklahoma City Police Station put it: *WHEN YOUR DAYS END, OUR DAY BEGINS.*

Both detectives were in the prime of their careers, Cook with nine years on the department and Mullenix with about the same. Together or individually, they had solved some of the state capital's most baffling murder mysteries.

"Looks like your everyday variety robbery-homicide," Cook recalled muttering to his partner as they initiated the crime scene probe. He would later admit that he really didn't know how wrong he could be.

The freshly-slain body of a thin, bearded man in his 30s lay crumpled on its right side at the rear of the store near the open doorway to the bathroom. He was dressed in jeans, cowboy boots, and a black short-sleeved shirt. There was so much blood, it looked as though it had been thrown at him from a bucket.

Police and the state medical examiner readily determined that the man had been shot twice, not stabbed. The bullet to his head had not been immediately fatal; it was the one to the rib cage that had killed him.

"Guess it's an understatement that somebody definitely wanted him dead," Mullenix observed.

A Circle K supervisor identified the dead man as

36-year-old night clerk Robert Bower. Apparently a drifter from Ohio, Bower had worked at the store for less than three months.

"About all we know about him," said the supervisor, "is what he put on his employment application."

A trail of blood droplets led from the floor behind the checkout counter to the short rear hallway by the bathroom where the corpse lay. Forensics experts recovered one .38-caliber bullet fragment lodged next to a *Penthouse* magazine rack at the front counter and another full .38 slug that had pierced a package of Eveready batteries.

Detective Tom Bevell, a blood spatter analyst, deduced that two shots had been fired at the clerk while he was still behind the counter. One fragment remained of the slug that tore through the victim's face; one shot had missed completely.

Terrified, the wounded clerk apparently bolted toward the restroom in an attempt to escape. The attacker pursued, overtaking him when the victim slipped and fell. A third shot ended Bower's flight and his life.

Indeed, as Detective Cook noted, the crime scene offered the appearance of a typical robbery-homicide, except that the cash register had not been touched; money remained in its trays. Surely a robber having used so much violence in order to get to the loot would not have left without it.

Could there be, detectives wondered, some other motive for the murder?

Authorities lifted Robert Bower's body onto a waiting gurney for removal at 7:30 a.m. They had sprayed, plastered, photographed, fingerprinted, and examined the Circle K and surrounding area for nearly five hours. They questioned the three witnesses who discovered the murder and canvassed the residential neighborhood for additional witnesses.

Although they tagged numerous evidence bundles containing bullets and fragments, hair tufts, clothing threads, blood samples, and other trace materials, they admitted that they had not uncovered a single clue to offer them a straight pathway toward solving the crime.

"It looks almost like a hit, a deliberate execution," officers said.

But why?

It was a question detectives continued to ask in the days that followed as they upturned every rock in the criminal underground searching for an answer. They also delved into the dead man's background on the premise that his killer might be lurking in the shadows there. Homicide detectives cannot afford to overlook any angle.

Information released to the press on Robert Bower revealed that his was a shadowy past. Acquaintances allegedly informed police that he was quick-tempered, argumentative, and occasionally violent, personality traits that intensified with his use of cocaine and LSD.

Two years before, Bower allegedly left a wife in Texas and had not returned. In Oklahoma City, he had apparently moved into an apartment with his girlfriend and another man named Claude Taylor. Taylor and Bower had argued over rent. Taylor moved out in a rage, threatening when he left that he would "get even."

A check of police records made Taylor appear even more likely as a suspect. He had been previously arrested and questioned about another Oklahoma City homicide, but he had not been charged. Acquaintances allegedly informed police that he had spoken of "needing a gun" following his eviction from Bower's apartment.

Spurred on by the prospect of a quick solution,

detectives tracked Claude Taylor to nearby Ardmore, Oklahoma. Hopes quickly faded. One officer noted with disappointment that Taylor's alibi was so tight it would have held helium.

So it was back to the beginning, sorting through the victim's past. Was his death the result of some kind of drug deal gone sour?

"He was odd-turned," a security guard who often stopped at the Circle K for coffee said of the victim. "Sometimes he stood behind the counter and just stared into space."

On September 10th, two days after Bower's untimely death, a telephone call to Crimestoppers gave the stalled investigation another boost. Two teenage boys had supposedly stopped at the Circle K at 2:06 a.m., minutes before the slaying occurred. They were armed with a .38-caliber pistol.

Detective Cook quickly obtained a search warrant and swept down upon the startled teenagers. They adamantly denied involvement in the murder. Subsequent ballistics testing eliminated the .38 revolver seized with the search warrant.

"They were looking for trouble," a detective said, "but they didn't find it that night at the Circle K."

Several other suspects emerged as the days turned into weeks, then months; but none of them panned out. The hot winds from Texas shifted around and blew ice from the north. The Oklahoma earth, already scorched by the summer, shriveled beneath winter's harsh breath.

Early in 1986, just before the first greening, an itinerant preacher erected a revival tent on a vacant lot not far from the Circle K and hung out a big sign in red lettering: SATAN IS AMONG US.

Police were still working on Robert Bower's homicide.

In early March 1986, weather forecasters called for

a warming trend. The temperature was well on its way to a high of 66 degrees on the morning of March 5th. At approximately 8:30 a.m., residents of an Oklahoma City housing addition known as Summit Place were jarred to alarm by a teenager running across the lawn shrieking, "Blood! There's blood everywhere! Call an ambulance! Quick!"

By 9:00, patrolmen, detectives, and their vehicles jammed the driveway, lawn, and adjacent street of the ranch-style house on N.W. 115th Street. Frightened neighbors stood in small groups on their porches and lawns. The word spread quickly. That nice young Bellofatto man and his wife had been shot to death in their sleep, the neighbors whispered. Their son found their bodies when he came home from spending the night with a high school buddy.

Veteran Oklahoma City Homicide Detective Ron Mitchell arrived at the murder site. He wended his way through the neatly kept house to the rear master bedroom. Out of habit, he paused at the doorway to scan the room for an overall impression. Later reports would detail how 41-year-old Lee Bellofatto and his 32-year-old wife Vonda lay face down on pillows on their blood-soaked water bed.

Police and medical investigators soon determined that Bellofatto had been shot once in the head at point-blank range. His wife had received two shots to the head. Bullets recovered from the victims and from the crime scene were reportedly of .44 magnum caliber. Clint Eastwood in the "Dirty Harry" movies had made the .44 magnum revolver famous. "The most powerful handgun ever made," Dirty Harry had noted.

Detective Mitchell and his on-scene investigators Sam Sealy, Bob Horn, and Willard Paige represented nearly a half-century of police experience. While first appearances suggested the motive for murder was apparently burglary, all four detectives said they refused to accept the burglary motive on face value. To begin with, the only thing disturbed throughout the house was a dresser drawer hanging open in the Ballofatto bedroom. Jewelry, a holstered .25-caliber automatic pistol in open view, and other similar valuables lay about in plain sight. Nothing appeared to have been stolen.

By sheer coincidence, one of the detectives happened to compare the scene to Robert Bower's murder at the Circle K six months earlier.

"We had a robbery there that wasn't a robbery," the sleuth quipped. "Now, we have a burglary that isn't a burglary."

Police gave special attention to the glass doors of the back patio. They were open several inches, suggesting the burglar may have broken into the house through that door. However, a length of broom stick used as a doorstop was positioned in the sliding track in such a manner that the door could only have been opened from the *inside.*

Police said there were no other signs of forced entry. The Bellofatto son, Sean Sellers, 15, explained that the doors were locked when he arrived home shortly after 8:00 a.m. He had had to let himself in with his keys.

"It doesn't make sense," detectives mused. "They were both shot in their sleep, but by whom? A burglar who somehow materialized through walls, shot them in their sleep for no apparent good reason, and then fled, stealing nothing?"

"Burglars just don't operate this way," said Detective Horn.

While other detectives and crime scene experts began the demanding and time-consuming task of collecting physical and trace evidence, Detective Ron Mitchell questioned Sean Sellers and Sellers' two teenage friends who had brought him home that morning. Sean was Vonda's only son and Lee's stepson. Detective Mitchell sat in his unmarked car with Sellers in front of the residence where the boy's parents lay brutally slain. The youth, dry-eyed, was a blue-eyed blond with a baby's expression molded innocently into his face.

The boy said that he had stayed the previous night in nearby Piedmont with his high school friend and his friend's teenage wife. They awoke late for school. After hurrying to get dressed, Sean remembered that he would have to obtain a note from his mother to excuse him from his first class.

"We . . . drove over to the restaurant [where his mother worked]," Sellers said. "But they said my mom wouldn't be there till nine, so we decided to come by my house . . . We pulled up. My dad's truck was here. I knew then that they'd overslept and that I was in trouble for not being there at seven-thirty.

"I used my key to get in. I walked into . . . into my folks' room . . ."

Sellers stared at the floor of the police car.

"I—I don't want to talk about it."

Sean Sellers' friends, Bobby Myers and Bobby's wife Cindy, supplied the same story. They said they drove Sean home to get a note, waiting in the car for him. That was all they knew about it until Sean burst out of the house yelling murder.

"Do you know anyone who might want to harm them?" Detective Mitchell asked all three youths.

"Yes. Carl Burton," they said almost in unison.

Carl Burton, went the explanation, was Cindy's father. When Cindy ran away from home to marry Bobby Myers, Burton came to the Bellofatto residence looking for Cindy and throwing his weight around.

Detectives easily located Carl Burton. Just as easily, they verified his alibi. He could not have been the Bellofattos' murderer.

Detective Mitchell remarked that, to him, the double slaying reeked of having a motive much closer to home than any Carl Burton or any happenchance burglar might provide. He had been particularly taken aback by the ease with which Sean Sellers spoke about his recently deceased parents. While the boy's story rang with undeniable truth, backed up by Bobby and Cindy Myers, something rang hollow in the youth's calm, almost detached manner.

The boy, police noted, had not shed a single tear.

Operating largely upon intuition, Detective Mitchell and the other sleuths launched a swift but routine probe into the private life of the victims' adolescent son Sean. It didn't stay routine long.

On the day of the Bellofatto slayings, Detective Bob Horn learned from a teacher at Sean Sellers' high school that Sean had been involved in a fist-fight the previous year over his claim that he worshipped Satan.

Just the day before, the teacher said, the principal had seized seven pages of a chilling essay from Sean's school locker. The essay found its way to police files.

"Power is life, power is joy, power is indescribable," Sellers had written. "The Dragon seemed at first to scamble my emotions until through a twist of fate everything turned clear. The love I felt for everyone around me disappeared overnight, replaced by a strong abhorition [sic]. I hated everyone and everything . . . I am free. I can kill without remorse and I feel no regret or sorrow, only love, compassion, hate, anger, pain and joy . . . I have seen and experienced horrors and joys indescribable on paper . . . The World of Darkness has touched me . . . Evil has

149

taught me good, good has shown me evil . . .

"Satanism taught me to reach down into my own heart and mind and soul, to find my true essence and let it permeate my environment . . . I became Ezurate, a Satanist . . ."

Satan? Evil? Demons? Detectives shook their heads in disbelief.

"He's a very bright young man," a drama teacher told investigators. "But I've noticed his moods changed a lot. Sometimes he has the opinion that everyone loves him. At other times, he thinks everyone hates him."

She paused, then continued, "About three months or so ago, he was terribly angry at his mother and father. He made the statement that he would be better off if his parents weren't alive."

That was far easier to understand than a bunch of garbage about Sellers having turned himself into some kind of demon named Ezurate.

"Most police are skeptics," said Detective Curt Jackson of California's Beaumont Police Department, who is a satanic crimes consultant. "But you have to understand, it doesn't matter what *you* believe, it's what *they* [satanists] believe."

The day after police questioned Sean Sellers' teachers, on March 6th Detective Mitchell summoned Bobby Myers to the Oklahoma City Police Station. He expressed his opinion that both Sellers and Myers knew more about the Bellofatto homicides than either was admitting. He permitted Myers to narrate the same story he had told the day before. Then the detectives interrupted sternly.

"Bobby, I know who killed Vonda and Lee Bellofatto," he said, "and I think you do, too."

The teenager looked startled, then uncertain.

"You know who did it, Bobby, the same as I," Detective Mitchell pressed.

150

"I'm afraid," Myers muttered. "I'm afraid of Sean. He did it. He killed them."

Mitchell's suspicions had paid off.

Police recorded Bobby Myers' statement in detail. It would later be played back for a jury. In it, Myers said that Sean barged into the Myers apartment during the night of March 5th. He was carrying a heavy black pistol wrapped in a towel.

"He told me that he'd taken off all his clothes except for his underwear, and that he'd sneaked into his parents' bedroom and shot Lee first and then shot his mom. But his mom raised up, and so he shot her again. He said that he took a shower and got dressed, then he came to my house."

Myers said he hid the murder weapon in an air conditioning vent, but later took it to his grandfather's house where he buried it at the bottom of the trash to be picked up.

That very day was trash pickup day.

Detective Mitchell and the teenager made a wild drive across the city to Myers' grandfather's house. Recovery of the .44 magnum was vital to the case. The detective arrived in time to recover the gun hidden among old egg cartons, potato peels, and other garbage. Another day and it may have been gone forever, buried beneath tons of soil at the dump.

On the way back to the police station with the recovered evidence, Mitchell took another long shot. Detectives had already remarked about the Circle K homicide and the Bellofatto murders bearing certain similarities if you looked deeper than just the surface. Both had been senseless; in each the obvious motive had not been a motive at all. Besides, officers had been picking up rumors for months that a high school student had killed Robert Bower.

Nothing ventured, nothing gained.

"I heard Sean did the Circle K killing, too," Mitchell began cautiously.

Mitchell noticed that Myers' hands started trembling. "Yeah," Myers replied at last. "I was there when it happened."

Detective Bill Cook had worked the Bower homicide down one blind alley after another.

"One break," he kept saying. "Just give me one break."

Bobby Myers provided that break. According to subsequent admissions presented in court, Myers said that Robert Bower's shady background and associations had nothing to do with his death. Bower was an innocent man caught up by chance in events controlled by—Satan?

The longer Myers talked, the more horror-tinged his story became. According to him, Sean Sellers was a practicing satanist who spoke of sacrificing someone to "see what it felt like." Sellers himself later remarked in public that "Bower didn't have any family or anything like that. He was the perfect kind of person that you would sacrifice according to the satanic bible."

After midnight on September 8, 1985, Myers and Sellers stopped at the Circle K on Council Road. Sellers had already said he was "going to kill somebody." He was armed with a .357 magnum that Myers had "borrowed" from his grandfather, a security guard.

The teenagers entered the store and talked at length with the clerk, Bower, with whom both boys were already acquainted. Myers returned to the car to wait, saying he had no idea what Sean planned. He watched through the windows as Sellers suddenly whipped out the .357 and fired twice at the astonished clerk.

The clerk ran. Sellers chased him out of sight into the back of the store. Myers heard a third shot.

Sellers came running out of the store and jumped into the car.

"He took three bullets, man. Three!" the youth exclaimed. "I can't believe I missed him on that first one. I can't believe it!"

Sellers relaxed as soon as they sped away from the crime scene. He then laughed. "We did it, man. And it feels good! Did you see the look on his face? That guy was terrified! Did you see his glasses fly off? He was dumb!"

The police would never find them, Sellers promised. Satan would take care of that.

March 6, 1986, had been a good day's work, detectives observed. Three murders solved, one of which had plagued investigators since the previous summer. But the day was not yet finished.

Detectives recovered the .357 revolver from Myers' grandfather's holster, literally while he was wearing it on duty. Ballistics testing soon corroborated everything Bobby Myers had stated—the .44 magnum was the murder weapon used to blast Lee and Vonda Bellofatto in their sleep; the .357 loaded with .38 silver tips had been the weapon used to execute Robert Bower.

Everything fell into place. Detectives Sam Sealy and Ron Mitchell confronted Sean Sellers with the evidence.

"I don't understand any of this," Sellers protested, assuming his look of baby-faced innocence. "Why am I here?"

"We've already talked to Bobby, Sean," Sealy said. "You're under arrest for the murders of your parents and Robert Bower."

After that, Sellers reportedly gave police his name and address and nothing more. Oklahoma County D.A. Robert Macy charged the 15-year-old as an adult with three counts of first-degree murder.

The young accused killer remained reticent with authorities, but his reticence dissolved with the media. The press quickly picked up on the story of the "Devil Child" who had first killed an innocent man, then murdered his parents after an apparent satanic ritual. Not shy in telling his story, Sellers appeared on *Geraldo, Oprah Winfrey,* the CBS News with Dan Rather, and in newspapers and magazines like *People.*

"KILLER SAYS SATAN MADE HIM DO IT," proclaimed national headlines.

In interviews, Sean Sellers himself outlined how his pact with the devil began with the Dungeons & Dragons (D&D) game when he was 13. While living in Greeley, Colorado, before moving back to Oklahoma, he bonded with other D&D players to hold satanic rituals in an abandoned building outside town. Police found skinned animals around the building, along with a spray-painted "666," pentagrams, and other satanic graffiti on the walls. A recovered notebook described satanic rituals: ". . . dig up graves, run naked through the streets, steal from a church . . . do dope, rape . . ."

Sellers said he sealed his pact with the devil by drinking his own blood.

"I kept a jar of my blood in the refrigerator at home, hidden behind the eggs, and I carried blood with me all the time and drank it a lot . . . I was like a vampire, I guess."

Over time, Sellers' involvement with satanism deepened and grew more complicated.

"I had rituals every night and invited the demons into my body . . . During one of the rituals, we decided to kill someone. I wasn't even Sean anymore. I was Ezurate . . ."

It was after this conversion that Sean murdered Robert Bower.

"I plunged into satanism with everything I had, 'cause that [satanism] had opened a new portal."

Near midnight of March 4, 1986, Sean Sellers told press representatives, he stripped down to black underwear and conducted a satanic ritual in his bedroom while his parents slept one doorway away.

"Something happened. The temperature in the room dropped about ten degrees. I got a shot of adrenaline and I felt my blood pressure go up. There was an erotic sensation . . . and sharp, clawed fingers touched me. I opened my eyes . . . there was this mist, and I saw demons flying."

Sellers then slipped down the hallway and shot his parents to death.

"I stood there and I looked at them. And my mother . . . there was blood running out the side of her head. I stood there, and I laughed . . .

"I loved my parents," he added somewhat incongruously.

On October 2, 1986, an Oklahoma County jury convicted Sean Sellers of first-degree murder in the deaths of his parents and Robert Bower. Sentenced to be executed, he became, at age 15, the youngest prisoner on Oklahoma's death row.

"He epitomizes," declared D.A. Robert Macy, "everything that is evil."

Sean Sellers still waits on death row in Oklahoma.

EDITOR'S NOTE:
Mary, Claude Taylor, Bobby and Cindy Myers, and Carl Burton are not the real names of the persons so named in the foregoing story. Fictitious names have been used because there is no reason for public interest in the identities of these persons.

"MY WHOLE FAMILY
IS DEAD!"

by Bill G. Cox

The telephone was ringing when Sheriff Gordon Morris entered his office in Lampasas County, Texas, on Monday morning, January 2, 1984. Mrs. Alma McGee, detention officer, was taking the call. In an emotional voice, the unidentified caller said, "They're dead, my whole family is dead!" She handed the phone to the sheriff.

"Come quickly," a man said. "This is James Haydon. I'm calling from a grocery store in Lometa. I just left my mother's house. My mother, father, and baby sister have been murdered."

"What a way to start a new year," Morris murmured, as he turned from the phone and sprang into action. He called Tim Angermann, chief criminal investigator. Together they sped to Lometa, 18 miles away from the county seat in Lampasas.

During his five years as sheriff of Lampasas County, Morris had become acquainted with the Haydon family. He knew the location of the home, a half-mile west of Lometa city limits. Morris had been a resident of the county himself for 10 years, serving as chief deputy to the former sheriff, and as justice of the peace in the county.

156

The two officers arrived at the native stone bunga-low and were met by James Haydon and three other men, whom he introduced as his friends. Sheriff Morris went directly into the house, leaving Anger-mann to question the slain family's son and the men who were with him.

Sheriff Morris entered the front door, and was im-mediately in the living room, where everything ap-peared normal, with no warning of the gruesome sight which he would soon discover.

Straight ahead of Morris was the dining room and kitchen. He went through the door and across the room. In the entryway to the kitchen, he found Edna Haydon lying on her back on the floor, her head was in a pool of blood that had flowed from several wounds to her face and head. It was apparent to the sheriff that she was already dead.

Off the dining room, the sheriff could see a hall that led to another room. Another bloody sight was the first thing he laid eyes on when he entered the adjoining room. Noah Haydon's lifeless body lay on the floor between the hall door and the master bed-room.

The dead man's head lay in a puddle of blood, and more blood had seeped from head wounds, making a grotesque circle around a spent cartridge. Sheriff Morris had yet to see the most shocking sight. Lying on the bed, close to where the man of the house had fallen, was the body of a small child. Morris would learn later that the girl was Amanda, the five-year-old daughter of the slain couple. All three of the victims were wearing their nightclothes.

Leaving the ghastly scene, the sheriff went to his patrol car and radioed for help. Texas Ranger Fred Cummings, Chief Deputy Bill Lott, and two other deputies, Ben Long and John Harris, soon re-sponded to the call. For the next several hours, the lawmen processed the scene, both inside and outside the house.

Investigating officers found splotches of blood in a dozen places in the six-room home. In one corner of the dining room there was a cabinet which looked to Sheriff Morris like a gun cabinet. However, there were no guns in it. On the floor in front of the cabinet door were several spots of blood, one of which showed a bootprint.

A diagram of the rooms was made by the sheriff, showing the position of the bodies, locations of the blood spots, and the exact position of several spent cartridges and full shells, all of them .22-caliber.

By late Monday afternoon the investigating team had recovered 107 items of evidence from the crime scene, including blood samples, a piece of rug matching the bloody footprint and other items to be submitted to the laboratory for analysis.

Deputy Lott was stationed at the residence to keep the curious and friends of the Haydons from inadvertently destroying evidence. It appeared to Sheriff Morris that the entire population of Lometa, 620 residents, had heard the tragic news and had arrived at the Haydon country home.

Morris notified Justice of the Peace Martin Adams, who had been the dead man's opponent six years ago in a bid for that post. Judge Adams responded to the call, arriving at the Haydon home. After a cursory examination, the JP set the approximate time of death about 24 hours earlier. He ordered the bodies removed to a Dallas mortuary for autopsies.

Adams pointed to the empty gun cabinet in the corner of the dining room, which he told Morris was hand-made by Noah Haydon. The judge told Morris that Haydon had reported some of his guns were stolen from the cabinet on December 22nd, while he and his wife were away from home.

"At one time, he had a right nice collection," Adams said to Sheriff Morris.

Ranger Cummings had arrived to assist Morris with the probe into the triple slayings. The Ranger was assigned to Lampasas County and also helped the adjoining counties when he was needed.

Meanwhile, Investigator Angermann had finished taking the statements given by James Haydon, 29, and the three men who were with him, tape recording each of their conversations to use for future reference. The Haydon son told Angermann that he was accompanied by the three men that morning when he came to his parent's home to pick up some personal things. He had found them and his sister dead. He said that he entered the back door of the home, and the minute he saw his father's keys on the top of the freezer, he knew that something was wrong.

He said his father always had the keys on his belt, along with a knife in a sheath, which was also gone. James described the knife and verified that some of the guns were missing from the gun cabinet, leading him to believe that theft of the guns must have been the motive for the triple murders.

The four men were warned not to leave the county. Angermann told them they might want to question them again.

The other officers had already begun their footwork, gathering information from friends and neighbors of the Haydons. They learned that 60-year-old Noah Haydon was a retired military man. He had served in the U.S. Army during World War 2 and the Korean conflict, retiring as a master sergeant. Haydon had worked at Fort Hood, located about 35 miles from Lometa, as an electronics technician, employed by a contractor. He also repaired television and electronic equipment at a workshop in one of the rooms in their three-bedroom house, the investigators were told by Lometa residents.

Noah and Edna Haydon were quiet people, not mixing much, but were well-liked by those who knew them. They had been residents of Lometa for about 20 years, and had no enemies anyone was aware of. They were considered good neighbors, always ready to help. One neighbor told Sheriff Morris that Haydon and his son helped him during an unreasonably cold spell during the Christmas holidays when everything was frozen.

"He wouldn't take any money for it, so I told Noah that he could go hunting on my place anytime he wanted to," the neighbor told the sheriff. "Haydon was an avid hunter, and owned a large collection of guns, including rifles, pistols and even a bow and arrow."

The investigation continued, with officers questioning the shocked residents of Lometa, who for the first time were sleeping behind locked doors. It was the first time a crime of this magnitude had hit their peaceful little town. The last had occurred 2½ years ago, when a fight erupted at a dance hall and one man was slain.

Until the Haydon killer was apprehended, shock and fear would stalk the small town, and wherever townspeople met, the triple-execution-style shooting was the topic of conversation, since the news had spread that the three victims were shot several times in the head.

One old timer expressed the feelings of many Lometans when he said, "This is a good, peaceful little settlement. It's appalling that something like this could happen here. I don't see how it could have happened, but it did."

Sheriff Morris and every lawman available were

working night and day on the mystery slayings. By Wednesday morning, Morris and most of his deputies had slept only three hours out of 48 since the deaths were reported.

Ranger Cummings stayed on the case, contacting most of Lometa residents, gathering information about the lifestyle of the Haydon family. One neighbor, who lived about five blocks from the slayings, told Cummings that he had heard a series of gunshots between 10:30 and 11:00 on New Year's night.

He said there were three in a row, one right after the other, then a couple of minutes passed before he heard a fourth shot. Then a few seconds after that he heard another shot.

From the information that had been gathered by questioning James Haydon about his father's gun collection, the sheriff put out a bulletin asking any person who had knowledge of the missing firearms to call his office.

Morris described the weapons as two shotguns, five rifles and a revolver. The 12-gauge shotgun was a Smith & Wesson; rifles missing included a .54-caliber single shot rifle, a Mauser 8 MM rifle, a Butler .222 Remington, a .22 Winchester, and a .31-caliber revolver; also, two hunting bows.

The sheriff assured the public that any caller would not be required to identify himself. Crimestoppers, Inc. also posted a $1,000 reward for information leading to the arrest of the perpetrator of the three slayings.

The lawmen huddled to compare notes. They were able to confirm the last time any of the Haydon family members had been seen was on Thursday, December 29th.

The report from the autopsies revealed that each of the victims had died as a result of multiple gunshot wounds to the head. Each of them had been shot four times. The 12 shots were believed to have been fired by a small caliber weapon, Sheriff Morris told the group of lawmen.

Morris had been in law enforcement in Lampasas County for 10 years, serving the past five years as sheriff. He first worked as a patrolman in Wilcox, Arizona, then went back to Texas where he worked in Highland Park until 1974, when he moved to Lampasas County and was appointed the chief deputy before being elected sheriff.

Morris theorized that since there was no sign of forced entry into the house where the murders occurred that the killer or killers had either been admitted, probably by Mrs. Haydon since she was closest to the door, or, they had used a key or that the door was unlocked, which the sheriff knew was not too unusual for the quiet town of Lometa. Morris feared that the citizens would not feel safe again until he had the killer or killers behind bars.

The Lometa School principal voiced the fears of residents when he learned of the tragedy from his school secretary. His first reaction was, "Not the little girl!"

He told officers, "After I got home in bed, I wondered if I'd locked my door. I have never lain there before wondering that. But I'll guarantee you, now I'll make sure my doors are locked."

When Amanda's kindergarten teacher was contacted about information that might possibly have been told at school by the five-year-old, she described Amanda as a model student, a bright little girl, who showed a lot of potential.

The teacher said she could tell that the parents spent a lot of time with her. Her daddy had been teaching her to use a computer. But the teacher could not remember anything the child had said which would indicate there was anyone whom the family feared.

As Justice Adams told officers, it was believed that the Haydons "had no enemies because they didn't go out enough to make any."

The sheriff continued checking all leads that came from telephone calls or from contacts made by other officers. Several leads were supplied by James Haydon, who kept coming into the sheriff's office every few days asking if any progress was being made on the case.

Morris was beginning to consider the Haydon son as a possible suspect as he followed up each lead that the man gave him.

But because the sheriff thought that Haydon might disappear if he knew of his suspicions, Morris always told him that he didn't have the slightest bit of evidence pointing to the killer of the Haydon family.

The sheriff again replayed the taped conversations with the son, which Investigator Angermann had made on the Monday of the discovery of the slayings. Then he made another visit to the Lometa crime scene.

Recalling the statement of James Haydon when he said he entered the back door and saw his father's keys on top of the refrigerator, Morris re-enacted the entrance into the back door. He walked into the kitchen from the back porch and looked toward the refrigerator.

It was impossible to see the top of the refrigerator from the kitchen door, Morris discovered. Then one of the close acquaintances of the Haydons told investigating officers that the Haydon parents and their son, James, were often at odds.

Another Lometa resident told the sheriff that, a few days after the murders, he had seen James Haydon with some guns. He was trying to sell them.

Another Lometan came into the sheriff's office and turned over a knife like the one described by Haydon as the one his father always carried on his belt. He told the officers that James Haydon had given it to him.

Meanwhile, Haydon continued to come into the sheriff's office to give bits of information which, when checked out, proved to be false. It appeared that Haydon was trying to divert the investigator's attention away from himself. Haydon brought a knife into the office and told the sheriff that he had found it at a friend's house. Haydon said it was his father's knife. He blamed the "friend" for the murder of his parents.

Then there was the matter of Haydon's past criminal record. When Morris checked into the record, he learned that James had been arrested at least five times, the first time in July, 1976. He had spent time in three jails in three different states. He had been charged with theft, burglary, possession of stolen property and rape. He had been released from a Louisiana prison in April, 1983.

Sheriff Morris called a meeting with Ranger Cummings; Inv. Angermann; and Ed Johnson, an assistant to the district attorney. They decided that the next time Haydon came into the office they would confront him with the evidence that they had and then grill him.

A second meeting was held the following day with three more officers from the district attorney's staff. They were District Attorney Arthur "Cappy" Eads, and assistants Ralph Petty and James Russell, all experts in appellate work and in drafting probable cause affidavits. Together they drew up the papers and considered that they had a case without loopholes.

But before the paperwork could be completed,

James Haydon made an appearance at the sheriff's office. The three lawmen—Morris, Angermann, and Cummings—listened to him for several minutes before saying anything. Then they informed him that they had some evidence against him, and told him that he was their prime suspect. Haydon became noticeably nervous. Sheriff Morris told Haydon what he believed had happened on the night of the murders, including the order in which he believed the three victims were killed. Haydon became even more nervous, but did not attempt to leave the office.

Halfway through the interrogation by the officers, Haydon began confessing to the crime. He agreed to give the sheriff a statement. The statement, which took over two hours, was taken down by Sheriff Morris. Haydon showed little emotion as he told his story:

"On the night of December 29, 1984, me and two friends went to a party at an apartment complex in Lampasas," James Haydon began. "At the party I drank several cans of beer and also took some speed."

The suspect said at approximately 2:30 a.m. the next day, December 30th, he and his two friends left the party. One of the friends got off at his apartment, and James asked the other friend to drive him to Lometa to his parents' home to pick up some personal items, which he consented to do.

Just before they arrived at the Haydon house, James told the friend to stay in the car. He told him if he heard any gunshots, not to pay any attention. The house had several rats in it and he might have to kill some of them, he said.

So the friend waited in the car in front of the house. It was a cold night, and he left the engine running, the heater on, and the radio playing.

James said he went to the house, and his mother

got up and let him in the front door. She began "hollering" at him because of some dogs that he had left at the house a few days ago. She said the dogs were going to have to go because they were making a mess inside the house.

Haydon said he never argued with his mother, but as they went into the dining room from the front room he was next to the gun cabinet. He said he got fed up with his mother's "bitching," opened the gun cabinet and got out a .22-caliber rifle. He knew his father always kept it loaded.

James said he pointed the gun toward his mother and started pulling the trigger. His father got out of bed, and as he was entering the hallway, James said, he stepped into the hall and shot his father several times.

Haydon said when the gun ran out of shells he got another gun out of the cabinet and shot his father again.

Amanda had awakened by then, James said. The five-year-old had been sleeping with her parents that night because it was so cold. She sat on the bed crying, he said. He said he placed the gun to her head and pulled the trigger four times.

After the shootings, he made four trips out to the car carrying guns and other household items including the knife from his father's belt and the money from his wallet.

"I asked my friend if he had heard any gunshots. He said 'No.' I told him I had to kill three big rats inside the house."

Haydon, who had given his shocking statement without showing any emotion, was placed under arrest immediately. He was kept in Lampasas County jail until he was taken before 27th District Court Judge C.W. Duncan Jr. at 4:37 p.m. on Thursday, January 5th, for arraignment on three charges of murder. The judge set his bail at $50,000 on each count, and Haydon was returned to jail.

Sheriff Morris and the other Lampasas County lawmen now got their first good night's sleep since Sunday night. Lometa residents breathed a little easier for the first time since the triple murder had been reported.

The sheriff admitted that during his 14 years in law enforcement he had never worked harder on any case. He told newsmen that he also had never had a case with such strong evidence against a suspect.

When the evidence was presented to the grand jury on January 25, 1984, the members agreed with the sheriff. They indicted James Haydon for the triple slayings.

The suspect went to trial for the murder of Noah Haydon on April 23, 1984. He was defended by three court-appointed attorneys, with Judge Duncan presiding. Haydon entered a plea of not guilty at a pre-trial hearing when the judge granted a change of venue.

During the first day of the trial, Judge Duncan delayed a ruling on a motion by the defense to suppress the statement made by Haydon on January 5th, the day of his arrest.

In the opening statements to the jury, District Attorney Eads told them, "Convicting someone of murder in the State of Texas does not mean you have to prove a motive. If you had to prove a motive, you would have to show why someone could do it, and we could not do that."

First witnesses called by the state included Sheriff Morris, Detection Officer McGee and Justice Adams. Mrs. McGee was asked to tell about the initial call she took from the defendant on January 2nd. Morris told the court of the crime scene, and the position of the bodies. He said he found 13 cartridges

167

of .22-caliber near the bodies of the slain Haydon family members. He testified that each of the victims had been shot in the head repeatedly with a .22-caliber rifle.

Also testifying for the state was the man who took the defendant to his parents' home on December 30th. He told the court that when he went with Haydon on the day the slayings were discovered, and after the call was made to the sheriff's office, that Haydon told him not to "say anything about the guns that he had taken from the home on December 30th."

The witness told the jury that he had known Haydon for only a month when they went to the same party on December 29th, where they smoked dope and drank. He testified that Haydon had not been drinking alcohol or smoking marijuana to the extent that he was "out of control" on that night.

The witness told the court that he took the defendant to his parents' home to sell a dog, but when he came out of the house he had an armload of guns but no dog. He said Haydon came out of the house carrying two .22 rifles and some other guns, some clothes on a hanger, a compound bow, a brown suitcase and a pair of boots. Later, Haydon gave him the boots, saying, "Here's a Christmas present for you."

In further testimony, the friend said that after they left the Haydon residence the defendant took him to work and kept his car so he could get an inspection sticker on it. When Haydon picked him up that afternoon, he said, the guns were gone.

Only nine of the 36 witnesses the state expected to call had been heard when in a surprise move, the defendant asked to plead guilty to the charges that he murdered his parents and sister.

Judge Duncan heard the guilty plea during a recess on Tuesday, in the second afternoon of the trial.

The judge sentenced the 29-year-old unemployed truck driver, James William Haydon, to three concurrent life prison terms. Haydon waived the right to appeal the sentence.

Judge Duncan ruled that because a deadly weapon was used during the offense, Haydon would have to serve a minimum of 20 years before being eligible for parole, even with good behavior.

Sheriff Morris took Haydon to Lampasas County jail and transferred him to Texas Department of Corrections the next day to begin serving his sentence.

When the trial had ended, Sheriff Morris was highly praised by District Attorney Eads. "I can't say enough good things about the Lampasas County Sheriff's Department and Texas Ranger Cummings," Eads said. "Without Morris' help, the district attorney's office would not have been able to prosecute this case."

"MICHIGAN'S MYSTERY OF THE 'GRADUATE FAMILY' SLAUGHTER"

by Christos Ziros

No one answered the ringing telephone in the Berkleys' apartment. No one could. They were all dead—savagely murdered. David was dead, lying outside in a nearby alley. Aline and Baby Jessica were dead, lying inside on a bloody bed. And the phone kept ringing and ringing and ringing.

It was some minutes past 11:00 p.m. on Saturday, December 18, 1982, in a section of the Cass Corridor area on the southern edge of Wayne State University in Detroit, Michigan. Christmas was only a few days away for most of the populace, but not for the three members of the Berkley family.

Earlier that day, however, Christmas had been on the 26-year-old David Berkley's mind when he'd phoned his parents in Maryland to settle final holiday plans. They were out, so he left a message with his sister that he would call again later. But he never did.

David had previously explained to his dad that he and Aline, his 25-year-old wife, wished to spend this particular Christmas with their infant daughter, 9-month-old Jessica, by themselves in their own dwelling. This was going to be their first Christmas as a new family. They wanted it to be special, a private observance.

Of course, David hadn't meant that they had no plans to see the rest of the family. The young couple definitely intended to travel with the baby after their private Yuletide celebration—first to visit David's parents in Bethesda, Maryland, and then Aline's, in Malibu, California. Their desire to get together with everyone for the holiday season was never in doubt.

During the call, David informed his sister that he had to tend to his research project for a while that evening. As a doctoral candidate in physical anthropology and a graduate assistant researcher at nearby Wayne State, he was keeping close tabs on an experiment involving animal corneas. He planned to be at the medical center laboratory between 8:00 and 11:00 p.m. The lab was just a few blocks away from the renovated West Hancock Street building in which the Berkleys rented a third-floor, two bedroom apartment.

As any loving husband and father would have, David in all likelihood gave Aline and Baby Jessica a quick "see-you-later" hug-and-kiss before jogging off to the lab. Assuming he did so, it was the last warm family moment they would ever share alive.

While David made the short trek to the lab, Aline had her own "project" to tend to—the traditional task of decorating the Christmas tree. The young wife—who was in her own right an honors student in third-year law at the University of Detroit—began preparing a batch of popcorn. When it was all ready, she started to string it. Perhaps as she did so, she may have been anticipating a cozy, old-fashioned Yuletide celebration, just days away, to be enjoyed quietly with her devoted husband and pretty little daughter.

The first deadly link in the tragic chain of events

171

was apparently forged within that 8:00-to-11:00 p.m. time frame while David was on his way back home from the medical center lab. Just a couple of blocks southeast of West Hancock, near a vacant house on the northern sidewalk of East Forest, three shadowy figures appeared out of the semi-darkness and approached him.

Suddenly, they were upon him. David tried to fend them off, but they overpowered him and forced him into the alley next to the empty building. He struggled valiantly against the knife-wielding assailants — to no avail. The odds were too heavily stacked against him. The vicious felons slashed and stabbed him again and again, until David crumpled to the cold ground in a bloody, lifeless heap.

A short time later, in the Berkley flat, Aline must have heard the sound of the door being unlocked. It may be impossible to report her exact thoughts, but it is reasonable to guess that she felt no alarm, expecting David to come in. After all, besides herself, he was the only other person in possession of a key, wasn't he? Who knows, then, what horror must have seized her when she saw three strangers burst into the apartment.

The savage trio showed no mercy. Even as Aline begged them to spare little Jessica, they snuffed out the lives of both mother and infant daughter. As David had done, Aline tried desperately to ward off the repeated knife thrusts, until she finally succumbed to the savage onslaught. As for Baby Jessica, they not only stabbed the helpless innocent, but smothered her, as well, right in her crib.

Even before finishing their grisly handiwork, the coldhearted killers began attending to another evil purpose. They found what they were after and, with the victims dead, the brutal threesome left the scene of their carnage.

It was after 11:00 p.m. that the telephone started ringing in the Berkley dwelling. David's father was trying to call. He'd gotten the message that David would be home from the lab by then, and he wanted to confirm the plans for the family get-together.

Each time the senior Berkley dialed, he could hear the indication that the phone on the other end was ringing, but no one was picking up to answer. The parent's concern increased with every unsuccessful attempt. He kept trying periodically on Sunday, but it was the same story—no answer.

Meanwhile, on that Sunday, December 19th, the gore-covered corpse of a slightly stocky white male was discovered in the alley next to an abandoned house on East Forest. Detroit Police Department homicide investigators who processed the slaying scene noted that the bespectacled victim wore an expensive down-filled jacket, blue jeans, two pairs of sweat socks, and walking boots with red and black laces. Whoever killed the young man had left no identification whatsoever on the body.

The only item on the victim that offered a remote hope of establishing his identity was the blood-drenched black T-shirt he was wearing. On that shirt, in red letters, were the words "Jessica's Daddy."

While the detectives of the homicide section's Squad Seven were expanding their investigation into the East Forest murder mystery, David's father was still trying to call, unaware that his efforts were in vain. He continued making intermittent attempts through Sunday and again on Monday, December 20th.

By Monday evening, the elder Berkley felt frantic with worry and decided that some kind of action must be taken. Obtaining the telephone number of the Detroit Police Department, he called with an urgent request that officers be sent to check his son's apartment at the West Hancock address. He explained that he had been unable to reach David and Aline since Saturday night.

The worried parent was disappointed to hear the desk officer say that the request might not be acted upon until some hours later. She did assure him that a patrolcar would be dispatched to the young Berkley's dwelling as soon as possible.

Of course, the desk officer was in no way being uncaring toward the distressed father. She was doing her job in a professional manner, following established procedures. The fact is, on any given day, the police receive any number of calls on matters ranging from deadly serious to incredibly frivolous, and priorities of response must be set. Assaults or robberies in progress demand immediate action. Missing-person cases require certain routine measures. Flying-saucer reports call for a grain of salt. And, at any given moment, a very limited number of patrolcars may be available to cope with an overwhelming number of calls.

On the other hand, it is perfectly understandable that the desk officer's statement did not sit well with David's dad. After all, routine procedure is the last thing any worried parent wants to hear about. Fears concerning a family member's safety bypass the logical mind and stir up the emotional human heart — and this father's fears had probably reached fever-pitch.

In considering what else he could do, the senior Berkley located the phone number of Sam Remsen, a friendly neighbor of David's in that same building in Detroit. It was late Monday when the anxious father called Remsen and asked him if he wouldn't mind checking David's apartment.

Remsen, who had a great deal of affection for the young Berkleys, was more than willing to help. He sought out the building manager, related the concern that David's dad had expressed over the phone, and the two men proceeded to the Berkleys' third-floor unit with the manager's passkey.

When the two men entered the unpretentiously furnished, once well-kept dwelling, they abruptly found themselves in the midst of a charnel-house scene. Words have no power to convey the shock that came over them as they saw the bloody corpses of Aline Berkley and Baby Jessica lying on the crimson-stained bedsheets.

It was 12:15 a.m. — ending Monday and beginning Tuesday, December 21st — when the gruesome discovery in the Berkley apartment was made. Regaining enough composure to act, Remsen and the building manager telephoned the office of the Wayne State University Public Safety Department, located only a couple of doors away from the homicide-scene building. The university police, in turn, called the Detroit Police 13th Precinct, less than a block away, on the corner of Woodward and Hancock.

Once again, Squad Seven sleuths had a mysterious homicide on their hands. Among the detectives assigned to respond to the call were Inspector Gilbert R. Hill and Sergeants Roy Awe and Chalmers Sanders. The probers made an initial survey of the Berkley dwelling and immediately determined that it had been ransacked. Having been informed that the Berkley family consisted of three members, and that only two were accounted for, the investigators had to wonder about the absence of that one particular member. That the husband and father of the slain woman and little girl was nowhere to be found could have paramount importance.

The investigative team set up shop to perform their grim duties. The bodies of the savagely murdered mother and infant daughter had to be photographed as they were found, lying on the blood-soaked bedsheets with several stuffed animals placed around them on the bed. A search for fingerprints and other physical clues had to be instituted. And the building residents had to be interviewed with an aim toward turning up possible witnesses.

Contrary to some popular misconceptions, a witness is not necessarily someone who has seen the actual crime being committed before his or her very own eyes. In a case like the Berkley family homicide, in which an on-the-spot eyewitness is unlikely, probers must hope to find what might be called secondary witnesses. These would be persons who might be able to provide information about the circumstances of the crime or about the characters and motivations of victims or perpetrators, or both.

What the Squad Seven detectives were looking for, then, was a witness who might have seen someone leaving the crime scene, or heard suspicious noises at the time that the murders were committed, or knew of persons who had expressed a wish to hurt the Berkleys for some reason or other. To find such witnesses, the sleuths would have to question building residents, before expanding the investigation into the streets.

Among the building residents, of course, were Sam Remsen and the manager. Remsen was able to fill in the investigators about the circumstances of the unanswered phone calls and the fears expressed by David Berkley's father. After doing so, Remsen excused himself for a brief while to telephone the senior Berkley and pass on the tragic news about Aline and the baby.

Apart from describing the shocking discovery of the bodies, all the building manager could tell probers was about the Berkleys as tenants. He said that the small family had just rented their two-bedroom unit in June of 1982, little more than six months earlier. He characterized them as "nice, quiet people" and added, "We had a tenants' picnic around that time and they got along with everyone real well."

As the homicide detectives interviewed various tenants who'd had some contact with the Berkleys, they were able to develop a description of the missing David. In a matter of hours, what would prove to be of vital important was information on the clothes he had been wearing when he was last seen in the building.

In the meantime, Mr. Berkley senior, still reeling from the shock of learning that his daughter-in-law and grandchild had been viciously murdered, called back Remsen to find out if David had been located yet. A police sergeant who was in Remsen's apartment conducting some follow-up questioning answered the phone. The officer reaffirmed the report of the murders of Aline and Baby Jessica and of the apparent disappearance of David. Then he started to ask Mr. Berkley some questions about his son.

Quite naturally, the parent was upset by the timing of these questions. To be sure, the officer was only following good investigative procedure, and the distraught father soon came to understand that a detailed description of David was needed if police were to find him.

Subsequently, Homicide Sergeant Sanders would point out to the press that probers needed all the data they could get on David, "because this was a brutal set of murders and daddy was missing, so we had to consider him a suspect."

David Berkley would not be considered a suspect in the slaying of his wife and daughter for long, however, thanks to Sergeant Sanders' own alertness. As the detective reviewed building residents' descriptions of the clothing the missing young husband had

177

been wearing when last seen, a bell rang in his mind. He remembered the unidentified body found on Sunday in the East Forest alley—the body now lying unclaimed in the Wayne County Morgue. In particular, he recalled the blood-soaked T-shirt with the red letters that spelled out "Jessica's Daddy." And, during the scene search, he noticed some family photographs on a mantel in the Berkley apartment. These pictures had been of a young couple and a baby girl.

That was it. The mystery of David Berkley's whereabouts was solved. The search for him could be called off. He had been the first to die, apparently, and his remains were already in the hands of the authorities on a slab at the morgue. And now, the enormity of the crime the Squad Seven detectives were investigating hit home hard. It was a whole family that had been wantonly slaughtered!

With this latest information in their possession, the sleuths were in a position to do some tentative theorizing about both the motive for the heinous crime and the sequence of the deadly events.

According to the probers' theory, David was probably a randomly chosen street-robbery target. When his assailants killed him in the alley, they must have found his keys and identification bearing his address. Here, then, was a perfect opportunity to score in the victim's home! They had the keys—it would be no problem to gain access. That was why no signs of forced entry had been found. The killers just strode in as if they owned the place, slew Aline and Baby Jessica, and then proceeded to carry off whatever valuable they could lay their hands on.

Of course, the possibility that the victims and killers knew each other could not—indeed, would not—be totally rejected. After all, the sheer savagery of the slayings did suggest a deep-seated hatred of the victims. Therefore, it was still necessary to keep looking for witnesses who might be able to establish a personal link between the Berkleys and their murderers, however unlikely it might seem.

At length, the wee hours of Tuesday yielded to the daylight, and police were prepared to make preliminary statements to the press. In charge of coordinating the homicide probe, Squad Seven's Sergeant Awe told reporters, "At this time, robbery appears to have been the motive. But we don't have all the answers yet."

After newspeople received a briefing of — as police put it — the "incredible viciousness" of the slayings, Inspector Hill urged possible witnesses with any knowledge about the monstrous crime to get in touch with the homicide section. "Whoever did this likes to kill people," he declared grimly. "This is a case of massive overkill."

Although the lawmen made a general statement about the things that were missing from the Berkley apartment, noting that the killers carried out some "bulky objects," they withheld specific details. The probers hoped that the stolen items might eventually be recovered and then be used to trace the murderers. Similarly, the sleuths held back certain particulars about the bodies and the two crime scenes — information that only the perpetrators of the hideous deeds could know.

The next order of business for the homicide probers was old-fashioned leg-work. Having interviewed the building tenants, they spread out to canvass the neighborhood for possible witnesses among the local residents, store-owners, passersby and street people. They also sought out friends and acquaintances of the victims, including classmates, colleagues, and teachers at both Wayne State University and the University of Detroit.

At WSU, David Berkley's peers and professors had

only the highest praise for the slain Ph.D. candidate. "He was quiet, congenial, serious, devoted to his work, but pleasant to be around," the anatomy department chairman said. "He was the kind of person you'd anticipate would make substantial contributions to science, in research and teaching."

Aline Berkley was spoken of with similar high praise at U-D. She ranked in the top 10 percent of her class and served on the *University of Detroit Law Review* in the prestigious position of editor of the "Case and Comment" column. "She was very intelligent, toward the top of her class, and yet she was not sure she could fit into what she considered the typical lawyer community," one of Aline's fellow students remarked. "She wasn't interested in the money chase, just how she could help people."

As the Squad Seven detectives delved into the background of the victims, what they learned drove home the feeling that the slayings of Aline and David Berkley were grievous losses not only for their respective families, but also for the community at large. It seemed to the investigators that the lives of the young couple had been cut short just as they were on the brink of bestowing upon society the rich gifts they had been developing in their education. And the probers could not forget Baby Jessica, who never had a chance to taste life.

Both Aline and David came from well-to-do, socially and professionally distinguished parentage. Yet, unlike some well-born young persons who may turn up their noses in disdain at the rest of the "low-born" world, neither of the young couple had ever displayed selfish, stuck-up or superficial character. Indeed, all who knew the pair offered one consistent description time and time again—Aline and David were loving, caring people who, through their chosen professions, sought to help others.

Making contact with the parents of each victim, the investigators learned that Aline Elizabeth Berkley was the daughter of an Emmy-winning television producer-director-writer and his wife. Aline's father, who has enjoyed great stature in the TV industry since its pioneering days, was involved in some of the early, high-quality drama shows, such as *Playhouse 90, Studio One* and the *U.S. Steel Hour,* as well as popular series such as *Dr. Kildare* and *The Man From U.N.C.L.E.* So it was that Aline grew up in an exciting, affluent milieu—the New York and Hollywood television circles. But she seemed unaffected by the wealth and status that surrounded her in these realms.

Even as a child, she was thoughtful and sensitive, according to a statement given by her mother. "You might say Aline was a loner. She was finely tuned to other people's feelings and always serious about the world around her," the pretty victim's mom said. "While she was in college, she tutored underprivileged children. Her perspective was always wider than that of most of her friends."

David Saul Berkley was likewise born into an affluent sphere as the son of a prominent Washington, D.C. lawyer and his teacher wife. The elder Berkley served as an assistant U.S. Attorney. He then went on to become a judge and deputy chairman of appeals in the Social Security Administration.

During David's high-school days, the young man's interests came to the fore when he obtained student-work assignments in Bethesda area medical labs. "He did some high-school-level medical research," the proud father said of the slain youth, "and assisted doctors at the National Institutes of Health."

It was in 1974 that the two young undergraduates, Aline and David, first met at Iowa's Grinnell College. They got to know each other, fell in love, and decided to wed. They carried out their plans in California, where they were married in a Unitarian ceremony. After a year's sabbatical from their courses, they transferred to the University of California at Santa Cruz. Upon completion of their undergrad work in 1980, David won a teaching fellowship at Michigan's Wayne State, while Aline was accepted at the University of Detroit's law school.

The young marrieds set out for Michigan in a dilapidated old Volkswagen that gave up the ghost when they reached Nevada. That didn't faze Aline and David in the least—they just sold it for parts and used the proceeds for bus fare to their destination. In Detroit, they lived in college-owned lodgings until Baby Jessica came along to turn the duo into a trio. In need of more dwelling space now, they settled into the West Hancock Street apartment. And there, as they continued their studies and began to enjoy life as a brand-new family, they were murdered.

On the one hand, investigators and residents alike were caught somewhat off-guard by this shocking family slaughter. One reason for this sense of surprise was the large police presence in the locality of the crime scene. Across the street from the victims' building is the Detroit Police 13th Precinct stationhouse, and the vicinity is almost always saturated with police vehicles. A couple of doors over is the headquarters of the WSU security police force. Not much farther away is the Metropolitan Police Academy. Thus, the immediate neighborhood, by its very makeup, tends to discourage street crimes.

On the other hand, however, it must be considered that West Hancock intersects Detroit's Cass Corridor, an area where saints and sinners cross paths on a daily basis. Here, honest, respectable folk find themselves in an urban stew with dishonest, unsavory characters. Rehabilitated houses maintained by decent citizens stand alongside deteriorating structures that shelter the dregs of society. Much has been accomplished in efforts to drive away the hookers, muggers and dope dealers. "But this neighborhood still contains a mixture of good and bad, poverty and affluence, hope and despair," Police Sergeant Kenneth Montgomery pointed out at the time of the Berkley murders.

Still, the victims' street did represent an island of stability in the area. In the final analysis, therefore, it seemed inconceivable to many observers that such a savage crime could be committed there. It made no sense.

Even as detectives continued wearing out shoe leather and quizzing possible witnesses, two grief-stricken fathers, one from California and the other from Maryland, traveled to Michigan. It was now Wednesday, December 22nd, and the heart-rending task of identifying the bodies of their slain children and granddaughter awaited them in Detroit.

That morning, Sergeant Awe met with the two men in a hotel room. The investigator was aware that one of the fathers had experienced some disturbing moments in dealing with the police procedures. He told the grieving parent, "I would like at this time to apologize for anything the police have done or will do in the future."

David's father was deeply touched by the sergeant's caring attitude. "At that moment," he would later tell press representatives, "I became appreciative of the police." He said of the sergeant, "He showed amazing sensitivity."

Sergeant Awe, Inspector Hill, Sergeant Sanders and all their colleagues who worked the case would continue to display that sensitivity throughout the entire investigation, earning the warmest praise from the victims' parents. A long time later, Mr. Berkley would remark, "I felt I had stepped into an episode of *Hill Street Blues*. The people in Squad Seven were so personally concerned. They told me they see so many murders that they have to harden themselves, but they couldn't harden themselves against a nice family and a little baby. I met Inspector Gilbert Hill, who said one way or another they were going to get these people. It was such a horrible crime."

How horrible it was became more known when the detectives received the autopsy report. David Berkley had suffered at least 36 stab wounds. Many of these were to his arms, indicating how fiercely he had tried to battle his assailants. The rest were to his upper body. His wife Aline had been stabbed 24 times. The lab tests also raised the possibility that she was raped. The infant Jessica had been stabbed three times and had also been suffocated.

Later that Wednesday, with the heart-breaking duty of identifying the bodies completed, the two fathers returned from the Wayne County Morgue with the detectives to police headquarters. They talked extensively about their children and grandchild, hoping to contribute something that would turn out to be useful to the investigators trying to solve the case.

"And maybe," Aline's dad told reporters, "it will help others to recognize people who are sick — like those who did this — and get some help for them before they turn to violence." Having also expressed an opposition to capital punishment, he added, "I feel no malice for those who did this to David, Aline and Jessica."

David's father offered another viewpoint. "The people who did this to them are animals and should be treated as such," he stated sternly. "I'm a firm believer in capital punishment and this would be a good case for it."

On one idea, however, the two parents agreed without reservation. The killers had to be found as soon as possible and had to be removed from society before they could kill again.

While the grieving fathers considered burial plans for their loved ones, detectives kept digging hard to find a lead to the killers. A possible break came when police at the 13th Precinct received an intriguing letter in an envelope bearing a December 20th postmark—that was the day after David's body had been found in the alley. The anonymous letter named three men and implied that they had something to do with the Berkley murders.

The investigators lost no time—they got in touch with the family of one of these possible suspects, and his mother brought the 19-year-old subject to the precinct house on Tuesday evening, December 28th. The other two men named in the letter were also rounded up and brought in for interrogation.

As it turned out, the 19-year-old had been implicated in the July, 1980 rape of a prostitute in the immediate area of the Berkley family slaughter. He had also recently been charged in an incident on December 8th of the current year, during which he'd flashed a knife at another hooker and then assaulted the officers who'd arrived on the scene to arrest him.

A careful investigation eliminated the other two men as possible suspects in the Berkley case and they were released. The 19-year-old was eliminated, too, but the authorities continued to hold him on the charge of assaulting the patrolmen.

"All three people named in the anonymous letter have now been cleared of implication in the killings," Sergeant Awe told the press. "But we have developed some new information and leads that we feel pretty strongly about at this point. We feel strongly enough

185

that we don't want to say any more about it right now."

On the following day, Aline's father posted a $5,000 reward for any information that would lead police to the slayers of his daughter, son-in-law and grandchild. The reward was offered through the *Detroit News* "Secret Witness" program. By January 1st—it was now 1983—the newspaper added another $2,500 to the reward fund, bringing up the total to $7,500.

On January 2nd, a brief memorial service for Aline, David and Baby Jessica was held at Detroit's First Unitarian Univeralist Church. The hour-long rites were kept simple. Three framed photographs of the family were placed on the altar next to a vase of white flowers, between two white candles. In special remembrance of the slain infant girl, Brahms' "Lullaby" was played on the organ.

In eulogizing the victims, the reverend declared, "There is a shame, the shame that anybody in whose veins courses the same blood as you or I, could stoop to that depravity . . . killing the hopes vested in two generations." He spoke of the accompanying despair and the fear that such a tragedy can happen again, but he urged that these negative feelings be replaced by "hope, forgiveness and renewal."

The Squad Seven sleuths continued to run down leads but found themselves no closer to any solid suspects. They acknowledged that they could sure use a major break in the case. "We're getting lots of tips and a lot of help from the community," Inspector Hill pointed out, "but we still need that critical piece of information."

Among the items stolen from the Berkley flat were a calculator, television and stereo equipment, watches and jewelry. The inspector avoided giving out a more detailed description of these, but he reaffirmed the probers' hopes that the items would be found and used to trace the killers. As yet, none of the articles had turned up.

Sergeant Awe, who remained in charge of the investigation for its first year, latched on to an unusual lead that suggested a kind of witchcraft aspect to the slayings. Following up on a claim that the Berkleys were a blood sacrifice made during a sacred date in the Druid religion, he spent a whole day with a University of Michigan professor learning about the sect.

The sergeant learned that Druidism dates back to pre-Christian, pre-Roman Britain. It was based upon beliefs in ancient Celtic gods, steeped in gloomy superstition, and marked by both animal and human sacrifices. Fascinating as this research was, however, the sleuth found no real evidence that modern-day Druids had anything to do with the Berkley murders. What this experience did emphasize was the necessity of tracking down every single lead no matter how improbable it might seem, if only to eliminate it.

Interestingly, it was not the supernatural, but a fear of it, that would play a small role in the case later. In fact, it would cause an irritating complication, but only for a little while.

Several months into the investigation, another development brought the first glimmer of real hope for a solution. It came after a young woman visited her brother, Buck Baldwin, in prison. Baldwin was serving a mandatory life-without-parole term for an unrelated slaying of a man in Dearborn, Michigan, in 1981. Baldwin's sister passed some intriguing information to him — something she discovered the last time she saw her boyfriend.

What his sister told him was positively inspiring to Baldwin. The convict quickly saw certain possibilities to improve his lot in life. Here was an opportunity to make a deal with the authorities to ease the hard time he was doing.

Baldwin sat right down and wrote a letter to the Wayne County Prosecutor's Office, putting forth a claim that he just might be able to help solve the Berkley family murder case. Here he was, after all, appealing his conviction and seeking a new trial. If he gave the cops some help, maybe he could get some consideration, in turn.

It was somewhat tantalizing bait for the prosecutor's office, and the authorities circled it for a bit, but refrained from taking a bite. They sent Sergeant Awe to have a chat with Baldwin. The detective found that the convict's story contained just enough information not known by the general public to merit attention. But Baldwin was holding something back — just enough to maintain what he felt was his bargaining power.

The choice for the prosecutor's office was to give up a murder conviction in one case in order to obtain uncertain information about another case. Nope, that was too much to ask for, as far as the authorities were concerned. They had this joker where they felt he belonged. No deal. But even though things seemed to be at a standstill, they told Baldwin they'd keep in touch. So the negotiations continued on and off.

Meanwhile, the probers of Squad Seven weren't sitting around swatting flies and waiting for Baldwin to come across. The investigation proceeded as though the convict's info didn't exist. They dug up whatever other leads they could, checked them out, and went on from there. And now Lieutenant Donald Parshall headed the probe, after Sergeant Awe suffered a knee injury at the end of the first year.

Lieutenant Parshall encountered his share of leads

that panned out only fool's gold. One wild-goose chase that stands out in his mind was a five-day trip out of state to Wisconsin. He and Sergeant Danny Knepp were following a lead that had come from an inmate serving time in a Milwaukee prison. The only satisfaction the sleuths got out of it was that they had eliminated another worthless tip. Someone had to do it.

For two and a half years, Lieutenant Parshall, Sergeant Awe, Inspector Hill, Sergeant Sanders and the rest of the Squad Seven investigators dug hard, eliminated more false leads, questioned and re-questioned witnesses, and handled whatever other cases were assigned to them. If they felt discouraged at times, they refused to let it sour them. The Berkley case was special—they were determined that it would never end up in the unsolved files.

"It's one of the most hideous crimes to kill a defenseless baby. It even shocked the people in homicide," Lieutenant Parshall would later remark. "It was just something everybody in the squad wanted to get the answer to."

It was at the end of those two and a half years that the sleuths of Squad Seven got their wish. They got the break that turned the probe into a "whole 'nuther ball game."

August, 1985, was the turning point. By then, the imprisoned Buck Baldwin realized that playing hard-to-get had gained him zilch. The deal he'd sought from the Wayne County Prosecutor's Office was not forthcoming. Meanwhile, his lawyer had been urging him to cooperate without asking for special favors. So Baldwin sent word to the officials that he'd had a change of heart. He would pass on to them the information his sister had given him about the Berkley case. Doing the right thing was more important than any deal.

His sister's boyfriend was the key Baldwin revealed. The boyfriend had told her about having been involved in some killings in late December, 1982. He and two other men had committed the crime to get money for drugs. Baldwin had never learned the identities of those other two men, but he could certainly name his sister's boyfriend. The man's name was Timothy Smith.

As things turned out, Baldwin did win a new trial on his appeal. He was convicted on a lesser charge, this time, which led to a reduced sentence of 10 to 30 years, rather than the original term of life without parole. But he still had something to be afraid about.

"Buck has done one act as a good citizen," his lawyer declared, "and now he stands in a position to die for it." The attorney was referring to the low regard convicts have for snitches and the possibility that Baldwin could be snuffed for giving police the info on the Berkley killers.

"He gave us a tremendous piece in our puzzle," Inspector Hill acknowledged. The inspector's only regret was that the process had dragged on so long, in view of how hard the Squad Seven detectives had worked on the case. But, with a solid lead in hand, he stressed, the probe would continue, full steam ahead. He added, "We haven't stopped working on this one since it went down and we won't until we get all the people responsible. We want to get all of them. This crime is one that just assaults our senses."

The detectives picked up 33-year-old Timothy Smith in late October but kept his arrest quiet. He was quick to see the handwriting on the wall and demonstrated a willingness to cooperate with police. According to Sergeant Sanders, a deal was made — Smith would be given immunity from prosecution for naming his two cohorts and testifying against them.

It was a sweet deal, but police quashed it when they found out that Smith lied in naming one of the other killers. Smith's excuse was that they were brothers, and he didn't want to see them both go to jail—especially since he was afraid of one of their female relatives who had powers of "voodoo magic . . . some kind of witchcraft!"

Smith's professed fear of supernatural forces sidetracked the probe for two weeks. It got on track again when Smith gave the correct name of the third suspect. And now, police were able to go after Smith's two partners in the Berkley murders—35-year-old Randy Talley and 31-year-old Jack Shepherd, who were half-brothers. Both these men, probers discovered, were also relatives of Buck Baldwin, who was shocked to learn that he had helped to finger his own kin.

On Friday, November 8th, police made Smith's arrest public and listed the charges against him as three counts of first-degree murder and two counts of armed robbery. But, with the breakdown of their original deal with Smith, they ran into a snag when they tried to bring charges against Shepherd and Talley. They would need corroborative evidence, independent of Smith's statement, to use in court against the half-brothers.

It was touch-and-go for the investigators until after the New Year rolled in. Then, on Tuesday, January 21, 1986, Smith and the prosecutor's office representatives came to terms. Smith's trial was about to begin, and he was aware that a conviction would net him some very hard time. At the last minute, he plea-bargained his way into a set of reduced charges—two counts of second-degree murder and armed robbery. In return, he would testify against

Shepherd and Talley. The recommended sentence would be 25 to 40 years, and he would serve it in a federal prison, because a sojourn in the state prison might prove unhealthy for a snitch — if not fatal.

During his sentencing, Smith heard Recorder's Judge Prentis Edwards deplore the fact that, "The punishment does not fairly reflect the crime." But the prosecutor's office conceded that the case against Shepherd and Talley hinged almost completely on Smith's testimony.

Within the next two days, Shepherd and Talley found themselves in custody. Some weeks later, on Tuesday, February 11th, the two men were brought before Detroit 36th District Judge Longworth Quinn Jr., who ordered that they stand trial for the Berkley family murders. The pair's trial was slated for May.

On Monday, May 5th, in Detroit Recorder's Court, jury selection was completed. It was to be a joint trial, but with two juries seated — one for Shepherd, one for Talley. Each of the half-brothers was charged with first-degree murder and armed robbery.

The next day, as Assistant Wayne County Prosecutor Joseph Koch made his opening statement to the juries, he did not hesitate in describing Smith, the state's star witness, as "a disgusting and revolting human being." He emphasized, however, that Smith was the key that would clinch the case against the two defendants.

In their turn, Defense Attorneys Jay Nolan and Robert Ziolkowski immediately tried to discredit Smith by characterizing him as an admitted killer and liar — someone who was ready to do anything to save himself, to shift blame away from himself. They sought to have a mistrial declared, claiming that the prosecutor inflamed the jury by focusing on the emotional aspects of the family killings.

Recorder's Court Judge Leonard Townsend denied

the motion for mistrial. He did admonish the jury panels to avoid making emotional judgments because of the "gruesome and offensive" nature of the crimes.

The main part of the trial got under way with the testimony of the chief witness for the prosecution. Smith testified for an hour, visibly shocking some of the jurors as he described the grisly events of December 18, 1982.

According to Smith's statement, David Berkley had simply had the bad luck to be chosen as a robbery target. Smith, Shepherd and Talley needed cash to buy drugs, and their choice of victim was quite random.

As the police sleuths had theorized, the trio found David's identification bearing his address and his keys after killing him. Then, Smith told the court, he and his pals proceeded to the West Hancock Street apartment, entered it, attacked and killed Aline Berkley and Baby Jessica, and ransacked the place.

Although Smith admitted stabbing David during the street attack, he denied having anything to do with the actual slayings of Aline and little Jessica. He claimed that he was preoccupied with gathering up the Christmas presents and other loot in the Berkley flat while his chums attended to snuffing out the victims.

Smith told the two juries that he and the half-brothers stole the Christmas presents and later divided them among their own respective families. The witness said that Shepherd took Aline's silver baby cup—which Aline was going to pass down to daughter Jessica as a kind of family heirloom—and gave it to his mother. And, Smith went on, Talley took a new silver baby spoon as a gift for his own infant. The trio also made $80, according to the witness, by taking the stolen TV and stereo equipment to a "dope house" and selling the items.

On Wednesday, May 7th, controversy rocked the courtroom when Smith's testimony about Aline's alleged rape came up. The postmortem lab tests had raised the possibility of rape, indicating that the victim had sexual intercourse not very long before being slain, but the prosecution had not included that crime among the charges, citing the evidence as being inconclusive. In his statement to police, however, Smith had asserted that one of the half-brothers did rape the young mother.

In spite of strenuous objections by the defense, the judge did allow Smith to repeat his original statement. Under questioning by the prosecutor, the witness testified that Shepherd had been the one who sexually assaulted the woman because "that was his thing."

As for the slaying of the infant girl, Smith told the court that Aline, before being killed herself, was "steady hollering . . . don't hurt her baby." Members of the two juries and other court onlookers cringed and the eyes of some filled with tears as Smith testified, "I saw Randy (Talley) stick the baby."

The defense lawyers hammered at Smith during the cross-examination. They accused him of being the lone killer and of having named Shepherd and Talley as his partners-in-blood for revenge. His motive for vengeance, the attorneys maintained, was that the half-brothers' female relative, whom he'd been dating, had played a role in leading police to him. She had named Smith to her brother, convict Buck Baldwin, during the prison visit.

Under redirect questioning by the prosecutor, Smith was offered a "last chance" to clear Shepherd and Talley if they had really not been participants in the Berkley family slaughter. The witness stood his ground, declaring, "No, they was with me."

On Thursday, May 8th, final arguments were presented. Prosecutor Koch stressed to the jurors that Smith's testimony was truthful, even as the witness had "just breathed out this horror so matter-of-factly." But, Koch also emphasized, "Your verdict" — that is, finding the half-brothers guilty — "does not mean Timothy Smith is a righteous and good human being. It means that Randy Talley and Jackie Shepherd were with him." He maintained that the two defendants were the chief assassins, unworthy of any mercy, and that Smith was "like a jackal . . . hanging on their coattails waiting to get his share."

When the opposing team came up to bat, Defense Attorney Nolan said of Smith, "Here's a man who'd identify anyone to save his own skin. The horror of this doesn't provide the evidence." Co-counsel Ziolkowski asserted that, when all the evidence was added up, it showed one man — Smith — could have committed the heinous murders.

On Friday, May 9th, the separate juries began their deliberations. Shepherd's jury came in with a verdict after two and a half hours; Talley's came in ten minutes later. The half-brothers were both found guilty as charged in the Berkley family murders.

Shepherd showed no reaction as he heard the verdict. Talley, who was standing with his back to the jurors, was seen by court observers to be mouthing obscenities.

As Judge Townsend thanked the members of the two jury panels for their service to the state of Michigan, some of them had tears streaming from their eyes. The judge told them that they could not have reached any other verdicts.

Prosecutor Koch expressed special pleasure at the fact that the juries had been able to make their determinations based on the testimony of a single witness—a man who was himself guilty of murder in the same case.

Timothy Smith began serving his plea-bargained sentence of 25 to 40 years in protective custody in a federal prison on Monday, May 19th.

On Tuesday, May 20, 1986, Jack Shepherd and Randy Talley appeared before Judge Townsend for sentencing. He sentenced the half-brothers to three life terms each, at hard labor, with no possibility of parole. Pointing out the absence of a death penalty in Michigan, the judge told Shepherd he was sorry he could not sentence him to "ride the lightning into the hereafter." To Talley, he said, "The only sentence that would be fair would be to take that one thing you have"—referring to the convicted man's life—"a short drop would do it."

As for the slain victims, perhaps their parents and families, who were close to begin with, derived some small measure of comfort in the knowledge that justice had been visited upon the killers. How close the two families were was shown during the trial, when they had sat together in the first row of courtroom spectators, facing the accused murderers. And earlier, when it had been necessary to decide how and where the remains of Aline, David and little Jessica would be buried, the closeness was underscored by the answer the families came up with. They decided to have the bodies cremated and then have all the ashes mixed together. Aline's father took half the ashes to California and David's father took the other half to Maryland.

That solution reflected the basic kind of wisdom that Solomon himself would have been proud of. "In a sense, they will be together that way," said David's dad. "I think that's the way they would want it."

196

"FAMILY MASSACRE ON THE MICHIGAN RESERVATION!"

by Arne Arntzen

Sheer horror greeted the Michigan State Troopers who stepped into the David Smith home, located two miles west of Wilson, on the Hannahville Indian Reservation. Headquartered at Menominee County's Stephenson post, in Michigan's Upper Peninsula, the troopers were responding to a call that had come in at 11:30 p.m. on Tuesday, June 14, 1988, alerting them that the Smith family had been hurt. But hurt was hardly the word for what had happened to the family.

When the officers arrived, they found the house lights on and the front door standing open. As they entered, they saw the still forms of four Smith family members lying only a few feet from the entranceway. Their clothing was blood-soaked and pools of blood had formed on the floor. Gory spatters stained the walls and ceiling.

Checking the unmoving figures for signs of life, the troopers found none. Sergeant Jim Meade estimated that the homicides had been committed within the past hour.

A search of the interior rooms and the premises failed to show any signs of the Smith's other daughter, 11-year-old Amanda. Establishing that the family car was missing, the officers surmised that the mass murderer had fled in it.

Entry into the building had been accomplished by breaking a window. Under the window lay a knapsack with several cans of beer.

The Menominee County Medical Examiner was notified of the homicides, as was the Michigan State Police Branch Crime Lab at Negaunee.

At about 12:30 a.m. on Wednesday, the dispatcher at the Escanaba Department of Public Safety received an urgent call from a frantic-voiced woman who reported a kidnapping on the 1200 block of North 22nd Street. When the officers arrived, she told them she heard a car stop in front of the house where she was visiting a relative, Peggy Loonsfoot. When she'd gone to the door and looked through the glass panel, she saw a man carrying a rifle get out of a white car. She recognized him as being Vincent Loonsfoot, who was separated from his wife Peggy. The witness yelled at Peggy that Vincent was coming and, when he approached the door, she tried to stop him. He pointed the gun at her and she fled upstairs. Meanwhile, he shouted at Peggy that he was going to kill her.

Pandemonium broke loose. The witness yelled from the stairs at Loonsfoot not to shoot Peggy, who was screaming with fright. The witness added to the confusion by shouting at them to quiet down. In all the excitement and tumult, Loonsfoot grabbed Peggy who was yelling, "Don't hit me! Don't hit me! I love you!" He dragged her out of the house. Once outside, he struck her in the face knocking off her glasses. According to the witness, he shoved Peggy barefoot, into the car and drove away.

According to what the Escanaba officers could piece together from the witness's story, Vincent

Loonsfoot had first gone to the David Smith home, where he'd shot all the family members except for 11-year-old Amanda, who had witnessed the vicious massacre. Amanda had escaped the carnage by running out and hiding in the back of the family car. But the young girl had been wounded in the chest by bullet fragments.

When Loonsfoot had completed his grisly chore, the officers determined, he'd come outside and found Amanda Smith in the car. He'd grabbed the girl and forced her to show him where Peggy was staying. Peggy was her aunt.

Arriving at the home in Escanaba, Loonsfoot started to force his way inside. Meanwhile, young Amanda jumped out of the car and managed to get into the building, where she hid on the second floor. In another room, Loonsfoot's 11-month-old daughter lay asleep.

When Loonsfoot had taken off with his wife, the neighbor called the authorities. Young Amanda, who was seriously hurt from the bullet fragments, was rushed to St. Francis Hospital and was immediately taken into surgery. Hospital personnel refused to comment on her condition at that time.

Detective Leon Wildey of the Gladstone State Police Post said that an FBI agent and state troopers hoped to question the 11-year-old girl as soon as possible concerning the slaughter of her family, as she was the sole survivor.

Questioning the neighbor of the abducted woman, detectives learned that she'd heard a lot of yelling and screaming in the house next door at about 12:00 a.m. on Wednesday. She said she wasn't acquainted with the occupant of the house, who had just moved in about a week previously. Thinking that the noise was a family quarrel, she'd opened her window and shouted to them to quiet down. She said she saw a man enter a white car and drive away.

Relatives of the murdered Smith family believed that Loonsfoot was not to much concerned about his estranged wife as he was about their 11-month-old daughter, and it was the child that he had come to get. He was very fond of the child and proud of her and he loved to hold her in his arms. Relatives believed that in all the shouting, confusion and excitement that prevailed when he entered the house, he momentarily forgot what he intended to do and fled with Peggy as his hostage.

Vincent Loonsfoot was described as a 25-year-old Native American, a man subject to moods and aggressive behavior patterns. Standing 5 feet 7 inches tall and weighing 155 pounds, he originally came from Bark River and was thoroughly familiar with the woods in the area. He'd married Peggy two years earlier; it was her second marriage and she was the mother of two children from her first.

Probers learned that her marriage to Vincent Loonsfoot was not a happy one. He was addicted to alcohol and used drugs. Six weeks earlier she had separated from him and in May, unknown to Loonsfoot, she'd called her brother, David Smith, to take her away from Baraga and bring her back to Delta County with her child. When Loonsfoot learned about what had transpired, he threatened to kill the entire Smith family — Peggy and her sisters and brothers.

A check on Loonsfoot's police record showed that he had been arrested in Montana for assault, battery, and armed robbery in the early 1980s. He served six years in prison for that offense.

He was also charged with assault and battery in Delta County. The case never came to trial and the charges were dismissed.

At 5:00 a.m. on Wednesday, the Smith car was discovered at a dead-end dirt road near the Delta County landfill near Danforth, about a mile west of Escanaba. Sheriff's deputies noticed from signs around the car that both occupants had gotten out the driver's door. The officers followed the footprints—one pair indicating a woman barefoot—to a railroad track a short distance away. The footprints led them along the track in a westerly direction for about two miles, where they left the tracks and entered into a heavily wooded area.

Early in the morning, the Menominee County Medical Examiner began his preliminary examination of the Smith family corpses at the crime scene. He observed that the victims had been shot twice—once in the body, once in the head. He assumed that each shot had been fired into the head of each victim to assure they would be dead. There were no other marks, bruises, cuts or lacerations on their bodies. He determined the time of death to have been shortly before midnight, Tuesday, June 14th.

The crime technicians from the Negaunee State Branch Crime Laboratory also arrived early in the morning. After setting up their instruments, they took photos of the victims and close-ups of their wounds. A fingerprint expert dusted the room with black fingerprint powder, hoping to raise latent prints. The floor, sofas and other furniture were vacuumed for possible fibers and other evidence.

The team worked throughout the morning and what evidence they were able to uncover was carefully labeled and packaged and would be tested and analyzed. Two guns and ammunition had apparently been taken from David Smith's gun rack and presumably used in the mass slayings.

Reaction to the multiple murder and kidnapping among the inhabitants of Escanaba did not appear to include fear or anxiety. According to the director of the Department of Public Safety, Wayne Heikila, most people didn't seem to be overly concerned. The police were not flooded with calls from the citizens.

When questioned about the incident, an elderly man said he was sorry about the murder of the family and if this Loonsfoot guy was guilty he ought to be executed. There is no death penalty in Michigan. "Sure we have crime in Escanaba, and I don't recall anything like what happened in Wilson occurring here. I've lived here all my life and it's a good place to live with good people, good schools, churches, an excellent hospital, the best harbor in Upper Michigan, a growing community college and good law enforcement. For a city of 15,000 people, we live comfortably in our own lifestyle. People like it here. They're stable."

One woman interviewed about the search for the slayer said she wasn't worried. "We've got a good police and sheriff department. They'll find him. My son, though, is concerned. He's locking the doors at night. He's thinking in terms of *Rambo*—you know, Loonsfoot wearing camouflage clothing."

But the 380 inhabitants at the Hannahville Indian Reservation were stunned and shocked at the massacre of the Smith family. They couldn't understand how anything like this could happen.

Although Loonsfoot wasn't a member of their reservation, they regarded him as a loving parent, albeit subject to moods that often led to violent displays of anger, but they couldn't conceive of him deliberately slaying the Smith family.

The school superintendent said he was puzzled and bewildered about the mass slayings. He thought that perhaps Dave Smith had had words with Vince that could have led to the homicides.

Because the homicides occurred on the Hannahville Indian Reservation land close to Bark River near Wilson, the Federal government assumed jurisdiction of the case and assigned FBI Special Agent Hal Helterhoff to head the investigation. He has had considerable experience in conducting such searches, recently having completed several operations successfully in Missouri. Two SWAT teams, heavily armed and specially trained for search missions of this nature, were flown to Escanaba with Helterhoff early on Wednesday morning. Headquarters were established in Escanaba and search operations began.

A Coast Guard helicopter was flown in along with three FBI planes. Tracking dogs from the Marinette Police Department also arrived at the search scene.

Convinced that Loonsfoot and his hostage were traveling on foot in the woods near Escanaba, the team designated a location four miles square as the search site. Perimeter checkpoints were set up. Others were established along the Wisconsin Central railroad tracks, according to Gladstone State Police Detective Wildey.

Aiding the SWAT Teams in their search on Wednesday were two officers from the Escanaba Department of Public Safety who were familiar with the densely wooded and rugged terrain. Also joining the manhunt were the sheriffs departments of Delta, Menominee and Dickinson Counties, the Michigan State Police, and the Escanaba Department of Public Safety.

Meanwhile, the Coast Guard helicopter and the three FBI planes were flying over the search scene, their crews hoping to catch a glimpse of the two fugitives. Tracking dogs were sent to the area where the footprints had been discovered leading from the abandoned Smith car to the railroad track. The scent was picked up late in the afternoon, but the trail had to be abandoned when a thick fog rolled in. Arrangements were made to continue the search in the morning with a fresh canine unit sent in from Detroit.

With the aid of aerial photography, searchers conducted a grid search, marking off on the map various places after they had been checked to the satisfaction of the search parties.

The abandoned Smith car was towed into the Escanaba Department of Public Safety garage. There crime technicians would check it out for possible evidence.

The bodies of the four Smith family victims were removed from their home and transferred to the Marquette General Hospital, where the autopsies would be performed. Investigating authorities said that no motive had been established for the brutal mass murders.

By this time, between 30 and 40 law enforcement officers from various police and sheriffs departments, together with FBI agents and two SWAT eight-man teams, were involved in the manhunt. The search continued into the night. Neither the searchers combing the area where it was assumed the couple were hiding, nor the crews of the helicopter and planes had made any sightings of Loonsfoot and his hostage.

An engineer operating a Wisconsin Central train that ran through the Danforth district reported that he had seen a man walking along the tracks near Hermansville about an hour before the homicides occurred. But the sighting was not confirmed.

The report did raise the possibility that Loonsfoot could have hopped the train as it was traveling through the Danforth area and eluded the searchers. Checking with the railroad officials, the authorities learned that the train would have been going too fast at that point for anyone to possibly get aboard it.

Questioned by reporters about the search, FBI

Agent Helterhoff said that the operation was progressing about as anticipated. Investigators considered it from various angles and came up with four theories regarding the search. One was that the suspect had another car hidden somewhere within the search area and left, taking his estranged wife with him. Another possibility was that he stole a car and fled. A third consideration was that he killed Peggy and then committed suicide. The fourth theory was that the pair were concealed somewhere in the search area and were capable of living off the land.

Loonsfoot, Helterhoff said, was known to be a survivalist with the knowledge and skill to get along in the woods. "If he's any survivalist worth his salt," the FBI agent said, "we will have a hell of a time getting him."

FBI Agent Helterhoff told reporters that it was not unusual for a search of this nature to last several days, but with a hostage, it could be of shorter duration. Peggy Loonsfoot was reported to be three months pregnant and barefoot, making it difficult for her to travel. If Vincent Loonsfoot were alone, he could move about more quickly, and if he had food and water, it could take a long time to apprehend him. Eventually he would be worn down, the agent said.

According to the Delta County Prosecuting Attorney, federal warrants were issued for the suspect's arrest charging him with murder. Kidnapping charges might be filed locally later by his office.

On Thursday, a tracking dog picked up the scent of the two fugitives in the woods near the railroad tracks, followed it for a short distance, and lost it.

By this time, 11-year-old Amanda Smith was able to talk to the officers in the hospital. She told them on the night of June 14th, the family was visiting friends and returned home shortly before 11:30 p.m.

Her father, 29-year-old David Smith, who was carrying two-year-old Laura in his arms, unlocked the front door and stepped inside.

Suddenly, he was shot, as was Laura. They fell on the floor. Her mother, Sherri, 27, was screaming and she was shot, falling on top of her husband. Ten-year-old Amy was crying and shot, she too, fell on the floor. Amanda said she witnessed the entire shooting from the partly open front door. Then she ran and hid in the back of the family car.

She heard four more shots fired and then the man she recognized as Vincent Loonsfoot came out and approached the car. He found her and forced her to direct him to where his wife was living in Escanaba. He had a gun.

The girl was scared, she said, thinking that he would kill her so they drove the distance to Peggy Loonsfoot's.

When he went after Peggy, Amanda said, she got out of the car and hid in a bedroom on the second floor of the house. She was hurt in her chest and, after Vincent forced Peggy into the car and they drove away, Peggy's relatives took the child to the hospital.

The manhunt continued all day Thursday, the weary searchers combing designated areas assigned to them. When each was covered, the areas were marked off on the grid photo. No sightings of either Loonsfoot or Peggy were reported by the time darkness set in. Neither the pilots nor their spotters had caught sight of the fugitive and his hostage from the air in the three planes they were flying.

Meanwhile, following up a tip received by the Menominee County Sheriff's Department, deputies discovered Loonsfoot's van about 1.7 miles east of the crime scene. The van, a yellow and black Chevrolet, was found at about 10:00 a.m., Friday, on a logging road. An effort had been made to conceal it with tree branches. FBI agents were notified and they received oral permission to search the vehicle from a Federal attorney.

The van was equipped with a CB radio. Inside the back were some empty ammunition boxes, styrofoam coolers, a camouflage duffel bag and a khaki-colored tarp.

Agent Helterhoff was elated at the discovery. It established how Loonsfoot arrived at the Smith residence and eliminated the theory that the suspect had stashed the car somewhere in the search area and had used it to escape with Peggy.

The van was impounded and towed to the Escanaba Department of Public Safety garage. There crime lab technicians checked it out for possible evidence.

Because the Smith car had been discovered in the Danforth area not far from the Delta County landfill, the search was centered there, and the road leading into the landfill was locked, causing some inconvenience to people in the city. The area was thoroughly combed by the searchers struggling through thick brush, dense woods and occasional swampy marshes. After days of intensive searching, the weary officers were convinced that the couple was not there. The search was shifted to another location. The landfill road was reopened and things returned to normal.

By this time, checkpoints set up early in the search had been moved, tightening the search area. It now included a three-square-mile perimeter; the grid in Helterhoff's office covered a good portion of the enlarged photograph.

As the search progressed, so did rumors about it increase. Many of them were circulated by people listening to police scanners. There were reports that sightings had been made of Loonsfoot and his wife and that they had managed to escape the police net. There were other rumors that Peggy had been murdered by Loonsfoot because she was becoming a drag on his efforts to escape detection. But authorities did not confirm these reports; they merely stated that the search was proceedings as planned.

FBI Agent Helterhoff announced that the authorities appreciated the interest displayed by the public in the manhunt and the tips and leads phoned into his office. He said that public participation in supplying information to investigators was a big factor in the success of a manhunt.

Saturday's search proved to be equally frustrating. The weary officers kept doggedly on with the manhunt, struggling over the rough terrain, thick brush and dense forests, wading through swamps, battling mosquitoes and other insects and failing to catch the slightest glimpse of the fugitive and his apparent hostage. Some members of the search party had to return to normal duties they'd been neglecting. Still the exhausted trackers kept on from dawn till dusk with tracking dogs and planes overhead trying to spot the elusive couple.

On Sunday afternoon, funeral services for the David Smith family were held in Spalding, attended by about 150 friends and relatives of the victims. A representative of the Michigan State Police and the FBI also attended.

The four caskets were arranged in a semicircle. Photos of the family recalling happy days had been placed on the caskets, bringing back memories to the grieving friends and relatives. In Mrs. Smith's coffin, Amanda had written "Mom" on a drawing of a heart.

The services were brief. Outside, Menominee County Sheriff deputies and Hannahville police were stationed in case Vincent Loonsfoot should appear at the funeral. He did not.

There was no graveside service. A lone hearse brought the caskets to the Spalding Township Cemetery because Loonsfoot's threats against the entire Smith family posed a continuing possibility of danger, even at the gravesite.

On Monday, six days after the Smith family slaying, FBI Agent Helterhoff, in charge of the manhunt, admitted that there were still no sightings of either Loonsfoot or his hostage. He said the search area was so large that it was possible for the couple to get in and out without detection, and they could have eluded the searchers and been miles away by now. He assumed that they were still on foot; there had been no reports of a stolen vehicle in the Escanaba area.

In the meantime, the authorities expressed a belief that the murders were planned. The theory was that after gaining entrance into the Smith residence through a broken window, Loonsfoot appeared to have sat in the kitchen waiting for the family to return. He had taken two rifles that belonged to Smith—a .22-caliber repeating rifle and a .30-.30-caliber carbine—with ammunition for the weapons. When the Smiths entered the house, according to probers he had shot them one by one.

Agent Helterhoff declared that Loonsfoot was a very, very dangerous man and a danger to society.

In another development, on Monday, tracking dogs of another type were brought in to aid in the search. Designated as "cadaver dogs," they were trained to detect the scent of dead bodies. For them to pick up the scent of a dead person, the individual had to be dead at least six days. These canines had a high rate of success in locating cadavers. Helterhoff told reporters that he was not overlooking the possibility that either one or both of the Loonsfoots were dead.

At this time, Captain Bill Beveridge of the Escanaba Public Safety Department told reporters that the full names and whereabouts of Peggy Loonsfoot's other family members were being withheld for their own protection.

Monday's manhunt failed to produce any sightings; the "cadaver dogs" failed to pick up a scent of dead bodies. The search would continue the next day.

By now, law enforcement officials and the FBI were becoming uncertain as to how long the manhunt for Loonsfoot would continue. Search parties hadn't made a single sighting of the suspected murderer-kidnapper and his hostage wife.

Discouraged by the lack of success to apprehend Loonsfoot, Helterhoff said that he would evaluate the situation from day to day.

Taking another approach, investigators began interviewing Loonsfoot's friends, relatives and close associates, hoping to gain some helpful information. But nothing of value came out of these interviews.

The SWAT teams had come to rely heavily on the officers from the Escanaba Department of Public Safety to guide them over the rugged terrain and woods. Terrain and woods. The local officers were quite familiar with the area, since they'd begun deer hunting there in their teens. Helterhoff described the search as a joint investigation from the beginning, stressing that these officers were of considerable help in the manhunt.

In the days that followed, nothing new developed in the prolonged search. No sightings of the couple were reported; no scent was picked up by the "cadaver dogs." Thus the searchers believed that Loonsfoot and his wife were still alive.

Then came the break law enforcement officers had hoped for. The Delta County Sheriff's Department in Escanaba received a call from a relative of Loonsfoot's in Baraga: Loonsfoot had called from a pay phone in Escanaba, asking the relative to come to Escanaba and drive him to Canada. The kinswoman refused and told Loonsfoot to give himself up to the sheriff. Then she called the sheriff's department to report Loonsfoot's call.

Sheriff Robitaille relayed the information to the Escanaba Department of Public Safety and police cruisers immediately began searching for the suspect. At 3:45 p.m. on Friday, June 24th, Vincent Loonsfoot, accompanied by Peggy, walked into sheriff's headquarters. Loonsfoot turned himself in to Sergeant Terry Loisenring, who read him his constitutional rights and confined him in a cell in the county jail.

Peggy Loonsfoot was questioned before being admitted to St. Francis Hospital for observation. According to Sheriff Robitaille, she had lost weight, was bruised, and had a black eye. Other than that, she appeared to be in fairly good condition, but hospital authorities would not comment further.

At a press conference held in front of the Escanaba Department of Public Safety building by the director, Wayne Heikila, and FBI Agent Hal Helterhoff, reporters were told about the events leading up to Loonsfoot's arrest. "We had him pinned down and trapped in the search area, and he finally just got tired and hungry and surrendered," Helterhoff said.

After the press conference, Loonsfoot was transported under heavy guard to the Marquette County Jail to await developments in Federal Court.

Appearing in Federal District Court on Friday before U.S. Magistrate Timothy Greeley, the defendant was ordered held without bond in the Marquette County Jail on a warrant accusing him of committing a major crime on Indian land.

Loonsfoot's arrest brought a sense of relief to the surviving Smith relatives, all of whom had been threatened with death by Loonsfoot. "Now," one of them said, "we can return to normal living again. It's been a frightening experience."

A detention hearing was held on July 7th before Magistrate Greeley. Several witnesses were called to testify, among them being Benjamin Walker, a 12-year veteran of the FBI. He had interviewed Peggy Loonsfoot on three separate occasions—on June 24th and 30th, and July 1st. She told him that Loonsfoot had decided to leave the search area, get a car by murdering the occupant, and take her with him to Canada. He made three attempts, she said, all of which failed.

The first attempt was at Hyde, about seven miles from Escanaba at Durfee Park. A truck driver had parked his truck in the wayside park and Loonsfoot was preparing to shoot him, but the driver drove away before Loonsfoot was in position to carry out the attempt.

On another occasion, Peggy said, they were behind a market in Escanaba when a woman clerk came behind the store to a dumpster after leaving her car. Loonsfoot intended to shoot the girl, said Peggy, but there were too many people around.

The last attempt occurred on one of the back roads near the search area after darkness had set in. Loonsfoot ordered Peggy to get out on the road and flag down a car as it approached her. He would then shoot the motorist. Afraid that he would indeed kill her if she didn't carry out his orders, she flagged down a car.

But the woman in the car panicked as she approached Peggy, put the vehicle in reverse and drove away rapidly. Later, the driver reported the incident to the police, the FBI agent said.

There were times, Peggy mentioned during the interviews, that the searchers were close to her and Vincent, and once only about 250 feet away. At that point, her estranged husband put a knife to her throat to prevent her from screaming for help. They watched the searchers moving about going farther and farther from where they were hiding.

According to Peggy, the couple lived on wild strawberries and raspberries and drank water from ponds and streams. They were hungry and tired, and Vincent was always on the alert, fearful of being caught. He was moody—she never knew what he would do during these periods.

In one of the interviews, Peggy told the FBI agent that the first day of her abduction, she made an attempt to kill Vincent. Waiting until he was asleep, she said, she took the .30-.30 rifle, aimed it at his head and pulled the trigger. It didn't go off and he woke up, saw what she was doing and hit her in the face with the gun. He had unloaded the shells from the gun before he went to sleep.

Every day during the time they were in the woods, Loonsfoot would attempt to sexually assault her. It was noted that the State of Michigan has a law which provides that a spouse can be charged with sexual assault.

Agent Walker also told the court that when he interrogated Loonsfoot shortly after his arrest, the suspect informed him where he had hidden the weapons he took from the Smith residence. He had hidden the .30-.30 in back of a restaurant on Lincoln Road in Escanaba, where agents recovered it.

Loonsfoot also told Walker that a second rifle and a knife he'd been carrying could be found at a

213

railroad crossing near Ford River. Law enforcement officers recovered both items.

The only remaining weapon that Loonsfoot had with him during the manhunt, a fillet knife, was not recovered.

At the conclusion of the hearing, Loonsfoot was ordered held without bail in the Marquette County Jail pending further legal procedures by Federal authorities.

Appearing in Federal Court in Grand Rapids, Vincent Loonsfoot was charged with a 20-count indictment in the mass murder of the David Smith family. The indictment included four counts each of murder during the commission of a felony, premeditated murder and murder with malice aforethought.

Loonsfoot was also charged with one count each of burglary with intent to commit murder involving the 11-year-old daughter of the David Smith family, two firearm violations, and two counts of theft for stealing Smith's rifles and car.

Appearing in Federal Court on Thursday, July 7th, with his attorney, Tom Casselman, Loonsfoot stood mute before U.S. Magistrate Timothy Greeley, who read the list of 20 counts against the defendant. Greeley asked Loonsfoot if he understood the charges. In a quiet voice, the defendant answered that he did, to each count. The magistrate then entered not-guilty pleas in his behalf. Loonsfoot was ordered held without bail, pending a pre-trial hearing set for July 20th.

At the hearing, Defense Attorney Casselman requested a psychological evaluation of his client, raising the defendant's desire to seek an insanity defense. Magistrate Greeley ordered two psychological examinations, one from August 5th to 8th, requested by the defense and conducted by a psychologist from Ann Arbor, and the other by government psychologists at Springfield, Missouri. The tests would take about a month.

During the hearing, Magistrate Greeley stated that the government would not seek the death penalty in the case based on the belief that it is unconstitutional under federal law.

At another pre-trial hearing on Wednesday, August 3rd, Vincent Loonsfoot's circuit court trial was set to begin on December 5th at the Federal Courthouse in Marquette. The trial was expected to last for two weeks, according to Defense Attorney Casselman.

When it was determined that the defendant was sane and capable of assisting his attorneys in the preparation of his defense, trial proceedings began as scheduled on December 5th in the Federal Court in Marquette, Michigan.

Because of the complexity of the case, attorneys for both the prosecution and the defense asked the presiding judge, Robert Bell, to decide the fate of the defendant instead of having a jury trial.

In his opening statement, Defense Attorney Casselman told Judge Bell that his client could not have premeditated the crime because he was on an alcohol-cocaine binge on the night of June 14th. "His judgment control was impaired," the attorney maintained.

One of the first witnesses to testify for the prosecution was 11-year-old Amanda Smith, daughter of the slain David Smith.

In tears and crying at times, she said that she watched everything from outside a partially open door at her home. Her father walked into the house carrying her 2-year-old sister, Laura, in his arms. Then Amanda heard shots being fired and saw her father fall to the floor. Her mother screamed and ran into the house with Amy, Amanda's 10-year-old sister. There were more shots, she told the judge.

Peggy Loonsfoot began her testimony on Tuesday, December 6th, the second day of the trial. She told the court that she had not been aware that her brother David's family was murdered at the time her estranged husband came to her house and, at gunpoint, forced her to flee with him in the Smiths' family car.

She walked barefoot through the woods for 10 days with Loonsfoot, she testified, living on wild berries and drinking pond water. On one occasion, she said, they saw a search party about 250 feet away, and Loonsfoot put a knife to her throat to prevent her from screaming for help. She also testified that she tried to shoot him while he was sleeping with the .30-.30 rifle he was carrying. She aimed it at his head and pulled the trigger. The gun didn't discharge, but the click woke Vincent and he saw what she was doing. He seized the gun and hit her in the face with the stock of the weapon. She wasn't aware that before he went to sleep he unloaded the shells.

Peggy also testified that her estranged husband made three attempts to kill motorists for their cars to drive away from the searching areas, but these attempts failed. There wasn't a day, she testified, that Loonsfoot didn't attempt to sexually assault her.

Assistant U.S. Prosecuting Attorney Thomas Martin then introduced as evidence a tape-recording of an interview Loonsfoot had with federal agents shortly after his arrest.

Sitting quietly and displaying no signs of emotion, Loonsfoot listened to his own recording, which played back his voice at times weeping or speaking softly, describing how he came to his brother-in-law's house, found the doors locked and broke a window to get into the house. The tape went on about how he sat in the kitchen, drinking beer and snorting cocaine, waiting for his estranged wife to appear.

Sometime before midnight, according to Loonsfoot's taped narrative, the family returned. When David Smith entered the house carrying the infant Laura, he switched on the light and told Loonsfoot that Peggy was not there. In the recording, Loonsfoot told the agents that he warned Dave Smith to tell the truth. It was then that Smith moved and Loonsfoot said he panicked, thinking Smith was going for a weapon, and Loonsfoot began shooting.

In the recording, the defendant broke down and cried as he told the federal agents, "I wanted my family back and would have done anything to get them back." He also said that the drugs he was taking made him hate people.

Another witness, Loonsfoot's relative from Baraga, told the judge that during the evening of June 24th, she'd received a call from Vincent, who was in Escanaba begging her to drive him to Canada. She refused and advised him to give himself up to the authorities. Then she called the Delta County Sheriff's Department, advising them of the phone call.

At the conclusion of her testimony, the prosecution rested its case. The defense said it had no witnesses to testify on behalf of his client and also rested. Closing arguments by both sides were then presented.

After a brief period of deliberation, Judge Bell announced his verdict. He found the defendant guilty of four counts of first-degree murder, one count each of kidnapping, use of firearm during the commission of a felony, and committing a crime of violence while possessing a firearm.

As the verdict was pronounced, Vincent Loonsfoot listened quietly, displaying no emotion. U.S. marshals then remanded him to the Marquette County

Jail to await sentencing.

Defense Attorney Casselman had no comment on the judge's verdict. Assistant U.S. Attorney Thomas Martin described the verdict as just, while a relative of David Smith and Peggy Loonsfoot told reporters that he was satisfied with the judge's decision.

On February 27, 1989, Loonsfoot, dressed in prison garb and heavily guarded by U.S. marshals, appeared for sentencing before Judge Bell. The convicted man appeared nervous as he glanced at spectators attending the proceedings. His attorney told the judge that after the trial, Loonsfoot had telephoned relatives of the slain Smiths to express his remorse and to say he was sorry for his actions.

After hearing these remarks, Judge Bell proceeded to pass sentence on the convicted killer. He sentenced Loonsfoot to four concurrent life sentences without parole, 12 years for the kidnapping of Amanda Smith, 5 years for the use of firearm during a felony, and another life sentence for possession of a firearm.

When Judge Bell asked Loonsfoot if he had anything to say, he answered, "I can't think, sir."

Loonsfoot's attorney said that his client intended to address the court to apologize to Peggy, the Smith family and his own family for the sorrow and grief he had caused them, but now he was too nervous to speak.

Addressing the defendant, Judge Bell said, "This is tragedy for the victim, the family and the Indian Community, and certainly a tragedy for Vincent Loonsfoot. Some things can not be undone.

"Particularly troubling is that you, Mr. Loonsfoot, were out on parole at the time of the killings," Judge Bell added. Then he recommended that Loonsfoot be given drug and alcohol treatment.

With sentencing concluded, Loonsfoot was remanded to the Marquette County Jail by U.S. marshals to await transfer to a maximum-security prison, probably at Marion, Illinois, a maximum-security prison constructed to replace the federal pen at Alcatraz outside of San Francisco.

(*Left to right*) Floy Roberts, Mae Bell Roberts and Columbus Roberts, all victims of the Mars Hill, Alabama massacre.

The simple home in which the Roberts were murdered.

The Roberts family plot, one of the largest in the Mars Hill cemetery.

The Marshfield, Missouri Buckner family: (left to right) Michael, Jeanette, Tim, Steven (holding Dennis) and Kirk. Only Kirk survived the vicious mass murder.

James Schnick, the man who murdered the Buckners.

The Fairmont, Ohio home in which Georgis Davis, 46, her daughter, Cheryl Senteno, 25, and her son, Gary Mullins, 20, were shot to death.

Jose Trinidad Lonza was convicted of killing Davis and her two children.

Burgate House, the spacious British mansion in which the Cleaver family was slaughtered in September 1, 1986.

Thomas Cleaver, 47, and his wife, Wendy, 46.

Joseph Cleaver, retired publishing tycoon, and his wife Hilda. They were eighty-two years old when they lost their lives.

Joseph Stephenson, the former servant of the Cleavers, helped mastermind their death.

George Daly (with mustache) and his brother, John, helped Stephenson dispose of the Cleavers.

Michael Robert Tucker, 32, along with Bryan Mikesell, 23, killed Rickreall, Oregon couple Robert and Barbara Farmer.

Sacramental items used in Satanic rituals found in Sean's bedroom.

Sean Sellers, 15, Satanist and self-acclaimed "vampire" killed his parents while they slept.

Lee Bellafatto, 41, and his wife, Vonda, 32, as found by police.

Robert Bower, 36, Circle K convenience store supervisor, was the first victim of Sellers' bloodlust.

"ENRAGED LOVER MASSACRED A FAMILY OF FIVE!"

by Robert Carlsen

The man was nervous as he walked into the large department store. There was a security guard at the store's entrance who gave him a brief glance.

The man walked back to the firearms department to purchase some type of weapon. He wasn't sure exactly what he would come away with, but knew it had to be of sufficient caliber to kill somebody.

He decided on a .22-caliber rifle. It was cheap yet effective at close range. And that's what he would do. Blow them away at close range.

He threw the money on the counter and left in a hurry after the transaction. He went to his apartment and got the .38-caliber revolver. Then he hailed a taxi.

It was about 5:25 when the cabby left him off at the intersection of Fourth Street and Robinson Avenue in the city of Marrero, Louisiana, which is in Jefferson Parish near New Orleans.

His destination was one block away, a house on Robinson Avenue. He had a plan. He knew he could get away with murder without being caught.

He made sure nobody in the neighborhood saw

him as he skirted up the street to the house. In a nearby lot eight men were playing cards. They'd been there a good portion of the afternoon, and had no reason in the world to think that their game would be broken up by a deadly tirade.

The killer burst into the house and caught all who were inside by surprise. The eyes of the off-duty sheriff's deputy widened when she noticed that the intruder was brandishing a rifle. Without giving any of them a chance, he started firing.

Sheila Thomas, the 27-year-old sheriff's deputy, fell to the floor dead after receiving a bullet from the rifle in the brain and another in the left arm.

Sheila's four-year-old daughter, Shantel Osborne, was shot with the rifle in the right forehead. The bullet tore into her brain. He had fired at point blank range.

The little girl's father, Carl Osborne, received a rifle shot that entered his right ear and shattered his brain. He, like his daughter, was shot from a mere six inches away.

Myrtle Griffin, 44, Sheila's mother, died of two bullet wounds to the upper front of her chest. One bullet passed through her heart and the other through her lung. Both were fired at close range and both exited out her back.

The slayings occurred so quickly that nobody had a chance to do anything. The screams were brief, for the slugs were pumped into the victims in rapid succession. The expended shells dropped to the floor.

When the shooting erupted, Owen Griffin, 45, one of eight men playing cards near the house, rushed towards his home. His wife, stepdaughter and her husband and child were inside, and he knew he had to protect them. He ran to the side door, looked inside but saw nothing; then he ran around to the front door.

As he plunged into the house, the killer fired a bullet into the right side of Owen Griffin's face. It shattered his backbone, and he died instantly.

Only the little four-year-old girl was alive as the killer quickly hid the .38-caliber revolver in an air duct vent, and then placed the .22-caliber rifle under Sheila's bed covers. She had been living with her mother and stepfather in the house during this time.

As quickly as he'd burst in, he was gone. And not one of the other seven men who'd been playing cards with Owen Griffin saw what the killer looked like.

Four persons were dead. A little girl lay bleeding to death inside the house on Robinson Avenue. It was the worst slaughter in recent Louisiana history. And the killer had gotten away without being spotted.

Jefferson Parish Deputy James L. Johnson was one of the first lawmen to arrive on the scene. Captain Kevin Smith wasn't far behind, followed by 28 more.

It was 5:30 p.m. Nobody had seen the killer flee, and it was believed he might still be in the house. Deputy Johnson called for a K-9 unit, which arrived within minutes.

The dog cautiously entered the house and, after a few minutes, again appeared at the door. It was safe to enter, the officers now knew.

When Deputy Johnson and Capt. Smith entered the house, they were appalled at the carnage. The five bodies lay around the dining room table. Expertly, so as not to disturb evidence, the officers checked the victims for a pulse.

"Nothing here," Capt. Smith said as he gently placed the arm of a victim down.

"Wait a minute," Johnson said. "I've got something."

Deputy Johnson was holding the limp arm of four-year-old Shantel Osborne. She had been found in a chair near the table. She was rushed into an ambulance and then to the hospital.

Little did the investigators realize that she would be their only eyewitness to the killing. Despite the fact that there were many people nearby, nobody had seen the killer. Only Shantel knew his identity, and she would never be able to tell, for she was dead soon thereafter.

Crime scene investigators descended upon the death house along with hordes of newsmen. Marrero had never seen anything like this before. This kind of crime rarely happened in Louisiana or, for that matter, the entire deep south. A family massacred in broad daylight while others were nearby but helpless.

Bullet fragments, blood, brains, and shell casings were found on the floor of the house. The bodies of the two men, Carl Osborne, Shantel's father, and Owen Griffin, 45, were slumped together. Apparently when Griffin charged into the house, he was shot and fell on the already dead body of Osborne.

Sheila Thomas, Shantel's mother, and Myrtle Griffin, were found on the floor.

As technicians carefully poured over the house in search of any evidence such as fingerprints, other detectives busied themselves by questioning the neighbors and the seven men who had been playing cards with Griffin when the mass murder occurred.

"He rushed into the house and never came out alive," one of the men told detectives. "It was just before 5:30 when we heard the shots," he said. The witness related that he first saw Griffin run across the vacant lot to his house, going first to the side

223

entrance and then entering the front door.

"I heard more shots after Owen went in the house," the witness told investigators.

When hiding the guns, the killer had not only been careful, but meticulous. He knew the air duct vent cover could be removed and the .38-caliber revolver easily stashed in there. It would be difficult to find once the vent cover was replaced.

When he went into Sheila's bedroom to hide the rifle under her bed covers, he was careful not to step in any blood or brain particles. By not tracking anything into the bedroom, the cops wouldn't suspect he'd gone in there. And he was right.

There wasn't a speck of evidence in the house to indicate that the killer had done anything other than enter the home, blow his victims away, and then quickly leave. Naturally since no weapon was found near the crime scene, the assumption was the killer took the murder weapon with him.

There was no evidence to cause the investigators to start tearing into such things as the air vent or mattresses.

If the sleuths would have found the weapons stashed away in the house right after the crimes, they would have had a vital clue.

The detectives worked into the evening. An officer had been sent to the hospital to guard Shantel Osborne and talk to her if at all possible. The disappointing news came back that she was dead. The detectives' job would be that much harder.

After the seven card players were questioned, the search for witnesses branched out to other neighbors. Nobody saw the suspect. Nobody even saw or heard a car roar off after the shootings.

It seemed logical to the detectives that the killer would have wanted to make a quick getaway, if he'd had a car. Perhaps he'd parked it just a couple blocks away.

Detectives expanded their search into nearby neighborhoods in their effort to find a witness who'd seen a strange car speeding away from the murder scene. Although some leads were checked out, none proved fruitful. It just seemed like the killer appeared out of nowhere, and vanished in broad daylight just as quickly.

That left open several possibilities. Perhaps the killer lived in the neighborhood, or maybe he'd gotten a ride to the crime scene area from a friend, or maybe he'd gotten there in a cab. The first and third possibilities could be checked out. The second couldn't be worked on until a suspect was located.

Detectives contacted area cab companies and learned that shortly before the murders, a female cab driver had dropped a man off at the corner of Fourth Street and Robinson Avenue, just a block away from the murder scene.

Detectives pounced on the clue and learned that the man the cabby had dropped off had been carrying a .22-caliber rifle. The West Bank cab driver said the rifle looked relatively new to her.

Detectives reasoned that a man fleeing a murder scene while carrying a rifle would certainly be conspicuous. Perhaps he'd stashed the weapon somewhere in the house.

A relative of Sheila's was contacted, and the day after the murders another search was made in the house. The relative found the rifle under the covers of Sheila's bed.

It was a .22-caliber, and on its stock, the detectives noticed, Sheila's name had been written several times with a felt tipped marker.

Also in Sheila's bedroom was an incriminating 30-page notebook found in her closet. The notebook, in large, crude print, contained obscenities and threats to Sheila Thomas, the slain 27-year-old deputy.

The notebook didn't have the author's name in it, but detectives surmised from its contents that it was penned by a jealous, ex-boyfriend.

The notebook spoke of their relationship, and how Sheila took advantage of it. At least that's how the author had perceived the situation.

"And now you want to go and f— around," the notebook stated on pages five and six. "It do not work like that you and me will have, to bouth be dead bitch."

The improper punctuation and misspelled words in the notebook indicated to the detectives that its author had little education. Later in the notebook it stated: "But God know I made my life streight and now Sheila want to mess it up but no, she have to go to the wormes she took all I work for then leave to go and be with Carl but I just cannot take it eany more."

Detectives checked into the background of Deputy Sheila Thomas and learned that she did have a former boyfriend who would have fit the profile of the person who penned the crude notebook. His name was Leslie O. Lowenfield, detectives learned after questioning relatives and friends of the victims.

Lowenfield had come from Guyana and was not well versed in the use of the English language, especially the written word, the detectives were told.

As the investigation continued, Dr. Alvaro Hunt performed autopsies on the five victims. All were shot at close range with a small caliber weapon, Dr. Hunt told the detectives. In some of the cases it was possible to determine the caliber of the weapon used.

Detectives already had determined that the weapon was some type of automatic .22, as shell casings had been found at the murder scene.

Dr. Hunt said that some of the wounds didn't appear to be consistent with a .22, and that a second weapon might be involved, but it was impossible to determine its caliber from bullet fragments found.

Detectives obtained a photograph of suspect Lowenfield, put it in a montage, and the female taxi driver picked him out as being the man she'd dropped off at the corner near the murder scene shortly before 5:30 p.m.

Det. James Trapani, who spearheaded the investigation, knew that Deputy Thomas and Carl Osborne were probably the primary targets of the killer, if it indeed had been Lowenfield.

Det. Trapani learned that Deputy Thomas had, for the past two years, been assigned to jail and courthouse duties. She was a guard and escorted prisoners to court. She was well known and well liked at the Jefferson Parish courthouse. She was present daily in at least one of the court's 15 divisions.

For that reason, detectives questioned her work associates and learned that Deputy Thomas had a very good friend, also assigned to prisoner escort. The friend told detectives that she knew Leslie Lowenfield; and that five days before the mass murder, Lowenfield had said he was going to kill Sheila Thomas or "blow her brains out," as he put it.

Detectives learned from one of Sheila's cousins that on the evening of August 29, 1982, Lowenfield had appeared at her (the cousin's) apartment and said he was going to kill Sheila Thomas and Carl Osborne, the father of Sheila's baby, as well as Myrtle Griffin, Sheila's mother.

Det. Trapani and other investigators learned

Lowenfield's address and descended upon the apartment. Nobody was there, and neighbors said they hadn't seen Lowenfield since the afternoon of August 30th.

An all-points-bulletin was put out for the suspect but he was nowhere to be found in Marrero, Gretna, or New Orleans. Leslie O. Lowenfield, 28, had simply vanished after committing the murders.

The search for Lowenfield dragged on with no results. But Det. Trapani had his men working on several fronts, and while the search for Lowenfield was on, detectives were trying to trace the rifle which was one of the murder weapons.

Their hard work paid off when they turned up the department store clerk who had sold the gun. The clerk said she probably could remember the man she'd sold the gun to because not too many sales were made on August 30th.

Detectives showed the store clerk the photo montage, and she picked out the photo of Leslie O. Lowenfield as being the man who had purchased the murder weapon.

Another link in the chain of circumstantial evidence was in place. Det. Trapani knew that he would have to build the case on circumstantial evidence because there was no eyewitness to the five murders. He knew it would have to be an air-tight case if he was going to bring in Lowenfield and get a murder conviction.

The hours ticked by, the days passed, and still there was no sign of Lowenfield. It was a week after the murder that Lowenfield's second murder weapon was found.

By then another relative had moved into the house to tidy things up and take care of the property preparatory to the settling of the estate.

He found the .38-caliber revolver in the air vent.

He turned it over to a deputy sheriff, who in turn gave it to detectives.

The fact that the killer knew enough to hide the revolver in the ductwork indicated to detectives that the slayer had to be somebody familiar with the home. Again, Lowenfield met the qualifications.

Ballistics experts studied the bullets that had killed the five victims and determined that all the shots were fired from either the automatic rifle or the .38-caliber revolver.

No fingerprints had been found on either gun to link Lowenfield to the weapons.

The search for Leslie O. Lowenfield dragged through September when the FBI got into the act because it was believed he had fled the state.

Lawmen got reports of Lowenfield surfacing in different parts of the country, and every lead had to be checked out. They all proved false.

For awhile it was believed Lowenfield had gone to Florida, but no trace of the suspect could be found in that state. Florida appeared to be the most promising possibility because while checking airline, train and bus depots, detectives learned that Lowenfield had purchased a bus ticket for Florida for August 29th.

But that was the day before the murders, and detectives learned that the ticket wasn't used. As they would eventually find out, the purchase of the bus ticket by Lowenfield was just part of a plan to fabricate an alibi for himself for the time of the murders.

It was October 5, 1982 when FBI agents Michael J. Henehan and Thomas F. Sinnott were working the Brooklyn, N.Y. area at 11:30 a.m. The agents had familiarized themselves with Lowenfield as well as other fugitives wanted by the bureau.

When they spotted him walking down the street,

there was no doubt in their minds who he was. The agents followed Lowenfield for a short distance and called for other backup units. When they determined it was safe to make the arrest, it was done without incident.

The month-long manhunt for Leslie O. Lowenfield had finally come to an end.

Lowenfield was held at Riker's Island Prison in New York pending his extradition to New Orleans. During his stay at Riker's Island, he wrote several letters in which he said he didn't intend to shoot the four-year-old child. In the letters, he described how Carl Osborne had grabbed the tot and tried to use her as a shield just before the girl and her father were shot.

The letters were turned over to detectives, who realized that they were just as good as a confession. Lowenfield apparently didn't expect the letters to be used as evidence against him. If he'd known they would be given to detectives, he probably wouldn't have penned them.

A handwriting expert compared the letters, the notebook that had been found in Sheila's closet and other known samples of Lowenfield's writing, and determined that the same hand had penned them all.

Detectives learned that Lowenfield planned to use as part of his defense the story that he'd taken a bus trip to Florida 21 hours before the murders and that he was in Jacksonville at the time of the slayings, looking for work.

Det. Trapani knew that because his case against Lowenfield was strictly circumstantial, he would have to disprove Lowenfield's alibi.

Detectives set about tracking Lowenfield's movements from the time he left New Orleans to his arrival in New York. It was a time-consuming task but their efforts finally paid off.

Detectives found a witness who said that Leslie Lowenfield had telephoned her after the murders from a location in Alabama.

"This was the day after the killings," the witness told detectives.

Leslie Lowenfield claimed he left for Florida on a bus 21 hours before the killings. That being the case, how could he be in Alabama the day after the murders?

He couldn't, was the logical conclusion. He'd lied about leaving on the bus, detectives knew from the start, but now they had proof that he couldn't have been in Florida as he'd claimed.

Leslie O. Lowenfield was eventually extradited to Jefferson Parish from New York, and he went on trial in May of 1984.

Assistant District Attorneys Arthur Lentini and Greg Gremillion sought the death penalty and presented the case in much the same manner as detectives had unearthed evidence. They did battle with two highly competent court-appointed attorneys who defended Lowenfield.

Testifying at the trial were the department store clerk who sold Lowenfield the .22-caliber automatic rifle, the cab driver who dropped him near the murder scene, the seven men who had been playing cards with one of the victims, and witnesses who knew Lowenfield, had threatened to kill Sheila Thomas and Carl Osborne.

Dr. Hunt told of the grisly manner in which the five victims were killed. The defense made a great deal of the manner in which the two murder weapons were found in the house after the crime investigation was completed.

"You had all the police rank out there that night," one defense attorney said at the trial. "You had everyone from Sheriff Harry Lee on down and all those police overlooked the two guns," the attorney criticized.

The attorney also argued that it was incredible to think one man could have hidden the two guns so quickly and effectively and fled the scene before police arrived one minute after receiving the 5:30 p.m. telephone call at headquarters.

The attorney suggested that more than one person would have to be involved, and that Lowenfield was not one of the individuals.

Lowenfield took the stand and called all of the state's witnesses liars. He said the cab driver was lying, the department store clerk was lying, and he denied writing the threatening notebook which had been found in Sheila Thomas's closet.

But the most damning state witness against Lowenfield was the woman who testified that she'd received a telephone call from Lowenfield from Alabama the day after the murder.

"I never met her," Lowenfield said on the stand about the witness. "I never saw her before she came in this courtroom Saturday and testified. I guess someone coached her on what to say."

The woman had testified that she had met Lowenfield in the spring of 1982 and had been in his apartment and he had telephoned her frequently that summer. Lowenfield denied it all.

He had to deny it, because it shot holes through his alibi that he was in Jacksonville, Florida looking for work in the shipyards at the time of the murders.

Lowenfield insisted he left New Orleans at 8 p.m. on August 29th, arrived in Jacksonville on August 30th where he couldn't find work, and caught a bus to New York. He arrived there September 1st. He said a cousin showed him a story in the newspaper about the Louisiana mass murder.

The jury was faced with the task of either believing all the state's witnesses or else believing Lowenfield. There was no middle ground; no chance that facts were confused, Lowenfield simply called all the state's witnesses liars. One of his attorneys contended that the department store clerk who had sold the gun identified Lowenfield because she was hysterical over the fact that she'd put the murder weapon in the killer's hands. She would have identified anybody the police suggested, the defense attorney told the jury.

In closing arguments, the defense urged the jury not to rush to a judgement. The defense said it was a rush to judgment which had brought the case this far and had put an innocent man on trial.

On Monday, May 14, 1984, the jury got the case and deliberated for eight hours without reaching a verdict. Judge James Cannella dismissed three alternate jurors.

The jury began deliberations on Monday at 11:50 a.m., and at 8 p.m. sent Judge Cannella a note stating that the panel was weary and wanted supper and rest.

The sequestered jury took the rest of the night off, and resumed deliberations Tuesday.

The whole while defendant Lowenfield remained in the packed courtroom and chatted amiably to a capacity crowd which at times even laughed at some of his jokes. Deliberations dragged on Tuesday, and Judge Cannella called attorneys into his chambers to tell him he was about ready to declare a mistrial because the jury obviously couldn't reach a verdict. But he gave it more time, and about an hour later the jury returned with its verdicts.

They found Leslie O. Lowenfield guilty of three counts of first-degree murder in connection with the deaths of his former girlfriend, Sheila Thomas;

Carl Osborne, the father of Sheila's daughter; and Myrtle Griffin, Sheila's mother.

Those three persons, the jury determined, were the primary targets.

The jury found Lowenfield guilty of voluntary manslaughter in connection with the shootings of four-year-old Shantel Osborne, the daughter of Sheila and Carl, and of Owen Griffin, who had burst onto the scene to help.

After returning the verdicts, the jury began deliberating at 8:20 p.m. about whether to recommend death in the electric chair or life in prison for the first-degree murder convictions.

After deliberating seven hours, the jury decided Lowenfield should die. As jurors were discharged Wednesday and led out of the Gretna courtroom, Lowenfield, in handcuffs and leg irons, was led back to the Jefferson Parish jail by three armed deputies.

He smiled at his two court-appointed attorneys and said, "Hey, see you guys later."

On May 29th, Judge James Cannella sentenced mass murderer Leslie Lowenfield, 30, to be executed three times in the electric chair.

It was not an easy task for the judge, and his voice cracked during the proceedings. His judicial aides even left the courtroom. They didn't want to hear the sentences three times.

He told Lowenfield three times that an electrical charge will be sent through his body "until you are dead, dead, dead."

Judge Cannella admitted after the sentencing that it was one of the hardest things he ever had to do in his life. He was shaken by the experience.

"That is an enormous emotional experience," Judge Cannella said, "to read that and then to read it three times. I'm just glad that under the new state

234

law, the jury determines life or death in a first-degree murder conviction, and I just make the formal pronouncement."

The triple death penalty is believed to be the first of its kind in Louisiana.

"I know there are some inmates in Angola currently under a single death penalty and life sentence for multiple murder convictions, but I have not heard of a triple death penalty," an assistant to the state's Secretary of Corrections said.

Under Louisiana law, the case will be automatically appealed. Lowenfield is currently awaiting the outcome of that appeal.

"A WHOLE FAMILY WAS MASSACRED FOR REVENGE!"

by Peggy I. Mullins

Mt. Vernon, Illinois is situated in the southern part of the state in Jefferson County. Here Carolyn and Robert Odle lived with their four children. Although the couple had been divorced, they had only recently remarried and were going to church. They were trying hard to make a real success of their marriage. The future looked promising for the couple.

Both Carolyn and Bob were well liked by all their neighbors. Bob's employers considered him to be very dependable, and they placed a lot of confidence in their employee. He rarely took off from his work, and always did his best and was always on time.

On November 8, 1985, however, Bob Odle did not appear for his 4:00 p.m.-to-midnight shift. His supervisor waited for him to call and explain, but they did not hear from him. This surprised the company, because they knew that Bob Odle had always been very reliable. They began to wonder if something could have gone wrong for him.

After they had waited for some time and still no word from their employee, company superiors relented and called the Mt. Vernon Police and reported their fear at 6:30 p.m. Officers in a squad car re-

236

sponded to the call and went to the Odle residence. They walked around the house and peered into the windows, but saw nothing unusual. When the officers knocked on the doors, nobody answered, and they soon left.

The hours went by and the company waited patiently, but Bob Odle still did not report for work and neither did he call in. At long last, the company again called the police at 9:08 p.m. and once again officers hurried to the Odle residence and looked around and knocked on the door. But they failed to see anything unusual.

As before, the officers saw the two cars. One sat in front and one on the property, but everything seemed to be okay. The officers again left the area. They had not seen anything out of the ordinary.

After some more time had passed, the company called again, but this time they called the Jefferson County Sheriff's office. The call was placed just a bit after 10:00 p.m. When the office received the call, Sheriff Bob Pitchford and Police Commander Captain Robert Smith drove to the Odle home.

The two officers walked around the house looking into the windows to see if they could see anything unusual, but there was nothing. Knocking on the door drew no response.

Finally, Sheriff Pitchford managed to shift himself into a position so that he could just barely see into the high bathroom window. As he twisted his head and shaded his eyes to get a better look, he did just manage to peer into the bathroom. He finally saw something that made him wonder.

The two men shifted themselves into a better position so that the sheriff could lift Captain Smith into a position so he could shine a flashlight into the bathroom. Smith soon caught a glimpse of a pair of legs, which later turned out to belong to Bob Odle.

As a result of what the officer had seen, they tried to open the door, but found the residence locked tight. Looking around, the officers could find no proof of a break-in. So the sheriff and Smith broke into the Odle residence and found five bodies lying here and there.

Blood was everywhere, and the two officers had to be very careful where they stepped. Looking around, the lawmen could see that somebody had made an effort to clean up the area of blood. The officers searched for signs of life, but the people were all dead.

Moving on through the house, the lawmen found four of the bodies in one of the bedrooms. Also, the police discovered an Old Hickory wooden-handled butcher knife. In addition, the men also found a pair of gray socks, the bottoms of which appeared to be bloodsoaked. Also found was a pair of white Nike shoes with blood on the tops and bottoms.

The officers immediately called the coroner and the State Crime Lab and personnel from these departments soon arrived on the scene. The coroner went to work with a preliminary check of the five bodies.

Police secured the scene and began to look over the entire area for any clues that would help them discover what had taken place in the Odle residence. Crime lab technicians began an inch by inch check for fingerprints. They took pictures of the five bodies and all the rooms in the house. They checked outside for any type of tire marks of which they might take a plaster cast, but found none.

Later, an inquest was held into the deaths of the five members of the Odle family. After testimony by Police Chief Ron Massey, and Pathologist Dr. James R. Miller, it was found that the deaths were all homicides. It was brought out during the inquest that all the victims except one had been stabbed again and again. One victim had been strangled with a piece of clothing. He was the youngest member of the Odle family. The six-member panel deliberated less than 25 minutes and reached its verdict.

The five victims of the Odle family were identified as Scott Odle, 10; Sean Odle, 13; Robyn Lyn Odle, 14; Carolyn Odle, 39; and Robert Odle, also 39. This left only one son Thomas, still living.

Coroner Dr. Richard Garretson told the inquest jury that he had pronounced all five of the family members dead at 11:15 p.m. on November 8th. The bodies had then been taken to the Good Samaritan Hospital for autopsies.

As the coroner handed the panel color pictures of the Odle family, he said that he found a macabre scene when he entered the Odle residence and pronounced them all dead. He said that the bodies of Sean, Robyn, and Carolyn were discovered stabbed and lying on the bedroom floor. Scott, the one who was strangled, was found lying on the same floor. However, Robert had been found stabbed and lying in the bathroom floor off the master bedroom. Dr. Miller, the pathologist, told the inquest jury that all the members of the Odle family except young Scott bled to death. This was the result of the multiple stab wounds which had cut the vessels in the victim's neck.

The pathologist said that Carolyn's and Robyn's right jugular vein had been cut and their carotid arteries severed; that Robert's right and Sean's left jugular vein had been cut; that young Scott had been strangled with a shirt and a pajama bottom tied very tightly around his neck.

Meanwhile, investigators prepared to launch a full scale probe into the deaths of the five family members. They began a neighborhood canvass to question all the neighbors who had known the Odle family and any friends who had been close to them.

One neighbor who lived not far from the Odle home said that the whole area was shocked by the multiple slaying.

"Did you see or hear anything at the Odle house that seemed unusual?" asked a detective, as he sat in the woman's living room.

"I didn't hear anything. I just thought they were having a party," answered the neighbor. "I can't believe this."

"How well did you know the Odle family?" asked a detective.

"I had the little kids over once in a while to play cards. They loved to come," said the neighbor, as she struggled to keep from crying.

Moving on about the neighborhood, investigators questioned another friend of the Odle family. He told them that he was absolutely stunned over the killing of the five Odle family members.

"Isn't this terrible?" said the Odle neighbor. "It's shocking. I loved Bob; he was sweet as can be."

As detectives questioned him, the neighbor told them that the Odles had been separated, but they had reconciled only recently.

"They were getting along so good and going to church," said the neighbor.

Investigators continued to canvass the neighborhood in the hope that somebody would be able to give information that would help clear up all their questions about the case.

"I would call them a quiet family. They never mixed with any of us," commented one neighbor of the Odle family. "I'm shocked to think this could happen. This block is the quietest block around. We're all old women that live around here. I didn't hear any screams or anything. It must have started early. I was afraid over here. Something was telling me that something was happening."

Another friend, a former classmate of Carolyn and Bob Odle, talked with detectives. He also said that he was a co-worker with Bob Odle for several years.

"We worked different shifts," the Odles friend told probers. "I worked in the days and he worked nights as a mechanic keeping up all the vehicles and equipment we use in Mt. Vernon. He was really nice, easygoing; never said a bad word about anybody and would go out of his way to be nice to you."

"Tell me," asked one detective, "did Bob Odle have any hobbies or other activities?"

"By the time he drove back and forth to Centralia, worked nights and kept up with his house, car, and family, I don't see how he had much time for much else," said the friend.

Meanwhile, Coroner Garretson described the crime scene to the press.

"It appears the bodies had been moved," said the coroner. "At least four of them had been moved from the kitchen or another part of the house and then just kind of stacked on available floor space."

"The young girl had apparently been stabbed in the living room and died in the bed in the master bedroom, then fell off onto the floor," continued the coroner.

"There was a lot of blood, and it was apparent the kitchen had been cleaned up extensively," added the coroner. "Towels were laid on the carpet. All the wounds were in the neck. They were stabbed repeatedly."

Police Chief Ron Massey praised the law enforcement men for their work in the case.

"Citizens came forth, too," said Chief Massey,

"and gave us the information that helped establish the time element."

As detectives continued to delve ever deeper into the case, they received a tip from an Odle neighbor who had seen someone on the Odle property. Detectives asked the neighbor if he had recognized the person whom he had said was coming around the south side of the Odle house on the morning in question.

Although probers were well aware that just because a man was coming around the side of the Odle house did not mean that he had killed the family. Yet, the officers wanted to question him and determine if he knew anything at all about the slayings.

Checking the identification of the man, police learned that he lived in Mt. Vernon, and they went immediately to his home. The probers told him they wanted to talk with him at the police station about the Odle family slaying.

He went with police to the station where detectives questioned him about why he was at the Odle residence. He said that he had gone there to talk to Bob Odle about helping him get a job. But when he knocked on the door, there was no answer.

For the next three hours, probers grilled the suspect and asked about his actions for the entire day in question. The man was able to account for his time and detectives soon learned that he was telling the truth and told him that he could go.

This action brought the investigators back to where they started, without any suspect whatever in the gruesome slaying. But detectives were determined to solve the case as quickly as possible.

The weary probers now turned their attention to Coroner Garretson, who told them that judging from the evidence at the crime scene, he believed that Robert Odle was slain first. His body had seemed to have been dragged through the master bedroom and into the bathroom, his legs propped on the edge of the bathtub. His eyes were open and his glasses were undisturbed as he had worn them.

Investigators asked the coroner who had been killed next. The coroner said that he believed it was Carolyn Odle. She had been found in the northeast corner of a bedroom with her head pointing toward the southeast.

Scott, who was believed the third one to be murdered, was discovered with his head on his mother's arm. Sean, thought to be the fourth victim, was found lying across the legs of Scott. Believed to be the last to die, Robyn appeared to have been thrown against a wall with her head pushed into her chest in an unnatural way. As they pushed ahead, detectives next questioned a crime scene investigator. Slowly, he pulled items from a bag and said they were from the Odle home. They included bloodsoaked articles of clothing, a bottle of cleaning fluid, a dish towel, a mop, six kitchen floor tiles, hair samples, and some pictures. One item was the Old Hickory brand chef knife that had been found on top of a jewelry box on a dresser in the master bedroom.

The detectives questioned Dr. Miller, the pathologist, about the knife, and he said that the stab wounds on four of the victims other than Scott Odle could have been made by that knife. Questioned about pain, Dr. Miller said that the victims would have felt the pain as long as they were conscious. The sharpness of the knife would have governed the amount of force required to do the damage to the victims.

The probers quizzed a co-worker of Robert Odle who told them that she had known Carolyn Odle for about three years. She had been with the victim on November 8th, from about 8:30 to 11:15 a.m. Together, they had gone to a school to get ready for a Parent-Teacher Organization chili supper.

The detectives continued to move through the neighborhood where the Odle family lived, talking to several persons who had known the luckless family, but none of them could answer key questions.

In addition, probers questioned other Odle family members, hoping that one of them would recall something and give them a lead that would help break the case.

One relative told detectives that Tom Odle, the couple's oldest son, was seen driving his father's car, a brown 1978 Mercury Marquis.

"What's wrong with that?" asked a detective. "Older sons all over America drive their father's car every day."

The kinsman told investigators that he knew something was wrong at the time he saw Tom Odle driving the car, because it was absolutely off limits to him. Tom Odle was not allowed to drive his father's car.

Lawmen considered this information and then became suspicious that something could possibly be wrong. They decided to ask the Odle boy about his driving his father's car when it was off limits to him.

Officers began an intense hunt for the Odle boy and asked several of his friends if they had any idea of where he was. Most of Tom Odle's pals told probers that they did not know where he had gone. Then detectives received a tip that Tom could be in Covington, Kentucky, since he had some good friends there.

Officers alerted police in the Covington area to be on the lookout for the Odle boy. Meanwhile, lawmen received a lead that led them to a Mt. Vernon motel. Looking into the matter, detectives discovered the Odle car on the motel parking lot.

Quickly, the investigators made the decision to stake out the auto rather than trying to rush the motel immediately. Chief Massey noted that this action was to avoid the possibility of a hostage situation.

Patiently, detectives waited and watched the motel for any sign of the Odle boy. About 9:50 a.m., Deputy Sheriff Mike Anthis and Division of Criminal Investigation Agent Charles Parker saw Tom Odle and a young girl come out of a room at the motel and head for the Odle car. The lawmen immediately moved in and placed Odle under arrest.

Afterwards, Odle was questioned for three hours by Anthis and Parker. Early Saturday afternoon, he was placed in the Jefferson County Jail and Resident Circuit Judge Lehman Krause ordered him held without bond. Chief Massey told the press that Odle had picked up the girl sometime during the previous night after having driven around the town for a while. The two of them had spent the night in the motel.

Chief Massey said that the girl had no connection with the case and didn't know anything was wrong until she called friends and learned that police were looking for Odle.

A few days later, detectives questioned a man who had been in the Jefferson County Jail at the time Tom Odle was brought in. He told detectives that Odle had told him what had really happened at the crime scene.

The man told probers that Odle had said that he and his father were alone in the house and were having an argument. Odle said that he went into the kitchen and obtained a knife and hid it under his flannel shirt. Odle had said that he then realized what he was doing and turned back to hide the knife behind the couch or somewhere else.

The man then quoted Odle as saying the next

thing he knew was he saw his father bleeding and his father saying, "I love you. I want to help you."

Also, Odle had told him that his father fell to the floor and he had become scared. Then he had attempted to clean up the mess which took about an hour. The man said that Odle had told him that he then hid behind a door and waited for his mother to come home. The man told probers that he couldn't actually recall what Odle had said he had done then.

The prisoner said that Odle had stated that his mother had asked him if he was going to kill her. The man told probers that Odle had told him he used drugs a couple of days before November 8th, and had smoked a joint early that day. Yet, he was not high at the time of the argument with his father.

"I never saw Tom cry," said the prisoner. "Sometimes he shivered when he spoke, though." The prisoner told probers that he had known Tom Odle for about three years before mid-November and he used drugs at different times with him.

Next, detectives questioned a trusty of the Jefferson County Jail at the time Odle was taken in. He told lawmen that Odle had told him about the slayings.

"He said he kept stabbing them and stabbing them like he enjoyed it," said the trusty. "He said he was glad he killed his father and mother but wished he had taken the kids to his grandma's. He said his dad was always beating him and his mother was always yelling at him."

"He said he smoked three joints earlier that day," said the trusty.

Detectives asked the trusty if Odle was blaming the use of drugs for what he had done, and the prisoner said that he was not.

As the prisoner continued to answer questions, he said he thought Odle had a very freaky look in his eyes when he was in jail in mid-November and had a similar look later.

Investigators next turned their attention to a friend of Tom Odle who told them she had known Tom for about one-half to two years. She said their friendship had developed to the point where they were thinking about getting married. The young woman told probers that they were still friends when Odle left for military service in April, 1985.

Continuing, the woman said that Odle was in the service about six weeks and was then discharged. When he returned from the service, the young woman said she and Odle broke up their friendship. "I was young . . . I wasn't ready to spend my life with just one person," she said. The woman said that Odle didn't want them to break up. "I guess he took it really hard."

The young woman was asked if it were true that there was an abortion which had involved her and Tom Odle.

"Yes sir," replied the woman. Asked if Tom was against the abortion, she said that he had been against it.

The young woman told probers that she knew Odle used marijuana and LSD. She said that Odle's family tried to help him but Odle refused all their attempts.

"He needed to find a job. He needed to learn respect for his parents and he needed to help more around the house," said the young woman friend.

The woman told detectives that Odle never did realize his folks were attempting to help him. "I thought maybe he'd grow out of it."

The young woman stated that she knew Robert and Carolyn Odle had told their children to play only with certain people and had forbade them from having any friends in the Odle home.

The woman said that she talked her father into giving Odle a job in her father's business. However, Odle was discharged after three or four months because he failed to perform duties and lied about work he failed to do.

She told detectives that Odle beat his brother Sean.

"If Tom ever missed anything, he immediately took Sean back to his bedroom and would slap him around and threaten him. I think the children were too scared to say anything about Tom hitting them," said the woman.

When investigators completed their questioning, they made preparations to turn all evidence over to the State of Illinois for possible prosecution.

Tom Odle was then formally charged with the murder of his father Robert Odle, his mother Carolyn Odle, his brother Scott, his brother Sean and his sister Robyn.

Kathleen Alling, Jefferson County State's Attorney, said that she would oppose any attempt to set bail. Also, she stated that it was too soon to say whether she would seek the death sentence.

Alling and Assistant State's Attorney Rob Crego said that the suspect had left the house and picked up two of the children at school before they were murdered.

"I believe that based on the evidence the first murder occurred early in the morning — 9:30 or 10:00 a.m. — and the murders ended when the last two children were brought home from school by the defendant," said Crego.

"We do have evidence that he did leave the house and did pick up the children from school," said Attorney Alling.

Alling, asked about the motive, refused to make any comments, other than to state: "What we have so far is that there was a family disagreement on an ongoing basis over more than one or two weeks," said the state's attorney. When the press asked her about a confession, Alling remarked, "We have a statement that was taken by the police department by tape recording, transcribed, typed up, and he signed it. In his statement, he did take responsibility for the killing of the family."

Tom Odle was brought to trial before a jury of six men and six women. After the panel heard all the evidence, they took one hour and 50 minutes to find him guilty of killing the five members of his family.

Circuit Judge Donald E. Garrison sentenced Odle to the death penalty. The judge entered the nearly full courtroom at 9:20 a.m. and rendered his decision at 9:40 a.m.

"17-YEAR TRACK OF
THE FAMILY SLAYER!"

by Bud Ampolsk

It all began with a routine call. Before it was to end some 18 years later, it took on the unbelievably grotesque proportions of a "Nightmare on Elm Street" horror scenario. Its bloodstained history would leave at least three American communities in a state of benumbed shock. For those living in the well-to-do community of Westfield, New Jersey, things would never be quite the same again.

It was early in November 1971 that a series of notes and telephone calls were put through to teachers in the Westfield school system and to local tradesmen.

The message was, with a few minor variations, primarily the same: Please excuse the three children of local residents Alma and John List from classes until further notice. Please suspend mail and newspaper deliveries to 431 Hillside Avenue until further notice.

According to the then 45-year-old Joseph List, he, his wife and three youngsters would be away from their 18-room $500,000 Victorian mansion for an indeterminate period of time. In placing the messages, List was said to have variously mentioned a protracted vacation and the need to care for an ailing relative who was said to be residing in North Carolina.

List was a highly respected accountant. He had served in such worthy capacities as a Sunday School teacher in the Lutheran church where his family worshipped. There was no reason to suspect that anything sinister could touch the man, let alone be instituted by him.

The devoted husband and father possessed other impeccable credentials. He was reputed to hold an M.B.A. degree from the University of Michigan. He had been a successful insurance salesman before entering the field of accounting and was (in 1971) a former vice president of a local bank.

He and his family completely fit into the respectable conservative affluent suburban town that was Westfield in the early 1970s.

A month passed before anyone felt that something was amiss in the List household. Neighbors began reporting that the lights which had been left on at the Hillside Avenue address—a seemingly standard practice of suburbanites wishing to discourage housebreakers and vandals—were beginning to wink out.

In the ensuing days, concern grew. The neighbors contacted the Westfield police, asking them to check the List premises to determine if everything there was in order.

It was on a cold foggy, drab December 7, 1971, that a detail under the command of Westfield Police Chief James Moran entered the sprawling turn-of-the-century mansion.

Some 18 years later, Moran would say, "It's something I remember like yesterday. I walked into that house and saw that one kid was shot with nine bullets in him, just savagely.

251

"You don't forget something like that."

It was more than the numbing chill of the interior (the heat had been turned off to slow the decomposition of the bodies) that caused those who accompanied Moran on his tour of horror to shiver as if attacked by some nameless, malignant ague.

One of those who had been there at the moment of the grisly discoveries would write nearly two decades later, "The ballroom of the List mansion was one of the most beautiful rooms I'd ever seen. But on its hardwood floors was a scene more horrible than any I'd ever seen or imagined."

The man would go on to tell of how four bodies, rotted and blackening in the putrification of decomposition, had been discovered.

"I've never forgotten that sight," the man would continue.

"The smell struck me and the Westfield police officers I accompanied as soon as we entered. The bodies were those of List's wife and three children, all neatly laid out in a row on sleeping bags. Only later did we find the corpse of his mother upstairs.

"I remember one of the police officers telling me that the woman had been crammed into a bedroom closet and that they'd had to break her legs to remove her."

As the nauseated searchers continued their probe of the mansion-now-turned-charnel-house, they came upon one obscene discovery after another. Included were bunches of blood-soaked paper toweling which had been stuffed into paper bags in the kitchen. The walls had been hastily washed in an attempt to eradicate the gory stains which besmirched the house's walls and woodwork. The attempt had failed.

Propped on the dining room table was a letter (allegedly written by John List) reputedly explaining why and how he had killed his family.

Caught in the maelstrom of violence which had wiped out three generations of Lists had been Alma List, the missing accountant's 85-year-old mother, Helen List, 45, John's wife; his 16-year-old daughter, Patricia; and his two sons, John Jr., 15, and Frederick, 12.

One theory had it that the murders had occurred on November 9th, two days before List himself had disappeared.

The chronology espoused by those investigating the savage bloodletting had it that List allegedly began the carnage after his three children had left for school on the fatal morning. First to be shot to death had been the missing man's wife. Then, allegedly, John murdered his aged mother.

According to police speculation, there had been a temporary respite in the mortal proceedings. The alleged killer had awaited the return of the teenage children from their classes. It was thought that Patricia had been the first to enter the house and had been cut down by a single bullet when she did. John Jr. had been the next arrival. Because he had probably put up a valiant but futile struggle, the 15-year-old had been made the target of nine bullets. Twelve-year-old Frederick had been the last to come home and the last to die.

Police have never revealed the full contents of the five-page confessional letter allegedly written by List and addressed to the pastor of the Redeemer Lutheran Church in Westfield. However, local lawmen have reported that the note describes how the shootings had been carried out and the reasons behind them in graphic detail.

It was believed that the accountant had been in severe financial straits. This theory was shored up by information developed that he had taken out two mortgages on his home and that he had been dipping into his mother's savings account, estimated at $200,000.

There were also reports that John Sr. had been failing in a financial consultant business he'd set up.

Possibly compounding the missing man's animosity towards his next of kin, according to those with inside information of the contents of the "confessional letter," was List's sense of having lost control over the women of his family. He was said to have felt that his wife and daughter had been going down the wrong path and that his sons would not have understood their father's reasons for having slain Helen and Patricia.

At this point in the probe, local police only had these shreds of evidence to go on . . .

Five people had been coldbloodedly shot to death at the Hillside Avenue address.

Bullets recovered from the decomposed bodies indicated that a .22-caliber rifle and a 9mm pistol had been used in the executions.

The condition of the bodies and the continuing absence of John List led probers to believe that the slayings had taken place on November 9th at the latest and that the corpses had remained undetected until December 7th.

The sequence of the murders had been determined by the fact that while the bodies of Alma and Helen List had been dressed in indoor clothing, the three teenagers cadavers had been stretched out still garbed in their overcoats. The rationale was that the children had been intercepted as they arrived home.

No sight of John List Sr. had been reported since November 9th.

The enigma surrounding the missing bespectacled man's whereabouts thickened on December 9th when his car was discovered in a parking lot at Kennedy

Airport, just two days after police had first entered the Hillside Avenue home.

Now an APB was issued on the balding executive and churchman. Everything that was known about his earlier life was disseminated in hopes that it would produce leads. Included in the dossier was List's earlier service in the armed forces. It was learned that the erstwhile Westfield financial expert had entered the Army as a private during World War II. Later, during the Korean War, he served as a reservist. He'd left the Army as a first lieutenant.

But there was nothing in these facts which would keep List's trail from turning ice-cold. Both the police, who wanted to bring him in on the indictments for five counts of murder which had been lodged against him in absentia, and the FBI, which was tracing him for having unlawfully fled to avoid prosecution for murder, were stymied.

It was obvious that the fugitive had made excellent use of his month-long head start over his pursuers.

The fact that he had abandoned his car at Kennedy added to the confusion. Lawmen had to wrestle with other possibilities.

Perhaps List himself had become a victim. The area around Kennedy Airport has long been known as a mob dumping ground.

If List was still alive, he could be just about anywhere on earth. Flights from Kennedy not only stretched over the furthest reaches of the United States, but the airport served as the point of departure for all overseas flights from the New York City area.

There were numerous sightings, not only from the 50 states, but from Europe and South America, as well. None panned out.

The simple truth was that if John List Jr. resembled anybody at all, that person was "Everyman."

255

Outside of a jagged scar that had been left behind his ear by an earlier mastoidectomy, John List had few if any other distinguishing physical characteristics. Although his fingerprints were on file in Washington, as are those of all persons who have served in the Armed Forces, they would prove of little value unless List was apprehended on some other charge. As long as he kept his nose clean, he could probably go about his new business in complete anonymity.

As the search remained stalled, the Hillside Avenue home came to be thought of more as a haunted house than a mansion. It became a magnet to teenagers who drove by and dared each other to walk around the grounds and peer through the windows.

The macabre hijinks surrounding the property ended suddenly in 1972 when the house mysteriously burned to the ground.

The months slipped into years. Still there was little hope that John List would ever surface. People talked of the quintuple shootings which had wiped out the List family as they talked about the other "great unsolved crimes of history." The common thought was that the slayings would go down alongside the "Jack The Ripper" murders as a prime example of somebody getting away with murder. However, Chief Moran, as well as Frank Marranca, head of the homicide division of the Union County (New Jersey) Prosecutor's office, John C. McGinley, agent in charge of the Newark Office of the FBI, and scores of other lawmen throughout the country, felt somewhat differently.

Moran, for example, retired as Westfield Chief of Police in 1986. But he continued his quest. Three years after his retirement, he was still tracking down leads. He never gave up the "wanted" flyer which contained List's picture and pertinent facts concerning the fugitive.

Never mind that FBI agents from 23 offices had at one time or another gone out on wild-goose chases which had led nowhere. Never mind that there was nobody who could say with certainty that John List, Sr., was still alive.

Then, early in 1989, Marranca had an idea. It concerned the Fox Network weekly program, "America's Most Wanted."

Although most lawmen had expressed early dislike for the weekly show which graphically stressed sensational unsolved cases and urged civilians to contact the producers with possible leads, the enthusiastic public response had not gone unnoticed. In recent months editors and executives of "America's Most Wanted" were able to boast that the show had been responsible for eliciting information which had led to the arrest of 48 prime suspects in 48 major crimes.

Playing a hunch, the Union County Prosecutor's homicide division head contacted program representatives, asking them to do an item on the List case.

The talented sculptor worked from the only photos which were currently available of the fugitive. He improved such details as a receding hairline and the wrinkles which would have accrued over an 18-year span.

Later Ms. Roberts would say of the project, "The bust was an experiment. Our show hinges on the indelible image of the human face. In this case, all we had was precious few photographs almost twenty years old. This crime was the most notorious in New Jersey history."

Now all systems were go for the cooperative venture. On Sunday evening, May 21, 1989, the List story was beamed to viewers on 125 of the Fox Television Network's stations.

Minutes after the List portion of the telecast was

aired Fox switchboards were deluged with tips. Over 300 callers came forward with their views as to List's current identity and where he might be located.

To FBI agents, at least 200 of the leads held promise of being "substantive." One, in particular, stood out.

This was the one which was to send three federal agents from their Richmond, Virginia headquarters to nearby suburban Midlothian, Virginia, home of 63-year-old Robert P. Clark.

There the G-Men showed Clark's wife a number of pictures they had of List. At first the thunderstruck middle-aged-woman refused to believe that the man she had wed in 1985 could be the John List, Sr.

Later, Agent McGinley of the Newark, New Jersey FBI office would say of the interview with Mrs. Clark, "She reacted with disbelief and shock when the agents showed her the pictures of List. But she was very cooperative and helpful in resolving questions about his identity. She brought out wedding pictures which showed a man who still resembled the pictures of List that were circulated after the murders."

Once she had been convinced of Clark's alleged other identity, his wife provided two Norfolk-based agents with the one item they felt they needed to complete the puzzle. This was the name and Richmond address of Clark's current employer.

A short time later, two agents were walking through the doors of one of the biggest accounting firms in the Richmond area. The third agent had stayed behind with Clark's visibly shaken wife.

At the firm's reception desk, the agents asked for Clark's employers and were told by the receptionist that the executives were out of town. They then inquired as to whether Clark was in.

The receptionist led the G-Men to a small office

where the 63-year-old suspect was seated at his desk.

Reportedly the agents asked the suspect, "Are you John List?"

They claim that Clark denied he was the man they sought. However, the receptionist who had watched the dramatic climax of the 18-year search being played out would report, "He (Clark) didn't seem surprised to see them (the FBI agents). He didn't say anything, other than he wasn't John List.

"They took him into custody and when they led him out, he turned his head and glanced at me and gave me this strange look. He looked full of anger."

An attorney who works in the office building and who viewed the arrest, said, "He didn't offer any resistance and he didn't look surprised."

The man who had over the course of 18 years apparently built an entire new life was taken in handcuffs to the Richmond FBI field office and fingerprinted. According to the FBI, Clark's prints were a perfect match for those of John List Jr. which had been in their files.

An official FBI statement noted, "Although he would not admit to his identity, List was positively identified by his fingerprints."

For retired Chief Moran, June 1, 1989, was a banner day. Said the former head of the Westfield Police Force, "That's the best thing that ever happened to me. How can a guy murder five people and walk away?

"That's what bothered me these many years."

The sense of vindication for the effort he'd put into the almost two-decade-long search was apparent as the triumphant Moran added, "We knew he had to be somewhere."

The suspect, who was described as "very calm and self-contained," was taken before United States Magistrate David G. Lowe in Richmond for a preliminary hearing. He was ordered held at the Henrico County Jail pending extradition hearings to bring him back to New Jersey to face further court proceedings.

As List was led from the courtroom, clad in a white sport shirt and slacks and with his manacled wrists attached to a chain which encircled his waist, he glared balefully through his thick-lensed eyeglasses.

With List securely in custody, authorities turned to piecing together his comings and goings over the past 18 years.

They claimed that while he had changed his name to Robert P. Clark, he had made no effort to alter his appearance or embark on a new vocation.

At the time of his arrest, List was earning $24,000 a year from his employers. He had been handling corporate work and clients' personal finances, including preparation of income tax returns.

He had posed as the upright citizen he had once been in New Jersey.

List had not run afoul of the law since having fled to Denver, Colorado, in 1972.

Those who had known him in Denver, where he'd remained until 1988, described List as a quiet, churchgoing accountant who impressed neighbors, pastors and acquaintances as respectable and altogether average.

Some referred to him as "an American John Doe" who lived in a modest home, worked steadily and spent his free time puttering around his garden and watching television.

Generally, the feeling about List was that he had always been friendly, generously doing odd jobs for neighbors, trading videotapes and books. But he had remained tight-lipped about his past. Acquaintances stressed that his life in the Denver area had centered around home, work and church, and that he seemed, if anything, like the antithesis of evil.

Said one woman, "I don't know what a guy who's killed five people is supposed to look like, but he was not that person."

Added a man who had been a Clark neighbor in Midlothian, "He worked hard in his yard, went to work every day, went to church every Sunday—the guy was so average. You talk about an average neighborhood, this is it. This just doesn't happen in my neighborhood."

A Denver pastor commented, "He was well-liked. He had gained the respect of the parish. There was nothing to cause us to be suspicious of his demeanor or his credibility. Somehow, some way, he was able to stabilize himself here."

The clergyman attributed the Clarks' move from Denver to the Richmond area to the fact that Clark's wife reportedly had relatives living in Virginia. He said he had recently received a letter from Clark (List) which gave no indication that anything was wrong.

One co-worker at the Richmond accounting firm called Clark "a nice fellow, almost too nice to be true. He even had a fraternal Order of Police sticker on his car."

With irony, a woman co-worker stated, "I would hold him up to my husband as a model because I heard him talk to his wife on the phone—he would say how much he loved her."

The pastor of the Lutheran Church the Clarks had joined after they had moved into the Midlothian bedroom community, 15 miles from Richmond, noted, "The congregation is stunned. I think we are all trying to reserve judgment. They have been kind to people. They have been faithful church members."

One Richmond friend seemed to sum up the feelings of many when he stated, "I only know Bobby

Clark. I don't know John List. But even if it's all true, this is not a man with a history of murder, but a man with murder in his history. It was one day after all these many years."

The friend stressed Clark's abhorrence of violence, saying, "He didn't even like football because he said it was just men out there battering their heads together, instead of using their brains. Clark liked baseball, the *National Geographic*, Walter Cronkite and documentaries.

"He is deeply religious. If he goes into a McDonald's for a hamburger, the man is going to bow his head and say grace to God."

Piecing together the events of Clark's (List's) life since 1972, sources close to the situation said that a resume he prepared for a position after moving to Richmond in 1988, listed a business in Wheatridge, Colorado, under the name of R.C. Miller. They said no such R.C. Miller is currently in business there, nor is there any evidence that it ever existed.

In 1973, a close friend from that time places Clark as working as a night cook at a Holiday Inn in Golden, Colorado.

Clark's name first appeared in a Denver telephone directory in 1974. He continued working as a restaurant and hotel cook. By 1977, Clark was seeking employment in accounting.

Noted one executive who interviewed him at that time, "He was an introvert galore, if there is such a thing. He spoke slowly, softly, almost under his breath."

The man recollects that Clark's clothes at the interview were ill-matched. "He was living hand-to-mouth, doing bookkeeping work," the man holds. "I had the impression he was barely eking out enough of a living to buy weenies and a room somewhere.

He was living meagerly and said he needed a full-time job."

An employer for whom Clark had worked in 1977 recalled that he had found him a little strange. He cited Clark's penchant for eating a solitary luncheon in his automobile while listening to classical programs on his car radio. Said the man, "We kind of liked him and felt sorry for him.

"I remember talking to him a few times about marriage, because I was having marital problems at the time. He said he'd been through that before and knew what I meant. I'd tell him I wasn't going to get into that kind of a mess again, and he said he wasn't going to either. He insinuated that it had been a bad experience."

The year 1977, had been a good one for Clark. His salary rose to $400 a week and he met his future second wife at a Lutheran Church function.

However, there were apparent discrepancies in stories he allegedly told friends concerning his past familial relationships.

One friend said, "When asked about his family, he would make some reference to Minnesota or Michigan. He would say that he had been married before but that his wife had been terminally ill and took years to die and that he took care of her. Her illness left astronomical bills, he'd tell me. We all made assumptions, such as the fact that he didn't have any children, since his wife had been so sick."

However, later in Richmond, another friend quoted him as having confided that his wife had been an alcoholic and a spendthrift who had died of cancer, and that he had a daughter who was "somewhat uncontrollable."

At a news conference held after Clark's arrest, his second wife reported that he had told her that his first wife was "a very sick, sickly lady."

263

During the same news conference, Mrs. Clark corroborated a neighbor's report that the woman had shown her a tabloid edition in 1985 which carried John List's photograph accompanied by a story of the Westfield murders.

Said Mrs. Clark, "I dismissed it because I felt it was not true. It still is not true."

The neighbor's fears for Mrs. Clark were rekindled when she watched "America's Most Wanted" on May 21st, long after the Clarks had moved to Virginia. She revealed that she had instructed her son-in-law to call the program's telephone number which had been flashed cross the screen to give the operator the Clarks' address and telephone number in Virginia.

It was also revealed that the Clarks had been beset by financial troubles since having made the Virginia move.

In her interview with the *Richmond News Leader,* Mrs. Clark was quoted as saying, "I find it impossible to believe my husband is a killer.

"I hope somehow this is not true, and if it is, he was so stressed out that something snapped.

"I am devoted to him. I hope that somehow, God will see us through."

For the people who suffered through 18 years of the malaise which gripped Westfield, New Jersey, between the gun deaths of the five family members of John List Jr. and the arrest of Robert P. Clark in Richmond, Virginia, on June 1, 1989, the sense of relief at the possibility that at long last the case has been broken, is great.

However, there are those who still mourn the dead.

This was shown shortly after Clark was taken into custody when somebody left a small card amidst the five graves which marked the final resting place of Alma, Helen, Patricia, John Jr. and Frederick List.

The message was simple. It read, "Now at last you

can rest in peace."

Robert P. Clark, identified by the FBI as John List has been convicted of five counts of murder and one federal count of unlawful escape to avoid prosecution for murder.

"THEY MOWED DOWN THE WHOLE FAMILY!"

by Benison Murray

The late Robert Linder claimed, "There walk among us men and women who are in but not of our world . . . often the sign by which they betray themselves is crime . . . of an explosive, impulsive, reckless type . . . the sign is ruthlessness . . ."

The psychopathic personality loved by family and friends always has his inevitable fall from grace excused. It is explained away, accepted as part of his psyche, or ignored in the vain hope that it will somehow be outgrown, matured out of or forgiven by some astute defense lawyer.

Police files are filled with examples of impulsive, ruthless behavior.

In 1960, a young man in his twenties went on a murderous spree with his girlfriend, potshotting at innocent bystanders until four lay dead. The motive? "Just target practice," wearily reported one police officer.

There was the infamous tower in Texas. There was the nightmare paths taken by a demon-ridden loner in New York.

To Tennesseans, these places were far away, the happenings made exotic reading. A hasty glance at the newspaper, a delicious shudder, then turn to the local bazaar, the Ladies Aid Bake Sale—things comforting and familiar.

A picnic is a familiar thing. Especially in a loved place with members of your own family. The Estis family, grandparents, son Gary, and his wife Diane with the two youngsters, were looking forward to the picnic.

It was a day made for picnics. June 23, 1982, was warm and sunny, perfect for fishing. And to cap it all, another son and his wife with their two girls would join them later in the afternoon.

Early up and with the whole day to look forward to, Mrs. Estis arranged hard-boiled eggs, potato salad, and iced tea for the blanket table. The picnic was also somewhat of a celebration. Mrs. Estis had just recovered from an operation on a brain tumor and her family, grateful the operation was successful, felt like celebrating.

The head of the Estis family had his troubles, too. During a simple gallbladder operation, liver cancer was discovered by his doctors. Still, it was great to be alive. Doctors were discovering new cures every day, and in the meantime, there was a perfect June day to be enjoyed.

The family's favorite fishing spot was at Vaughn's Landing at Duck River. Surrounded by high, brush-covered bluffs, it made an ideal picnic spot and afforded the Estis family a place where they could spread out their supper and let the children run like wild things.

That morning Hazel Estis buttered the bread while her daughter-in-law, Diane, prepared several ham and cheese sandwiches and placed them in the back of the car.

Gary, Diane's 30-year-old husband, went with his father to put fishing poles and a bait bucket, an igloo container with ice and soft drinks, towels for the children and a blanket in the car next to the lunch.

Others were aware of the Duck Creek location. Others knew of the camping possibilities, the fishing, the serenity of the high bluffs, the seduction of a June day.

When the family arrived at the picnic spot, they carried a neatly arranged blanket tent, a chair made from skinny tree limbs, various cans of food, soft drinks, some pans for cooking, and guns.

The two young men who had spent the previous night at the Duck River location had a hundred rounds of ammunition, two .22-caliber automatic rifles, a .22-caliber pistol and a pellet gun.

Concealed behind brush and tall weeds, they watched when the head of the Estis family, his wife Hazel, Gary, Diane and their two children arrived at the Duck River site.

Hidden as they were, the little family group was unaware of their observers high on the bluff.

There is something magical about the sound of water, they decided. Running water next to a campfire flickering in an early dusk produces a serene sense of well-being.

Right now it was, they agreed, too hot for fish to be biting. Better to wait an hour. Most of the crappy, bullgill and occasional catfish had sunk into the weedy depths away from the sun-dappled surface water.

But to catch fish was not everything. Just to stand on the white sand bar holding a pole and inhale the moist earthy air made magic. Wild roses tumbled in garnet confusion on the far side of the bank. Honeysuckle, with its cream and gold blossoms, ran rampant.

Little could be heard. The cacophony of vehicles passing on the nearby road perhaps, or the sound of bees frantic in the honeysuckle, the lift and suck of the creek against the gravel shallows, and the shrill, playful screams of the Estis children in some game or other. But little else.

The Estis family was not aware of the watchers. They weren't thinking of evil or malice.

The watchers secure in their 20-foot high vantage spot, took a certain satisfaction in their invisibleness. It was a god's-eye perspective. And like an almighty entity they could, if they chose, rain down death and destruction on the unsuspecting family below.

As expected, the other son, his wife and their two little girls drove out and parked above the picnic area where the rest of the family was. They got out of their car and started walking down the incline to the creek below.

They noticed bicycle tire marks on the weedy verge, but were more intent on their footing on the steep bank than on any other campers in the area.

The young couple waved at their family below, then sped down the trail after their two children who had run on ahead of them toward their grandparents.

The head of the Estis family stood on the sand and gravel bar with his line in the creek. He waved at them and shouted, "Get something to eat."

The four new arrivals took a sandwich, the two youngsters impatiently running off to join their cousins. The four children ran like so many mountain goats up and down the bluff, their voices ringing out in the still air.

Gary Estis, anxious to replenish the minnows in the bait bucket, started for the creek then veered off and climbed the 20-foot bluff toward the campers.

Conversation lagged for the 15 minutes it took Gary to get back down the bluff, slipping and sliding all the way down.

Hazel Estis took her husband's pole and threw her line in the creek to try her luck.

"Who was that up there?" Gary's father asked.

"Just a couple of guys," Gary answered briefly. "I know them, they—"

Suddenly there was a barrage of gunfire.

Gary grabbed himself, shouted "I'm hit!" and fell face down on the ground.

The Estis family raised terrified eyes, the children standing as still as little statues. They looked in disbelief at Gary on the ground.

The younger Estis couple began to run, herding the terrified children before them. They were sure they were all doomed to death from the lethal hail of bullets. The children scattered like lambs uncertain of shelter.

As the young woman ran, her heart labored in her chest. Sobbing aloud, she wondered if her husband was behind her or if he had been shot and had fallen beside his brother.

Her husband, after one shocked glance at his brother, heard his father call out an agonized plea to the unseen snipers, "Stop! Stop that firing."

It seemed the bullets being aimed at their little band would never end. Hazel Estis fell screaming, then tried to crawl toward her fallen son, Gary. Diane had fallen soundlessly. The head of the family, after his futile plea, was knocked backward with bullets in his chest and right shoulder.

As the surviving members of the Estis family ran for help, Gary's brother, sweat blinding his eyes, pulled his wife and the four children fleeing ahead of him to safety. They would make their way to a nearby market and call the law.

Behind them were a few more desultory shots over the four fallen figures, then an ominous silence.

The murderous bluff campers came slipping and sliding down from their vantage point to look at their handiwork.

One of them came up to the fallen Gary and fired a careful bullet into his head from a scant three-inch clearance. The shot sounded sharply in the sunny silence.

After grabbing one of the women's purses, the pair raced back up the bluff, wadded the blanket tent under a bush, thrust the two rifles and a pistol under another, and disappeared down a faint trail among the trees.

In spite of being seriously wounded, Gary's father was still alive. Cautiously, he raised his head, then got shakily to his feet. He staggered to his car, stumbling as he went, climbed into his vehicle and somehow got it started.

In spite of loss of blood, shock, and his terror in case the killers came back, the wounded man managed to drive a quarter of a mile to the nearest house for help.

He wondered if his other son, his daughter-in-law had made it out safely or if they had been gunned down by the killers on the bluff somewhere. He wondered if that was why the pair of men had left so hastily—to run down what was left of his family and kill them, too.

The head of the family made his way to a nearby house and sobbed out his story. He told of the three bodies left behind him and the six more he feared were dead, hidden in the bushes on top of the bluff.

Horrified, the people tried to lift him to a couch, then called an ambulance and the law.

"We got a man might be *dyin'* here!" the excited homeowner told the authorities.

As the gasping man was loaded into the ambulance to be driven to Columbia hospital's intensive care unit, he told the attendant, "They just stepped out and started shooting. Fire just started coming out all over."

Deputy Joe Chunn, the first officer to arrive at the Duck River location, took one look at the scene of carnage and radioed in.

Maury County Sheriff Bill Voss and other deputies arrived in minutes, surveying the havoc wreaked on the happy family picnic.

Voss grimly started rapping out orders.

The murderous story of what had happened was laid out pretty plainly for the investigators to see. The *why* of it was another matter.

The finding of this fell to Sheriff's Investigators Wendell Harris, Steve Thomaso and Guy Porter.

Voss moved carefully around the picnic site. Together with his men, he climbed the bluff to the concealed camping site.

There were more than a hundred shell casings scattered around where the blanket tent had been.

"I suspect one of them stood here behind this tree and used two rifles," he said pointing to the shells behind a young locust. "The other man moved off to the left upcreek and fired a pistol."

"What do you think of robbery as a motive?" Chief Deputy Wade Metheny asked him.

"Not much," Voss answered laconically. "These were poor people."

He moved toward the medical examiner. "I think the purse is an afterthought."

"Kids out potshotting?" mused one of the deputies. "An accident?"

Chunn snorted. "It's a mindless slaughter," he said.

"Yeah. It looks pretty cold-blooded to me," Voss agreed.

Assistant District Attorney General Jim Hamilton,

apprised of the situation, exploded. "It's not so deserted that you have any kind of 'Deliverance' situation. It's just a part of the river people go to fish and camp."

The surviving couple with their children stood trembling in shock and fatigue.

"When they started shooting we took off," explained the surviving son to the deputies. "My wife grabbed the kids and ran behind Gary's two. My family were shot in the backs—it was murder."

His wife, who had heard someone mention the purse, added, "Robbery might have been the motive, but they intended to kill us first because they never came near us."

What remained of the family was escorted home. Their dead mother, brother and sister were photographed *in situ* and removed for autopsy.

Regulation police photographs were taken of the crime scene, the camp up the slope and the scattered empty shell casings.

Blackjack, a bloodhound belonging to Deputy Fred Shelton, was brought in and, in short order, led Voss and his men to a tennis shoe print, two rifles and a pellet gun hidden in the bushes. Also found was the wadded blanket tent and the emptied purse thrown 200 yards away from the death scene.

A pair of boots stuffed with toilet paper and an old bicycle added to the forensic total bagged by the bloodhound. These were carefully preserved as evidence.

When the bicycle was lugged into the sheriff's department, Deputy Investigator Wendell Harris did a double take.

"I know who that bike belongs to!" he said with a shocked look on his face. "I'd know those wheels anywhere—it belongs to my nephew!"

Maury County investigators lost no time in going

to a modest home where they arrested William Kelley and Phillip Kelley, distant cousins and good friends, for the triple murder.

Sullenly, the two boys stood facing the officers while they were given the Miranda warning. Then they surrendered the .22-caliber pistol William had taken away from the death site.

Charged with three counts each of first-degree murder and one count each of intent to commit murder, they were held without bond in the Maury County Jail after pleading innocent at the arraignment.

Sheriff Voss said with a great deal of satisfaction that one of the suspects had given the authorities a "pretty good" statement, but he refused to reveal its contents.

One of the Estis daughters, tears streaming down her face, stood outside the jail and said, "It was my mama, brother and sister-in-law that were killed. My mama never hurt nobody."

On the Saturday after the senseless slaying, the Estis family gathered for the burial of their loved ones. The bodies of Hazel Estis, her son, Gary Estis, and his wife, Diane, were laid out in side-by-side caskets. Their friends, neighbors and relatives filed slowly by them for a last look before their burial.

The head of the family, now removed from intensive care, was unable to attend to see his wife, or his son and his son's wife for a last time. He was still in only fair condition from the savagely inflicted bullet wounds he had suffered.

The following Wednesday, the preliminary hearing for the two young men was held.

Chief Deputy Wade Metheny, when asked for the motive behind the slayings, said, "The best we can tell, they saw somebody and wanted to shoot them. That's about all we can come up with. They don't give any reason. They just said they started shooting."

Sheriff Voss repeated what he had said before. Robbery had entered into the killings, he stated, but only as an afterthought.

"Robbery was the aftermath," Voss said.

The surviving daughter-in-law, in an interview with the *Columbia Daily Herald* said, "We never heard them. We never saw them. We saw bicycle tracks on the ground as we drove up, and up on the bluff there was a tent, like people were camping up there. We didn't think anything about it.

"The family had probably been there all day," the stricken woman continued. "They would take supper with them. When we got down there and saw them they made us have a sandwich.

"It seemed like the last couple of years they stayed home a lot—she (Mrs. Estis) had an operation and was doing well. And now this."

Her husband, wiping his eyes with a washcloth said, "The last thing I heard my father say was, 'Stop, stop that firing.'"

Voss revealed that the Kelley who had given the statement to the department had been William. Phillip had refused to talk to the officers.

Phillip and William Kelley sat solemnly during the hearing which was interrupted once by a thunderstorm that knocked out the lights.

Sometimes they glanced at the witness stand where the tragic events of June 23rd were being related.

Hazel's son took the stand first and told of the Estis picnic that had ended in such unforeseen grief for his family.

Twisting his hat in his hands, he recalled that he and his family had joined his parents and brother's family after work at the fishing spot on Duck River that they had used before.

"I heard my father hollering, 'Boys quit that shooting.' Then I turned and heard shots upon shots," he said. "All I knew to do was run for my life."

The bereaved man continued, explaining that there had been no warning before the shooting started at Vaughn's Landing. He said he knew neither of the suspects.

Sheriff's Investigator Wendell Harris testified that he suspected the recovered bicycle found at the shooting scene belonged to his nephew because he recognized the unusual wheels.

Harris also said that the .22-caliber pistol used in the Estis deaths was confiscated when they arrested the Kelleys at the house.

Harris explained that Phillip had told him he and William had been taking speed and drinking cold drinks on the afternoon of the sniper's attack.

Harris told the court he had known Phillip "all his life" and quoted his nephew as saying that during the camping trip with William Kelley, "We started shooting . . . I don't know what happened."

Harris finally said Phillip told him, "William and I hid the rifles and the pellet gun in the bushes and William kept the pistol . . . I don't know why I did this."

After a two and a half hour preliminary hearing, both the Kelleys were bound over to the Maury grand jury.

A true bill was delivered by the grand jury and the trial for the Kelleys was held the last week of September and the first week of October, 1982.

A change of venue had been sought by the defense and granted so that testimony was heard in Giles County. Judge Robert Jones presided and Assistant District Attorney General Bobby Sands was prosecutor.

Again and again, the sad Estis story was recounted from the witness stand by the various witnesses for the state.

The jury heard how, after the survivors escaped, the killers came down the bluff to their fallen victims and shot Gary Estis in the head from a scant distance of inches.

They heard how the bloodhound, Blackjack, led officers to the concealed blanket tent that had been wadded up and hidden in the bushes, to the boots dropped as the killers fled, to the rifled purse, and, finally, the guns used in the killings.

The jury listened to the Estis family described as "just poor people who liked to fish" from the sandbar in the creek leading to the placid Duck River.

Perhaps the most damning testimony came from a young friend asked by the Kelleys for help that night. He told how the Kelleys said, "There's two more people we'll have to get before we leave town." This witness admitted he had lied earlier to officers because he had been afraid the Kelleys would kill him if he told of the conversation.

The ambulance attendant testified that the critically wounded Estis father had still managed to gasp out, "They just started shooting. Fire just started coming out all over."

Officers explained over a hundred rounds of ammunition had been fired at the death scene, the casings proving it. Of these, they said at least 12 round had been fired at the Estis family, the dead victims having been shot from a distance of 50 to 75 feet.

In his final argument, Prosecutor Bobby Sands told the jury the defendants were bushwhackers and had committed murders that were "cold, brutal and senseless."

Sands labeled the defense contention that the Kelleys were under the influence of drugs and therefore not responsible a "backdoor" John Hinckley defense.

Sands pointed out to the jury that the rifles used in the killing barrage were single shot and that the pistol used mercilessly on Gary Estis had to be reloaded before he was shot at close range.

Dramatically, Sands picked up one of the .22-caliber rifles introduced as evidence, pretended to load it, and pulled the trigger.

"They were hearing them yell and watching blood come out of them and continued to fire again and again and again and again." Sands pulled on the bolt, snapped it forward and squeezed the trigger until the hammer clicked each time he said "again."

"Testimony has shown it was a time of happiness for the Estis family," the prosecutor thundered. "It was also a time of death—death from bushwhackers—from a sniper attack. This has been a story of murder—cold, brutal and senseless."

Referring to the defense argument that the Kelleys were only shooting at turtles, Sands asked, "Do they think turtles walk and fall over off their feet and blood spurts out of them?"

There was a hiatus in the court and a dread hush momentarily fell over court officials, the defendants, the spectators and the jury. Then Judge Robert Jones, in a measured tone of voice, carefully instructed the jury as to their duties.

After a four hour deliberation, the jury filed back into the courtroom and handed in their verdict. The two men, William Kelley and Phillip Kelley, accused of killing three members of the Estis family and of wounding a fourth member with intent to kill, were found guilty on all counts. It was October 8, 1982.

Judge Jones told the jurors to prepare a choice the following day between a death sentence in the electric chair or life in prison.

Saturday, October 9, 1982, William Kelley and Phillip Kelley stood impassively and heard the sentence that determined their fate.

Both of them were given three life sentences, one for each of their dead victims, plus an additional 25-year prison term for their assault with intent to kill the surviving head of the Estis family.

With time, people will go back to the white sand and gravel sandbar in the creek that leads to the placid Duck River. The day of that tragic picnic will be almost forgotten. But not entirely, and never by what remains of the Estis family.

"RIDDLE OF THE 'GENTLE' MAN'S RAMPAGE OF DEATH!"

by Terrell W. Ecker

It sounded like another routine assignment on what so far had been a routine Wednesday morning for Gary Bowling. It was 11:00 a.m. on May 12, 1982, when the dispatcher told him to investigate an unknown problem on Blackbeard Drive in Holiday Harbor, an affluent Jacksonville, Florida, community of homes with six digit price tags. But it only sounded routine. After two years on the police force, 25-year-old Gary Bowling was on his way to his first murder scene, and it would be a scene that would sicken hardened veterans.

As the dispatcher had predicted, Bowling found a woman waiting for him on Blackbeard, but she climbed into his police car and said the problem, whatever it was, was at a friend's home a few blocks away. She directed Bowling to a house on Shipwreck Drive where the woman's husband was standing in the front yard waiting for them.

Also standing in the front yard was a realtor's SOLD sign.

The worried couple explained that the owners of the house, John and Nancy Weiler, had sold it because John, an engineer, had been transferred to

Pittsburgh. He was already living there and buying a new home for his family. Nancy and the girls, nine-year-old Kristy and four-and-a-half-year-old Kathy, were going to join him when the school year ended.

What had the couple worried was that there didn't appear to be anyone home although both cars were in the garage with the garage door open. It was the couple's turn in the nursery school car pool, but when the husband came by to pick up Kathy she hadn't appeared and no one answered his knocks on the door. This wasn't like the Weilers at all. It was so unlike them, in fact, that the couple had become worried enough to call the police.

The husband handed Bowling a key that Kristy, the nine-year-old—no, ten; today's her tenth birthday—kept hidden in the garage and led the officer through the garage to the kitchen door. After knocking and getting no response, Bowling unlocked the door, opened it and stepped into 37-year-old Nancy Weiler's kitchen. He was greeted by the hum of her range exhaust fan and voices from a television set that he could see playing in an adjoining room.

Bowling saw green vegetables and some partly cut up carrots on a counter top, and some browned chunks of beef in a microwave oven. From the kitchen doorway it looked like an ordinary household full of ordinary sights and sounds. But where were the people who lived here?

"Is anybody home?" the officer called out. No response.

The worried neighbor pointed out a hallway leading to the bedrooms and, leaving his wife outside, following quietly as Bowling cautiously made his way toward the back of the house, revolvers in hand, listening intently for any sounds of life—or of an intruder.

In the back of the house, near the master bedroom, Bowling turned a corner, stopped abruptly and turned to his companion. "You don't want to see this," he said. The man made his way back to the kitchen door and rejoined his wife in the yard.

Gary Bowling didn't want to see it, either, but he had no choice. Kathy Weiler lay face up in the hallway just outside her parents' bedroom, pale and pitiful with her knees upraised and her intestines protruding through a hole in her stomach. She was four and a half years old and wasn't going to get any older.

Bowling set his jaw and looked into the bedroom. Nancy Weiler lay face up in a pool of blood on the floor beside the bed, obviously the victim of a savage beating. Near Mrs. Weiler's lifeless head, Kristy was kneeling on the floor at the foot of the bed, her hands bound behind her back with nylon rope, her uplifted face resting against the foot of the mattress. Her expressionless right eye was open, the left one closed and blackened. In the middle of her forehead an ugly black smudge surrounded an obscene bullet hole. Kristy hadn't quite made it to her tenth birthday.

After carefully checking the rest of the house and satisfying himself that there was no intruder present, Bowling returned to his cruiser and told the dispatcher to send his supervisor and homicide people to the scene. Then he secured the house and waited for them to arrive.

It was 11:17 a.m. when homicide detectives, crime lab technicians and several uniformed officers were dispatched to the scene along with Duval County's assistant medical examiner, Dr. Bonifacio Floro. By the time they arrived a crowd of neighbors had congregated in the front yard and driveway, and officers were put to work immediately identifying and questioning them.

Detective Charles M. Kesinger, a 41-year-old veteran with 10 years in the homicide division, was assigned to the case as lead investigator. In those 10 years Chuck Kesinger had worked many murder scenes worse than this one, but none had shaken him as much. The father of three teenagers reminded himself with an effort that a policeman can't get emotionally involved in a crime, that he must detach himself from the victims who used to be people and go about his work in a protective cocoon devoid of personal feelings. It didn't work, but at least he kept the principle in mind as he went about trying to reconstruct the murder along with Dr. Floro and Detective Mike Cobb.

The bodies were in full rigor mortis, indicating to Dr. Floro that the victims had been dead for 12 to 18 hours, which meant that the triple murder had been committed between 6:00 p.m. and midnight the previous evening, Tuesday, May 11th. And from the positions of the bodies and blood spatters, the pathologist was able to speculate with reasonable certainty on the sequence of the slayings.

Mrs. Weiler had been beaten severely about the face and head with a hard, heavy object, possibly a large handgun. The beating had begun while she was standing beside the bed and she had fallen to the floor where she lay face down. The youngest daughter, Kathy, had been shot in the back as she fled through the bedroom door into the hallway. The large caliber slug had followed a downward trajectory, exiting through her abdomen and spinning her onto her back as she fell dying.

Kristy had been shot through the chest as she lay face up on the bed with her hands bound behind her. The bullet had exited through her back and was lodged in the mattress. Then her body had slid or been dragged over the foot of the bed onto the floor.

As she knelt there, dying, the muzzle of the weapon had been pressed against her uplifted forehead and a bullet sent crashing through her brain, exiting through her left ear.

At that point Mrs. Weiler apparently had begun regaining consciousness. In any event, she had been rolled over onto her back and beaten again, this time beyond recognition.

The second beating had been so savage, in fact, that it had broken the weapon as well as Mrs. Weiler's skull. Along with the bodies, the killer had left two pieces of the trigger guard and the medallion from a Ruger Blackhawk .357 magnum revolver. If the murder weapon ever was found, it wouldn't be hard to identify.

One of the many unanswered questions facing the detective at that early stage of the investigation was why Mrs. Weiler hadn't been shot. The weapon obviously had been a six shot revolver, but a painstaking examination of the scene by state crime lab technicians, including ballistics expert John Warniment, indicated that only five shots had been fired—two into Kristy and three at the fleeing Kathy, only one of which had hit her.

But the most important questions, of course, were who had killed them and why. The scene provided no clues to the killer's identity nor to his motive. All three bodies were fully clothed and bore no signs of sexual molestation. The house had not been ransacked and, in fact, was meticulously neat and clean. Neighbors confirmed that that was always true of the Weiler home. Whether anything was missing would have to be determined at a later time by the absent husband and father, John Weiler—a prospect that caused Detective Kesinger's already aching heart to sink farther.

While evidence technicians continued processing

284

the scene and Dr. Floro headed for the morgue to prepare for the autopsies, Detectives Kesinger and Cobb turned their attention to the neighbors. By then other officers had questioned all of the neighbors and knew that none had seen or heard anything suspicious the previous evening, but four of them did have information of interest.

One neighbor said he had been in the Weiler home Tuesday night. He said Nancy Weiler had come to his home to borrow a card table to use at Kristy's 10th birthday party Wednesday—today. He had carried the table into the Weiler home, and while there had fixed a minor problem with a bathroom door. Kristy hadn't been there, he said; she had been at a dancing class. Nancy and Kathy had walked him back to his own yard where they had stood for a few minutes chatting with each other and with another neighbor who happened along, then Nancy and Kathy had gone back into their house. That had been about 7:30 p.m.

The other neighbor verified the conversation and the time.

A third neighbor said she had brought Kristy home from the dancing class and had watched her walk uneventfully into the house around 7:45.

The fourth neighbor was Paul Crowley, who lived next door to the Weilers. Crowley said he hadn't seen or heard anything suspicious Tuesday night, but had been away from home, bowling, from 6:00 to 9:00 p.m. During that time, he said, a relative had used his garage work shop and might possibly have noticed something. Crowley said he would get in touch with the relative and have him come by later that day and talk to the detectives.

In the meantime, Kesinger went to his office in the downtown Police Memorial Building to perform a dreaded duty. John Weiler, at work in Pittsburgh, had to be informed that his wife and daughters wouldn't be joining him after all. Imagining himself hearing such a message from a strange voice over the telephone, Kesinger decided that at least he would arrange for Weiler to hear the crushing news from a friend's lips. He would call Weiler's office and ask the secretary to put a friend of Weiler's on the phone. Kesinger would explain the situation to the friend, then wait patiently to answer any questions Weiler might have.

With the statements he would make to the secretary and the friend firmly in mind, the detective dialed the Pittsburgh number.

John Weiler answered the telephone. Chuck Kesinger hung up.

After regathering his wits about him, Kesinger steeled himself and dialed the number again. Weiler answered again. Kesinger talked him into putting a friend on the phone, told the friend the news and waited. After a few moments Weiler came back on the line, but all he managed to say before breaking down was "Not my whole family."

It was 5:15 p.m. when Kesinger arrived back at the murder scene and found police divers searching in vain for the murder weapon in a canal behind the Weiler home. In the house crime lab technicians were still at their tedious tasks. So far they had collected nearly 200 pieces of evidence, but nothing that would identify the killer or suggest his reasoning or a possible motive.

Kesinger saw a three-quarter ton pickup truck parked in front of Paul Crowley's house next door. Thinking it might belong to the relative Crowley had mentioned, the detective walked over and knocked on the door. Crowley let him in and ushered him into the kitchen where his relative sat at the table — all 340 pounds of him.

"I suppose they call you Tiny," the detective said with a friendly smile. The rotund 37-year-old shipyard welder admitted just as amiably that his friends did indeed call him that but said he was Allen Lee Davis. Crowley told Kesinger that Davis possibly could have been the last person, other than the killer, to have seen the victims alive.

"Correct?" Kesinger asked Davis.

"Yes," the welder admitted. "But first, if I'm contacted by a police officer I'm supposed to show these." He handed Kesinger some papers indicating that he was on parole after having served time in prison for armed robbery. The detective perfunctorily examined the papers, handed them back to Davis and asked him to describe his activities on the previous evening, especially anyone or anything he might have noticed at the Weiler house.

Well, Tiny Davis said, he arrived at the Crowley home about 6:45 p.m. Tuesday and went to work in the garage. He saw Nancy and Kathy Weiler talking to a neighbor in the yard. A few minutes later Kathy came into the garage, talked to him for a few minutes and went home. A short time later Nancy and Kathy both came into the garage. He showed them a clock he was making, took them into the house and showed them a clock he had made for Crowley. Some small talk, and they left.

A few minutes later, Davis explained, Kristy came into the garage and asked him if he would come over to her house and fix a bathroom door. He said he would and walked over to the Weiler house, entering through the garage. Nancy Weiler was cooking supper—cutting up some carrots and things. She said the door had been fixed, so he left, secured the Crowley house, got into his truck, lit a cigar and drove home.

And that was it, Davis said. Hadn't noticed anything suspicious. Hadn't seen anyone else, except that neighbor in the yard.

At that point Crowley got up and left the room briefly, returning with an open magazine. "I saw on TV that possibly a gun was used next door," he said. "I know this looks bad but I'm missing a gun."

Crowley put the magazine on the table facing Kesinger. It was opened to a photograph of a large revolver. "My gun is exactly like this one," he said.

Kesinger looked at the weapon in the photograph. It was a Ruger Blackhawk .357 magnum. Crowley said it had disappeared sometime during the past few days from the top of the refrigerator right there in the kitchen. And it had been loaded, he said. Loaded with five cartridges. As many gun owners do, he habitually had kept an empty chamber under the hammer as a safety precaution.

Kesinger asked Tiny Davis, "Have you seen the gun?"

"No, I haven't seen the gun," Davis replied. "I can't be around guns. I'm on parole."

Assured that Davis had no objection to a search of his truck, Kesinger searched three police cars before finding a consent to search form. Davis signed it without hesitation and went to watch the divers at work in the canal. The detective had state evidence technicians search the truck and inventory its contents. The only thing they found of interest to Kesinger was a roll of small diameter nylon rope.

It looked exactly like the rope that had bound Kristy Weiler's wrists.

When the inventory was completed, at 7:15, the lawman asked the welder about the rope. Davis explained that it was merely an aluminum recycling aid. He used it to tie down plastic bags containing empty aluminum cans.

"I guess it don't look too good," Davis added reflectively.

Kesinger was noncommittal. He knew from long experience that in the early stages of an investigation, something looking like evidence pointing to a suspect frequently turns out to be a coincidence complicating the life of an innocent person. And that, most likely, was the case here. Davis just didn't impress Kesinger as a viable suspect. Still . . .

"Would you like to take a polygraph?" the detective asked. "We can eliminate any possibility if you care to do so."

"Yes, I'd like to do that," Davis replied. "I'd like to clear it up."

At 8:15 Kesinger and Cobb escorted Davis into one of the homicide division's interrogation rooms and made him as comfortable as possible while waiting for a polygraph operator to arrive. The department's own experts were tied up or otherwise unavailable at the moment, so Lt. Derry Dedmon was called from neighboring Clay County. Kesinger asked Davis if he'd like a cup of coffee and had to make some when Davis replied that he would.

"You understand that you don't have to do this, now?" the detective asked. "You're not under arrest and you don't have to answer any questions or take any test. You're free to leave at any time."

Davis replied, "Well, if I left now it would look pretty funny."

Kesinger walked into the main homicide office—a large open room filled with rows of detectives' desks—and put on a pot of coffee. He made some phone calls while the water worked its way through the grounds and into the pot, and returned to the interrogation room with a cup of coffee for Davis at 8:40. Derry Dedmon arrived at 8:55.

At 9:11 p.m. Dedmon and Davis disappeared into

a polygraph examination room. Thirty minutes later Dedmon emerged and told Kesinger and Cobb that the session had ground to a halt. Davis had flunked the test. Then, advised that Dedmon didn't believe he was telling the truth about certain things, Davis had refused to answer any more questions. Wouldn't speak at all, in fact. He simply ignored Dedmon.

By that time two of the department's own polygraph experts, Detectives Ray Smith and Patty Pavelka, were on hand. They studied the Clay County lieutenant's polygraph charts and agreed with Dedmon that Davis had failed the test.

Kesinger and Cobb went into the room and asked Davis if he would object to a search of his apartment. Davis replied cooperatively that he wouldn't mind at all. He signed a consent to search form, gave Cobb the key to his apartment and explained how to get there. Cobb left to get a warrant and carry out a search that would produce little of interest except a pair of boots with possible bloodstains on them.

Kesinger then introduced Detective Pavelka to Davis in an effort to get another polygraph test going, but Davis clasped his hands together on his ample belly and ignored the inquisitive lady. After 10 minutes of that she left, and Kesinger managed to get Davis engaged in a pleasant, general conversation. They talked mostly about the welder's work and wages, some about his personal habits such as the fact that he didn't believe in drugs and seldom drank.

With an atmosphere of cooperation restored, Kesinger brought the subject back to Davis's activities of the previous evening. Davis patiently went through them again, telling exactly the same story he had told earlier.

"Did you ever leave the kitchen?" Kesinger asked.

"I've never been in any part of the house except the kitchen," Davis replied.

"Let's take a short break," the detective said. "I know you're tired."

After a five minute coffee break Kesinger asked Davis, "Do you remember everything that happened while you were at Nancy's house?"

"No," Davis replied.

The detective continued, "Do you remember only bits and pieces of what happened while you were there?" When Davis replied in the affirmative Kesinger asked, "What are those bits and pieces?" and waited for an answer.

Davis was silent.

Kesinger asked, "If I described the way the victims were found in the home, do you think that would help your memory?"

"I'm not sure," Davis replied uncertainly. After Kesinger had described the way the bodies were found Davis said simply, "I can't remember going into the back of the house."

Kesinger then asked him flatly, "Did you do those murders?"

Davis sat bolt upright and announced firmly, "Allen Lee Davis wouldn't do anything like that."

Kesinger looked him in the eye and asked, "Could the other Allen Lee Davis have done it?"

Davis sank back in his chair. "I don't know," he said.

It was then 1:15 a.m. and the two men took another break. Kesinger used it to discuss the situation with Detective Ray Smith, whose "way with people" he admired. Besides being a 16-year police veteran and thoroughly experienced polygraph expert, Smith is a devout Baptist deacon who genuinely cares about people. And whatever else suspects and witnesses may be, they are people.

291

Kesinger introduced his colleague to Davis and left them alone. Noting that the interrogation room was getting hot and stuffy, Smith suggested a walk and a change of air, say a trip to the third floor snack bar for a cup of coffee. Davis agreed, and the two men rode an elevator to the third floor of Jacksonville's handsome Police Memorial Building and walked into the snack bar. As they got their coffee and settled at a rear table, Davis said that he, too, was a Baptist. Baptized at the age of 19, he said.

Deacon Smith's response to that was sincere. "Mr. Davis," he said, "if you've done anything about what you're down here for, the first thing you need to do is make sure you get straight with the Lord. Don't worry about these people and what they're saying to you; you get straight with the Lord."

"I'm afraid it's too late for that," Davis replied.

"It's not too late until you're dead," the deacon assured him.

After giving Davis a moment to digest that thought, Detective Smith got down to police business. "Mr. Davis, I ask you to think back to last night when you went over there to the Weiler home. When the little girl came and got you, when you followed her back over there, where did you go from that point?"

"Well, we went in through the garage," Davis said. "I went into the kitchen area and I talked to Mrs. Weiler. She was cooking some greens and cutting up some carrots."

"Okay," Smith said. "Now that you got the picture in your mind, where did the little girl go?"

"Well, she was at her desk cutting out paper dolls or doing something with the scissors."

"Where was the other little girl?"

"She was taking a bath."

"Did you see her taking a bath?"

"No. I just assumed that's where she was."

"Then what happened?"

"Well, I remember talking to her and then my mind kind of went blank."

"Do you remember leaving?"

"Yes, I remember leaving out through the garage because I had to step over a tricycle. And then I went and got in my truck and left but I don't remember how long I was in there and I don't really remember what happened."

Smith mulled that over while thinking back over what Kesinger had told him. Chuck had said something about a gun in a box on a refrigerator, hadn't he?

Smith said, "Now there was a gun on top of the refrigerator and it was in a box?" he asked carefully.

"No," Davis said. "The gun was in a holster."

In a holster? Smith continued, "Remember back now. Did you take that gun with you when you went over there?"

"I don't remember taking the gun over there," Davis replied. "I could have because I heard that it's missing, but I don't remember taking it over there." Davis paused for a moment, then added, "I don't believe that Allen Lee Davis would do anything like that."

"Well, I don't think he would either," Smith said. "But I'm wondering if there might be two people inside of Allen Lee Davis. Have you ever heard of Dr. Jekyll and Mr. Hyde?"

Davis replied, "Yes, there could be, because I don't think Allen Lee Davis would do anything like that."

For all practical purposes that was the end of the conversation. Smith tried to keep a conversation going and Davis tried to participate, but Davis's statements always trailed off into, "I just don't believe

Allen Lee Davis would do anything like that."

Back in the first floor homicide office, Smith repeated the gist of the conversation to Kesinger and said he was puzzled by two things Davis had told him. That gun on the refrigerator, for one thing—the gun in the box. "You did say that gun was in a box, didn't you?"

"No," Kesinger replied. "The gun was in a holster.

And there was something about a bath. Smith hadn't heard anything about one of the victims taking a bath, but Davis had told him that one of the little girls was taking a bath when he was there.

That startled Kesinger. "The only indication we had of a bath was in the back part of the house right next to the master bedroom," he said. "We found about four inches of clean water in a tub as if somebody was preparing to take a bath, but Davis couldn't have seen that if he never left the kitchen area."

Kesinger escorted Davis across the street to the Duval County Jail and booked him in on three first-degree murder charges. He didn't have much of a case against the suspect, however, and the investigation was still in the process of getting cranked up.

The autopsies did little more than confirm what already was believed. Kathy and Kristy Weiler had died of gunshot wounds and their mother had been beaten to death. Dr. Floro counted 25 blows to the woman's head and neck. The wounds, he said, were T-shaped—the shape of the butt of a revolver with the handle grips removed. None of the victims had been sexually molested.

The grips from the handle of a Ruger Blackhawk .357 magnum revolver were found at the murder scene along with the manufacturer's medallion, two pieces of the trigger guard and five expended bullets. A crime lab comparison of the spent slugs with live ammunition provided by Paul Crowley indicated that the bullets had come from his box of ammunition.

The murder weapon couldn't be found in spite of an extensive and sometimes hairy search. As the search expanded from the canal behind the Weiler home to neighboring ponds, alligators had to be moved from one pond to another for the safety of the divers. The alligators didn't particularly like playing musical ponds, and one large fellow proved impossible to catch. Guards had to be posted to watch for the uncooperative critter while colleagues searched his murky domain for the murder weapon. It never was found.

The killer's motive proved equally elusive. There had been no forced entry to the house, and as far as Mr. Weiler could determine there was nothing missing except his family.

Nor was there any direct evidence pointing to the killer's identity, but after Davis's arrest circumstantial evidence started dribbling in. One important development resulted from television coverage of the crime.

A Holiday Harbor housewife saw Davis on television and recalled that while taking her customary bicycle ride on the evening of the murder, she had seen Davis walking along Shipwreck Drive near the Weiler home. She had noticed him because, in his work clothes, the huge man had looked so out of place in that affluent neighborhood. And she remembered that there had been a dark object in his hand, but she couldn't describe it.

A few days later the housewife submitted voluntarily to hypnosis. In a hypnotic trance she was able to describe the object in the man's hand in considerable detail. She described a large revolver.

Another crucial piece of evidence came from Mary Lynn Henson, a state crime lab microanalyst and fiber expert. She reported that a fracture analysis proved that the nylon rope used to bind Kristy Weiler's wrists came from the roll of identical rope found in Davis's pickup truck.

Another crime lab analysis revealed that blood found on a pair of boots from Davis's apartment matched Nancy Weiler's blood but not Davis's.

As the weeks went by the evidence mounted. It was all circumstantial, but there were 200 individual items of circumstantial evidence. Assistant State Attorney Stephen Kunz, a sharp young prosecutor who had specialized in New Jersey organized crime cases before moving to the Sunshine State, wove those 200 items into a solid case against Allen Lee Davis.

On February 4, 1983, a capital jury found Davis guilty of three counts of first-degree murder. On February 9th the jury listened to arguments for and against the death penalty, deliberated for 35 minutes and recommended that the wayward welder be sentenced to die.

On March 2nd Circuit Judge Major B. Harding sentenced Davis to die in the electric chair, thereby making Davis the 200th resident of Florida's branch of the Federal Haven for Murderers.

EDITOR'S NOTE:
The name Paul Crowly is fictitious and was used because there is no need for public interest in his true identity.

"GRISLY SLAYING OF
A FAMILY OF FOUR!"

by Gary Miller

The hopes and dreams of many immigrants coming to the United States are made possible with long hours, sweat, a lot of hard work and some luck. For Korean businessman Young Man Kim, his dreams for the good life came true, and very little of it was because of luck.

He and his family came to the United States from Korea in 1977. Kim opened a food market with what money he had saved in Korea as a tailor, and he prospered in his new business. But for Kim, this was only the beginning of his future plans. With the money he made from the food store, he bought a small house for his family. Then he sold his store and invested the profits into a gas station.

Again, Kim worked without let up, pushing himself to the limits of his endurance, and, again, he began to turn an even greater profit than before. And with this increased prosperity, Kim decided to buy another house, bigger and in a better location, on Twenlow Street in Clinton Township, near Detroit, Michigan.

In early 1981, Kim was already making plans to start another business in California. He kept an eye on the business opportunity section of the paper and saw a liquor store for sale at a decent price. He began negotiations on the store but the deal suddenly fell through. For Kim this was merely a minor setback, something that one must expect in the daily routine of business dealing. He continued to search for opportunity, not willing to just wait for a good business proposition to fall into his lap by chance.

Before he had the opportunity to make his move, however, fate snatched his dreams, his hard work, his trust in America and smashed it into the ground in one ruthless, gruesome and bloody incident, an incident that would ultimately involve hundreds of police officers, detective teams, police technicians and ballistics experts.

Mt. Clemens Police Officer Harry Reynolds was filing his reports for the day of March 21, 1981 at 11:00 p.m., a Saturday. It hadn't been an eventful day for Officer Reynolds but, then, many days are not so eventful that it would remain etched in one's memory for many years to come. This day would be one of those that Officer Reynolds would never forget. He received the call around 11:10 and heard in a hoarse whisper, "Send police car."

Reynolds asked "What's the problem?" several times, but there was only an inaudible response. He thought perhaps it was a crank call.

Then, suddenly, the voice became clear again, a hoarse groaning whisper. "There's been a murder. I've been shot. I'm dying."

The caller then gave the street number of his address. Reynolds needed the name of the street.

"Spell the name," Reynolds said. The caller could only utter three letters, T . . . W . . . E, and there was no further response.

Officer Reynolds leaped from his seat and called his superior, Lt. Bill Prignitz. They then phoned a Michigan Bell operator and asked for a trace. While waiting for a call back, the two lawmen searched through street maps, but before they made any headway, the phone rang again and the operator told them the trace was successful. She gave them the address, which was located on Twenlow Street in western Clinton Township. Immediately, the lawmen dispatched the address over the police radio.

Deputy Larry Duda who was patrolling the area flipping on his lights and sirens and sped to the scene. When he arrived at the house, the first thing he noticed was the porch lights were on and the front door was open. Duda searched the outside of the premises and, by the time he was ready to enter the house, another officer was on hand as a back-up.

The two lawmen, with guns drawn, entered the house. They passed through the foyer and called out, but there was no response. Everything as yet seemed in order. No furniture was overturned, no drawers had been pulled out. Deputy Duda noticed, however, that the basement door was open. He slowly approached the opening and then descended the stairs. The first thing that met his eye was a baseball bat on the floor. There was something on it, but it was difficult to see clearly. He bent down and looked closer. There was no longer any question. Something terrible had happened there. There was no mistaking the blood, skin and matted hair on the bat.

Right next to the stairway, Duda saw the teenage boy. His face was unrecognizable. Duda checked his jugular for a beat. The boy was still alive.

"Call an ambulance. Quick," Duda ordered. He then continued on into the next room. There was another body, a child no more than 10 years old. Again, his face had been severely battered. A check for a pulse showed there was no need for assistance. The boy was dead.

With grim determination, the deputy continued on into another basement room. There were weights and other physical equipment supplies in this room. There was also the body of a middle-aged woman, later identified as Myung Ja Kim, 39, the wife of Young Man Kim.

If the previous sights had Duda reeling in horror, the brutal battering perpetrated on Mrs. Kim was even worse. It was obvious she had taken the full impact of the bat. Her face was completely obliterated. Her eyes and nose had been smashed to mere bloody masses. There was no need to even check, but Deputy Duda placed his finger along her neck. She, too, was dead.

There was another body in the weight room, that of a teenage boy. He, too, was horribly battered, but he was still alive.

Within minutes an ambulance crew arrived and were led into the basement. Duda, meanwhile, continued searching through the house for more bodies. In an upstairs bedroom, he found the fifth, that of Young Man Kim, 39. Kim lay on the bed. Unlike the others, his face had not been bludgeoned. But an obvious gunshot hole in his head and the blood on the sheet testified to his condition. He, like his wife and son, was dead.

These three victims were taken to the morgue for an autopsy while the surviving members of the family were taken to the hospital. Detectives from Macomb and Wayne Counties pulled together and canvassed the neighborhood.

Lt. Ron Tuscany, together with sheriff's deputies, worked throughout the night trying to obtain one clue. They questioned neighbors and friends of the victims and learned, with no surprise, that the victims were well liked, friendly, quiet and peace loving.

"They were very good people," a neighbor remarked. They were "not the type to be afraid of anyone. They were real easygoing, generous hard working people. They all just loved America."

Evidence at the scene had not as yet been processed, but detectives were working on one theory. The savage manner in which the victims were slain seemed to indicate vengeance. A statement made by one neighbor fortified this theory. According to the neighbor, Mr. Kim had recently planned on leaving the area to move to California. More importantly the family had reputedly gone to Korea the previous summer "to pick up a large sum of money," which Mr. Kim had apparently made in a secret business venture.

Police wondered if this had something to do with the murder. If so, then the brutality of the deaths could be explained as a mark of gangland vengeance. With this possibility now facing detectives, they immediately stationed guards outside the hospital rooms of the surviving members of the family — just in case the killers realized there were survivors and decided to finish their work.

After spending the rest of the evening gathering statements from neighbors, the detectives returned to headquarters and compared notes. There was not one clue as yet that could lead detectives to any solid explanation for the murders.

A phone call to the medical examiner produced

301

the information that Young Man Kim had died as a result of a gunshot wound to the head. His wife Myung had been strangled and bludgeoned to death. And their son Hyung Kim died from hemorrhaging as a result of a severe bludgeoning.

Doctors at the hospital where the two remaining children of the Kims were being attended to had little hope for their survival. Fourteen-year-old Byung Sup had suffered a fractured skull as a result of the beating. And a portion of the skull had embedded itself into his brain. The bludgeoning was not limited only to his head. He also suffered a severed spinal cord from the battering. Even if he lived, he would be severely brain damaged and paralyzed. The other family member also had a fractured skull, parts of which had also been embedded into his brain. He also had been shot in the chest. Doctors gave him little chance of survival. The detectives' hope that one of them would regain consciousness and provide some information was dashed to pieces with this development.

By the following day, police had gotten no closer to either a motive or the identity of the killers than when the murders were first discovered. Forensic technicians found not a single fingerprint or clue that would help in the investigation. The possibility of robbery was ruled out for the present since many valuables had been left behind.

By the evening of March 22nd, Lt. Ron Tuscany was completely baffled by the murders. He told reporters: "The house was not ransacked; not one drawer was open. There was no indication of narcotics in the house and no signs of forced entry."

By late Saturday night, detectives continued to man the phones and try working up leads. Again, it was to no effect. When asked about their

302

progress, one weary prober sighed, "There's nothing new. Nothing at all."

The lawmen had already been up over 24 hours. Their eyes were red, puffy and burning from lack of sleep, their stomachs bloated from gallons of coffee. And they continued throughout the night.

Monday morning came and went without any development. Police spoke with Kim's business associates and employees and were told Kim always took his daily receipts home with him. Detectives now had to rethink the motive. No money was found at the Kim home, and, although evidence at first indicated the absence of a robbery, the missing cash and the fact that it was common knowledge that Kim brought the receipts home with him suggested the motive could have been robbery.

The rest of Monday morning all Kim's employees were questioned about their actions on Saturday night, and all had alibis for their whereabouts.

Again, forensics was checked. Nothing.

Then, at 4:00 p.m. Detroit Police Inspector James Younger found something among urgent messages he had received that morning while he was busy in meetings on the Kim case. Several times that morning, a friend and former colleague of Inspector Younger when he was working on the gang squad, had some information on the Kim slaying. Younger immediately phoned him and was told that two police reservists had some information which could be useful.

Younger drove to the home of one of the reservists. Both men were there. Younger was disappointed during the initial questioning. They told him only what was already known from news accounts. But then they mentioned something completely new.

As Younger recalled, "One of them told me he had been asked to run a license plate check on DXGJ052." Younger already knew that such a check would reveal the car owner's address. He also knew that this license plate was that of Young Man Kim. As Younger continued questioning the reservists, they told him about a statement their "friend" had made to them.

"We were talking with Korean Joe and Gregory Belton. We were bullshitting, talking all about working as a bounty hunter for the Feds. You need a license for that. It cost a couple grand. So Gregory got the money, and's ready to go, but Joe's tap city. He got this idea about robbin' this guy he worked for, Kim. He said he knows the guy's got money, so that's where he can get it. We figured he was kidding. We still don't know."

Younger asked them if they knew the real name of Korean Joe. They answered that it was Chung Yim. Inspector Younger decided to bring the two reservists down to headquarters for questioning. He contacted Detroit Homicide Inspector Gilbert Hill, and both lawmen interrogated the two witnesses.

One immediate problem with statements of the reservists was an obvious question. Why did they run the check on the vehicle when they knew that this Chung Yim had already spoken about robbing Kim? The reservists explained that they thought he was kidding about the robbery and they didn't know that Kim was the person who owned the license plate until they ran the check. By then Yim had already gotten the information that he had asked for.

Younger wanted to know why they didn't tell police their suspicions about the possible robbery once they knew Yim had possession of Kim's address. They explained they had thought it was only a game with Yim. They never realized he would actually go through with it. And, again, they repeated they still didn't think he was the one who actually killed Kim and his family.

After a while of questioning the witnesses, Detective Hill phoned Sgt. John Hart of the Macomb County Homicide Squad. "I think we got good information on the slaying in Clinton Township," Hill told him. Sgt. Hart and another investigator drove to Detroit Police Headquarters and interrogated the witnesses.

Another interesting fact emerged during the grilling. According to one of the reservists, he had sold his gun to Gregory Belton. In addition, the reservist said that Belton had test fired his gun into a trailer where they were stationed as guards. Detectives immediately prepared a search warrant for the site. Recorder's Court Judge Justin Ravitz signed the warrant and within the hour, evidence technicians removed the slug from the wall in the trailer. The bullet was sent pronto to ballistics, and there, the slug and the bullets removed from the murder victims were compared under a dual-lens microscope. They matched.

With this hard evidence backing them up, detectives obtained arrest warrants for Gregory Belton and Chung Yim. On Tuesday, March 24th, police focussed their attention on capturing the suspects.

Sergeants Chalmers Sanders and Tommy Alston sat on Gregory Belton's house in Edinborough until about 8:00 p.m. when they received a radio transmission from headquarters. Belton had just walked in to give information on the Kim slayings. The officers told him he was under arrest for murder, and Belton replied, "I guess I'm in trouble." Alston and

Sanders returned to headquarters to interrogate the suspects.

In the meantime, however, other investigators were working on the other two suspects. Detroit Lt. Gerald Stewart and Sergeants Herbert Simmons and James Bivens spotted Yim's car near his home in Stabelin West. A car chase ensued when police flipped their sirens and lights.

"He cut through several alleys," one lawman recalled. "We followed him for several blocks. Then he stopped in front of a party store and bailed out of the car, leaving the motor running and the lights on."

Yim then ran into the store. One lawman covered the front entrance to the store while the others barrelled around to the rear entrance. They entered with guns drawn. The investigators slowly inched up towards the stock room.

Detective Stewart suddenly noticed movement from behind one of the boxes. He yelled, "Give it up, come on out." Suddenly, the suspect jumped up from behind the boxes with his hands in the air.

Stewart and the other detectives began leading the suspect to the car, but in a quick jerk, Yim whirled around. Stewart aimed his gun and said, "Don't do that again. You could get shot!"

Yim replied with a resigned look, "It doesn't matter. I'm dead already."

Yim was then taken to police headquarters where he and Belton were questioned in separate interrogation rooms. Both suspects identified Willie Heard as their accomplice and gave investigators Heard's address. By 11:00 p.m. that Tuesday, police investigators rushed to Heard's home, but when they entered his apartment, all they found was a half-empty suitcase. They kept a stakeout outside his apartment, but Heard never showed that night.

As one detective later put it, "As soon as he heard on TV that the other two were arrested, Heard knew he was next and split."

The following day, detectives questioned all known friends and acquaintances of the suspect. They got a call from a neighbor of Heard's that the suspect was staying at his house and was ready to give himself up. By 4:30 p.m., Heard was placed under arrest at his neighbor's house and taken to police headquarters.

With Heard's arrest, police had all the suspects in the Kim slayings in custody, but they had a lot more work cut out for them. In order to bring the suspects to trial and obtain a conviction, the lawmen needed more solid evidence. The fact that Belton had been linked with the murder weapon by the police reservists was hardly what could be called solid evidence. There was always the possibility the reservists had not been completely truthful in their statements to police. They said Belton had purchased the gun from them, but Belton could easily deny this. Was there any proof that he actually bought the gun? Was there a receipt for the purchase? Questioning of the reservists revealed there was no written receipt, so Belton could easily deny making the purchase.

The physical evidence found at the scene was also practically nil: no fingerprints or any other clue linking the suspects to the murder. What the detectives did have were the suspects.

Sleuths knew that the savagery shown in the murders of the Kim family was a sign of the kind of people they were dealing with. The suspects had acted like animals and, unless they were mistaken, the investigators believed if they gave them the chance, the suspects would, like a pack of sharks, turn on each other if the pressure mounted. They were right.

Through some hard questions, they were able to elicit a confession from Yim, Belton and Heard. Belton and Heard confessed that they were in the car outside the Kim home on the night of the murders, but they denied having anything to do with the butchery. It was Yim, they claimed, who went inside and carried out the grisly slayings.

Yim, on the other hand, claimed that all three of them were inside the house, and Belton and Heard were responsible for the murders. During their confessions, the suspects told police that they had stopped at stores along the way to the Kim house to ask for directions. Sleuths checked with these stores, and the employees there recalled Yim asking them directions to Twenlow Street.

While the probers continued piling up their evidence against the suspects, doctors were losing their battle to save the life of one of the two surviving members of the Kim family. Fourteen-year-old Byung Sup Kim, who'd suffered a fractured skull and severed spinal cord, showed no signs of brain activity. The hospital monitor measuring brain wave activity was flat, and doctors pronounced the victim brain dead. On March 27th, only six days after Byung Sup's family had been slaughtered, a relative, tears streaming down her eyes, gave doctors permission to remove Byung Sup Kim from life support equipment. Within minutes, he was dead. The last surviving member of the family remained on life support systems but doctors gave him little chance of survival.

Over the following months, detectives continued mounting their evidence against the suspects, but weaknesses in the case against Belton and Heard seemed insurmountable. Detectives had no evidence to indicate the suspects were lying when they claimed they knew nothing about the slayings, that all they did was stay in the car while Yim went inside to rob the family.

Only Yim's statements refuted their version of events. If detectives had a case, it was only against Yim since he had been pointed out by several store employees who gave him directions to the Kim house.

The case against Heard and Belton would have ultimately been stymied if it weren't for the courageous and miraculous recovery of the last surviving member of the Kim family. Given little hope for survival, he finally passed the critical life-threatening stages of recovery.

When detectives first tried to question him, he could recall nothing about the incident on the night of March 21st. Doctors informed investigators that the victim was brain damaged as a result of the savage bludgeoning. They did, however, hold out hope that as the injuries continued to heal, the victim would begin to recall, the incidents of that night. As the days passed and investigators continued working to pull together a case against the suspects, the surviving member of the Kim family began to recall in brief flashes, the events of that evening.

According to the victim, Yim wasn't the only person in the house. Belton and Heard were also there and were just as much responsible for the slaughter. By the time Belton's and Heard's trial approached, the victim was able to recall much of what happened that night.

At the trial, he told the court that on March

21st, Young Man Kim had come home from work at approximately 6:00 p.m. and went upstairs to bed. The rest of the family watched television in the living room downstairs. They had only just switched on the TV when there was a knock at the door. One of the children answered, and Chung Yim stood at the entrance. The family knew Chung Yim as a former employee of Young Man Kim's. They found nothing wrong with his being there, and invited him inside. Yim then asked the mother, Myung Ja, where Young Man was, and she said he was sleeping.

Just then, according to the survivor, "Two black guys came in and put a knife at (Byung Sup's) throat and told everybody to go to the basement. They were led into the laundry room. One of the black men stayed outside the room apparently guarding it from any attempt to escape."

Within a couple of minutes, according to the survivor, "I heard a gunshot noise that came from upstairs." Then Chung Yim came downstairs again and asked Myung Kim where she kept her husband's money.

" 'I want to see my husband first. Then I will give you everything I have,' " the witness recalled her as saying.

Yim then took Myung upstairs where the witness heard them speaking in Korean. Myung was pleading with him not to hurt her family. Then the witness didn't hear anything at all.

A few minutes later, the witness wasn't sure exactly how long, someone opened the laundry-room door and, the witness recalled, "I got shot in the chest. It was very painful . . . I fell forward."

The witness somehow managed to remain conscious. He heard one of the children crying. "I heard a whipping sound, then . . . the crying stopped."

Over the next few minutes, the witness struggled out of the laundry room. None of the killers were in the basement at this time. The witness somehow managed to crawl to another room where there was a telephone. He then called the police.

By the time he hung up the phone, he heard the three assailants coming back down the stairs. He identified Willie Heard as saying, "That m . . . f . . . is still alive." The witness then apparently lost consciousness and fell to the floor. The next thing he remembered he was lying in a hospital bed. He was deaf in one ear; his jaw was wired together and he was paralyzed on one side of his body.

On November 10, 1982, Willie Heard, 26, and Gregory Belton, 35, stood before Macomb Circuit Judge James C. Daner. Daner then announced his verdict in the bench trial. He found both defendants guilty of first-degree murder. Daner said his decision was largely based on the surviving witness's testimony.

"If nobody had survived in this case," Daner would later note, "the prosecution would have had a monumental job."

On January 5, 1983, Belton and Heard were sentenced to life terms in prison.

Four months later, the last suspect in the Kim slayings stood trial. Chung Yim's defense was based for the most part on his claim that he understood little English and had been duped by Belton and Heard. According to Yim, he had arrived in the U.S. in 1977 and had worked on and off at various jobs. Once he had worked for Young Man Kim as a gas station attendant. He had also worked elsewhere in a car wash and at other gas stations. It was while working in one of these gas stations that he had met Gregory Belton.

Over the next few months, he left his home to move in with Belton. He then became friends with Belton's acquaintances, the police reservists. They had told Yim they were regular police officers and that they were going to be working as bounty hunters for the federal government.

With tears streaming down his eyes, Chung Yim told the court, through an interpreter, how he was approached on the night of the 21st by Belton. The two men went to the home of Willie Heard and, there, they told Yim that they were going to do some police business. Belton drove the car for several miles, then gave Yim the wheel, explaining that he wanted to drink some beer, and he couldn't drink and drive. Belton also gave Yim a piece of paper. Scrawled on the paper was an address on Twenlow Street and the name Young Man Kim.

Yim said he knew Young Man, having worked for him before, but he didn't link the name to the person. In Korea, Yim said, the name Young Man and Kim were very common.

On the way to the address, Yim told the court, he stopped several times for directions. Belton and Heard remained hidden in the car.

When they arrived at the house, Yim recalled, Belton and Heard told him to knock at the door. Yim couldn't understand why he was the one to knock. It was their police business not his. "That's your job as policemen," Yim recalled telling Belton and Heard.

They explained that it was only proper for him to knock on their door since the owners were, like him, Oriental.

When Yim knocked at the door and it was

opened by one of the Kim children, Yim told the court, "I was surprised by the people because I knew them. I didn't know at all whose house it was.

"As they saw me," he continued, "they were surprised because I didn't know how to get to their place. They greeted me and asked me to come in because there was no hard feeling between us at all."

Yim then related that he was brought into the kitchen where he was offered something to drink. Only a short time later, he heard a knock at the door and the next moment, he saw Heard walk in with a knife at the throat of one of the children. Gregory Belton was right behind him.

The two men ordered the family down to the basement.

"I was frustrated. I didn't do nothing," Yim told the jury. Myung Kim grabbed Yim by his lapels and asked in a desperate voice, "What's the matter? What's happening?"

Yim recalled he was shaking terribly and his heart was pumping. "I was afraid, yes," Yim testified.

After the family was taken into the basement, Yim recalled, Heard walked over to him. He had a gun in his hand and told Yim, " 'Let's go upstairs together.' "

They went to the upstairs bedrooms and Heard told Yim to begin searching for money. "I didn't think anything. I just said I wouldn't do anything," Yim recalled. He stood there for a few moments while Heard went into other upstairs bedrooms. After only a short while, Yim heard a gunshot.

Yim's version of what happened on the night of the 21st would have fit the events if it weren't for several inconsistencies pointed out by the prosecution. If Yim couldn't understand English and was, therefore, duped by the other assailants, then how was it possible that he had passed a written and oral examination for a Michigan driver's license? Also, the prosecution introduced witnesses who recalled speaking with Chung Yim. According to the witnesses, Yim had no problem whatsoever either understanding English or speaking it.

In addition, the surviving victim of the murders testified that Chung Yim was the person who shot him in the chest, that he was an active participant in the murder and that Yim was not, as he had earlier testified, "frozen in fear."

Assistant Prosecutor Thomas Landy argued that Yim "went there knowing he had to do what he did because he knew the family. He aided in committing four murders."

On Friday, April 22, 1983, a jury of six men and six women, found Chung Yim guilty of four counts of first degree murder in the slayings of Byung Sup, 14, Hyung, 8, Myung Ja, 39 and Young Man Kim, 39.

At his sentencing hearing the following month, May 6th, 1983, Chung Yim stood before Circuit Judge James S. Thorburn and said, "I have a lot of things to say, but don't know where to start. But there is one thing that I may be allowed to say, that I am innocent." Judge Thorburn then sentenced the defendant to four consecutive life prison terms.

"ONE WHOLE FAMILY WAS MASSACRED!"

by Benison Murray

Miami is many things to many people; it is a city of contrasts. It's a vacation mecca for those few fortunate enough to escape the snows of the North and make the winter trek. It is also a way station for entrepreneurs decked out in silk shirts open to the belt and with enough gold chains on them to sink the Saratoga. These worthies are dedicated to free enterprise—the drug trade.

On Southwest 8th you will hear more Spanish spoken than English, and Latino fast foods outsell anglo burgers two to one.

Violence has taken root here. Displaced Cubans, Colombians and representatives from a baker's dozen other Latin American countries jockey for turf in the easy-money cartel.

Most are honest. Each day they open businesses, clean hotels, and serve the public. True, there are families who have BMWs at the door, while others dream of their first Porsche. Some live in houses like spun sugar under elaborate tile roofs; others reside in roach hotels and wish for better digs.

In December 1986, Miamians were busy decorating for Christmas, so that the brilliantly lighted city from offshore looked like a Disney fantasy.

One of the beautifully decorated houses in the Miami Lake section of the city on Friday, the 12th of December, had been the busy scene for a pre-holiday luncheon attended by a dozen laughing, chattering women. Their hostess, Amparo Hurtado de Paz, a vivacious and well-known journalist, offered her own special chicken and vegetables with rice, for which she was justly praised. This was followed by a rich dessert of fruit-stuffed apples with Surinam cherries and ice cream. The hostess wore a chic black dress and appeared quite elegant.

Her friends knew her as a journalist, a female Don Quixote unafraid to joust with drug-traffickers or erring diplomats.

Friends marvelled at — but didn't envy — the nerve it took to publish articles in *El Espectador,* second largest newspaper in Colombia. Jousting with drug lords, her friends felt, could be as safe as stirring a nest of rattlers with a stick and about as predictable.

That pre-holiday Friday ended, as far as friends or neighbors knew, with Amparo de Paz tidying her house after her luncheon guests had gone. Her 10-year-old daughter, Alina, played in front of the house; her husband Carlos, still handsome at 43, walked with their son, Carlos, Jr., the father's arm draped about the teenager's shoulder near the lake behind their home.

On Saturday, the beautifully decorated house was curiously silent. Nothing moved. The eerie stillness continued all day Sunday. On Monday, Carlos Sr. failed to show up at his cleaning establishment.

Tuesday morning was the limit. A call was made to the authorities. The caller mentioned a foul odor and a silent house, an ominous set of circumstances in a neighborhood which held, besides the Paz family, such well-knowns as then U.S. Senator-elect Bob Graham and Miami Dolphins coach Don Shula.

When repeated knocks at the doors and a flat official voice repeating "Police Officers" brought no results, the silent house was entered by force.

The noxious odor mentioned to the dispatcher permeated the front room, giving a macabre quality to the huge gold and ribbon-decorated tree with the creche lovingly placed beneath it.

The 10-year-old daughter of the house, Alina, a sweet-faced child, was sprawled face-up near the piano she had learned to play. Dead, too, were Amparo and her husband, Carlos Sr. Dental records would be brought in to verify their identities.

Soon the town house belonging to the Pazes became a hive of detectives, the Miami medical examiner and police homicide photographers.

Windows and doors were dusted, as were all other surfaces which might hold fingerprints. The three members of the Paz family were officially pronounced dead. Photos of the bodies were taken from every angle, both black and white for official use and quick Polaroids in color for the homicide detectives' own records.

People from the neighborhood milled about outside the police tapes cordoning off the crime scene. They were questioned one by one and their names and addresses were taken by probers.

According to the neighbors, a teenage son was missing, as was a new Volvo belonging to the family. The worst was feared. Perhaps a kidnapping with the boy as hostage, suggested one neighbor. If so, little hope was held for his safe recovery.

But Metro-Dade detectives were tight-lipped, refusing to give the media information on how the family had died or whether there was a known motive. Later, queries as far away as Bogota clarified nothing.

The sub-director of the newspaper Amparo de Luz had worked for under her maiden name, said, "I don't understand what happened. She had been doing stories about the Colombian community in Miami and I never saw her write anything that could offend someone

"We are deeply shocked."

When told of the missing teenage son, he said, "We fear for his life."

The brand-new 1987 gold Volvo gave working detectives a point of departure for the probe. With a BOLO ("Be On The Look Out") put out on the vehicle, perhaps the missing son could be located along with his abductor, if such was the case.

On Wednesday in Colombia, the editor of *El Espectador,* Guillermo Cano, was savagely killed as he left the newspaper offices. Gunmen on a motorcycle blew him away, then escaped, careening wildly down the streets of Bogota.

According to officials, it was considered to be unrelated to the Paz family killing, but many people both in and out of law enforcement wondered.

But if Cano's killing in Bogota had no connection to his journalist's murder in Miami, Metro-Dade detectives found alternate avenues to explore. Patient questioning of neighbors and friends showed that no one had seen any of the Paz family members after the Friday when the party was held.

One neighbor told investigators working the case, that the slain family was quiet, but friendly and hard-working. Others said that Paz senior usually left his house early in the morning to open the family business, a dry-cleaning establishment.

Pending the autopsy reports, it was taken for gospel that the Paz family had been massacred on Friday—in a word, dead four days before discovery. God only knew where the boy's body would be found. With the whole Atlantic Ocean at the doorstep, it was possible he would never be found.

One neighbor also told detectives he had last seen Alina playing in front of the house with another little girl. His last glimpse of the elder Paz was of the father and son walking together in the back of the house, the father's arm lovingly across his son's shoulders.

One woman, a friend of Amparo's who had attended her festive pre-holiday party, was equally emphatic that no one was able to get in touch by telephone with the Paz family and no one had seen them after Friday. Other friends told investigators of the beautifully decorated house, the tree and the nativity scene placed beneath it.

Sleuths queried the women about Amparo's column in *El Espectador* and learned that it covered the Colombian community in South Florida. Recently it had printed facts about the Colombian drug trade.

Detectives asked whether Amparo had acted nervous or afraid—did she seem spooked that Friday?

On the contrary, one close woman friend told them. "She was beautiful and radiant, very happy. She was all prepared for Christmas. You know the food was delicious, there was no worry. Someone who was worried about anything could not give that kind of party."

But Metro-Dade detectives cultivated patience, an attribute prized above all other in a job devoted to asking the same questions, going over the same terrain with a dozen or more people.

If not worried, how about her being afraid, sad?

The only sad incident any friend could think of was the recent discovery of a heart condition in the Paz's teenage son. It had been discovered three years before when he experienced difficulty breathing.

This made the continued disappearance of Carlos Jr. even more disturbing. The doctor's name and address would have to be followed up. Was the kid on life-preserving medicine? If so and if he didn't have it, what were his chances of living? Would ransom be demanded by his abductors?

Various witnesses told detectives that the boy appeared in good health when last seen. With a chancy thing like a heart condition, however, who knew how long the teenager, especially if on maintenance drugs, would remain healthy?

Then a lead turned up that dated back to an incident in 1981.

Detectives were told that the elegant Amparo and an enthusiastic art collector had opened a posh art gallery in Coral Gables, calling it "Amparo's Gallery." Among those attending the Gallery's opening night were soon-to-become Colombia's president, Belisario Betancourt, Bogota's Colonial museum director, and several visiting Colombian art critics and artists.

"The whole (Colombian) society was there," one of Amparo's colleagues said. "It was a tremendous scandal."

The local Colombian society sipped champagne in fluted glasses at the Gallery's opening night.

But, suddenly, the genteel laughter and low purr of conversation was shattered by Amparo's partner. The man burst in with police, shuttered the establishment and stripped paintings from the wall. He trashed the reception. Amparo de Paz never spoke of it again, except to say that the man defrauded her and he was eventually deported. But where was he now? How about vengeful relatives?

Every lead had to be followed, Metro-Dade investigators knew, no matter how tenuous. It takes a lot of hate and maybe years of sullen resentment before you can blow away three people and one of them a child. The trick was to zero in on the motive.

That Amparo de Paz had no idea of her immediate future on the last day of her life was certain. Women who had attended the luncheon said she had cheerfully discussed painting, a field in which she was knowledgeable, and she mentioned a book she had just completed and a trip back to Colombia planned for the first month of the new year.

On Wednesday, the cleaners on Biscayne Boulevard was closed. A hand-lettereed placard was taped to the door: "Sorry, we are closed today due to circumstances beyond our control."

The Paz family — husband, wife and daughter — remained unclaimed in the morgue at the Dade Medical Examiner's office.

One friend very close to the slain woman wept as she recalled the last words of her happy and vivacious friend. Amparo de Paz had smiled and promised, "I will see you very soon."

Metro-Dade investigators laboriously secured information on the slain family. It was discovered that the column written by Amparo under her maiden name had been called, "Carta de Miami" (Letter from Miami). In this regular feature of *El Espectador,* her stories were generally mixed with information picked up from U.S. newspapers with tidbits of interest to Colombians.

More important to the men working the case, her column had caused alleged drug lords to threaten her life at least once. But, far from being intimidated, the petite journalist became more determined to write as she pleased.

"She was a very belligerent journalist, very aggressive and controversial," a correspondent for another Colombian newspaper said. "She always put her fingers in the fire."

Playing with fire paid very little, investigators found. It seemed a job done for prestige rather than cash. The money offered Amparo came to little more than $250 per month, but it made her a force to be reckoned with in Miami's large Colombian community and in her own mother country.

Detectives found that in spite of the threat to her life, Amparo de Paz used Miami as the source for what would be front-page news in Bogota.

Colombian politicians, industrialists and drug-traffickers who lived or kept second homes in Miami all came under the censorious eye of the fiery journalist.

Detectives shook their collective heads. Small wonder the woman's life had been threatened!

Metro-Dade cops had a copy of her last column, dated November 17th. Once translated, it proved to be a blasting attack on the drug cartel that runs the world's largest cocaine empire out of the city of Medellin.

Amparo de Paz had sent to her newspaper a thick file of copies of an indictment against the cartel which *El Espectador* published with banner headlines.

Her column, entitled, "Not one single member of the Medellin cartel in prison," was written shortly after the Miami grand jury indicted the drug ring's leaders on 39 drug-related charges.

The column reproduced statements in which U.S. law enforcement officials expressed their feelings over the fact that the cartel's leaders were still walking freely on the street.

Detectives also got a copy of an August 19th column entitled, "Unhappiness in U.S. Over Ochoa's Release." This column had Amparo mulling over the frustration of U.S. law enforcement officials over the release in Colombia of an accused and well-known alleged drug lord.

August 1st saw yet another drug-related column. This one covered drug smuggling and was entitled, "Drugs of Death."

But even with a free and aggressive press as Colombia has, reporters admitted to investigating Metro-Dade detectives that the one area they rarely investigate is the drug business. They expressed what the detectives already knew — Colombian drug lords have at their beck and call private armies of several thousand men who kill their enemies almost daily and ruthlessly.

It was a formidable enemy for one petite female journalist.

Amparo had also taken on the diplomatic enclave residing in Miami. She accused top consulate officials who had attended a cocktail party of supporting a certain political candidate for a coming Colombian national election.

Amparo Hurtado de Paz had already enraged Colombian diplomats with a 1983 column which revealed the purchase of the Coral Gables Colombian consulate for much more than the building's market price. The headline over the article read: "The Site of the Consulate in Miami: Intimacies of a Purchase." One diplomat responded by saying he had felt no animosity toward the diminutive journalist. "She was an excellent newspaperwoman," he said.

With questioning and interviews by Metro-Dade investigators, the Paz family, their antecedents and their everyday life left law enforcement officials with a lot of unanswered questions.

The partner in the ill-fated art gallery was eliminated as a possible suspect. The short-lived partnership was just another common occurrence, unpleasant but not lethal.

The threat from the drug trade was iffy, but pavement pounding and dogged detective work led probers to conclude that it was just that — threat. But with no teeth behind it.

As always, the family proper was looked into. A murder-suicide is not uncommon, and then there was still the missing teenager. No ransom note had been delivered, no body had been thrown from a car — in short, nothing had gone down that looked like a kidnapping or hostage situation.

There was plenty that pointed in another direction, however. There had been much hostility between the boy and his father, the investigators found. The age-old generation gap. The sullen displeasure of an adolescent physically but not emotionally ready for manhood.

Carlos Jr. was a high school drop-out. His grades left much to be desired. The focus was now on the youth as the perpetrator of parricide — the slaying of close relatives.

Metro-Dade Police Commander William Johnson said they believed the primary target of the young killer had been the father. "He was angry because his father was grounding him, setting deadlines and curfews," Johnson said. "The father was very strict."

This was ascertained when the young man was picked up and arrested in his father's new gold Volvo outside a teenage girlfriend's house. He had his passport in his pocket.

Commander Johnson also told the media that it looked as though the mother and sister were killed simply "because they happened to be there." The possibility existed that the mother and daughter may have walked in on the act of patricide—the killing of the father, Carlos Paz Sr.—in the dining room. Wrong place, wrong time.

Detectives found that the 18-year-old Carlos Jr. had been too young to buy a handgun, so he had to be content with a semi-automatic rifle to systematically slay each member of his family the same day the gun was purchased.

After receiving his Miranda warning, the dark-haired youth was charged with three counts of first-degree murder in the triple slaying.

The young man remained in jail on Thursday while his family was buried in Our Lady of Mercy Cemetery. That same day, during a hearing, County Judge Meek Robinette refused to set bond for the accused slayer.

Carlos Paz Jr. pleaded not guilty to the murders he was charged with. Circuit Judge Ellen Morphonios set trial for March 30th of the new year.

Later, the 5-foot-9-inch, 160-pound Paz Jr. was moved from the large open area where he socialized with two dozen other inmates. He went to a single cell where he was alone. His lawyer revealed that Paz Jr. had received an anonymous threatening letter from *within* the jail, making the move necessary for the safety of his client.

The work of the Metro-Dade investigators would pay off at the trial of Paz Jr. however.

In April 1987, Carlos Paz Jr. made clumsy attempts at acting insane to lay the basis for a plea in that vein. In one court appearance, he formed a gun with his fist, then pointed it at spectators and court personnel. He then blew on his finger, much as would a five-year-old playing cowboys and Indians. Nevertheless, Judge Ellen Morphonios, after hearing testimony from two psychiatrists, ruled that the good-looking Hispanic was competent to stand trial.

On July 20, 1987, the young parricide, slayer of his mother, sister, and father, was found guilty as charged and sentenced to life in prison plus 134 years to be served consecutively.

"THE INFERNO SHROUDED A TRIPLE MURDER!"

by Billie Taylor

Carter Cove in Yell County, Arkansas is so tiny you can't even find it on a county map. To call it a village is to use too big a word. It doesn't have a cafe, a movie, or even a car wash.

Carter Cove's only business, a family owned grocery store and service station, had closed a few years before when its owners, Jake and Mabel Horn, had retired.

The little store had been the center of the social life of Carter Cove. Folks sat on the benches out front, whittling, spitting, and catching up on the local news. Though the store was closed, folks still stopped at Jake's and Mabel's to visit and talk. The Horns were everybody's best friends.

Carter Cove doesn't have a police force either or even a constable. But they don't really need one, for there is no crime in Carter Cove.

There is no fire department in Carter Cove either. But the community is only a few miles from Plainview, population 752, and Plainview has a two-man fire department.

So when an early rising Carter Cove resident

saw smoke pouring from his neighbor's house about 6:30 a.m., March 23, 1983, he called the Plainview Fire Department.

Fire Chief Elmer Padgett and fireman Monroe Hunt and volunteers responded promptly. They were on the scene at 6:55 a.m.

The thick smoke and high licking flames verified fears that the house had burned internally for some time before the alert neighbor reported the holocaust.

The burning building was the home of Jake, 70, and Mabel, 66. The elderly Horns were not anywhere near the house. The chief feared the owners were trapped inside.

Chief Padgett entered the back of the house where the living quarters were located. After their recent and well deserved retirement, the Horns had remodeled the concrete block building to make a comfortable, warm and welcoming home.

Chief Padgett battled the thick smoke and flames until he reached the front entrance on the west side of the house. His groping hands found Mabel Horn, unconscious. He dragged her body out onto the lawn where crowds of excited neighbors had gathered.

Chief Padgett re-entered the house which was now an inferno. He was closely followed by fireman Monroe Hunt. Padgett crawled to the den again. He found Jake Horn in his recliner, unconscious. He rescued the second victim.

Meanwhile, fireman Hunt had done some hunting, just in case the Horns had had company. Tragically, they had. He found a third victim in a small bathroom. He managed to pull this man from the burning house.

Fire had destroyed most of the inside of the back part of the house by this time. The Plainview Fire Department and trucks from two other towns finally doused the flames, but almost the entire structure was destroyed.

A doctor had come to the scene. He noticed something extremely strange about the three victims. Two of them, Jake and Mabel, showed no signs of burns or fire. Each one's head was a battered mess. Their throats had been so severely slashed that their heads were only barely attached to their bodies. Only the third victim, identified by a neighbor as John Lewis "Sailor" Horn, 65, Jake's brother, showed signs of burns and these were only minor. His head too was a battered pulp, his throat slashed, his head almost severed. Each victim also appeared to have stab wounds in the chest area.

Authorities were immediately notified and by 8:00 a.m. Yell County Sheriff Denver Dennis and Deputies Loyd Maughn and Nub Knight, along with Prosecuting Attorney Investigator Joe Jones, as well as Coroner Mike Cornwell were on the scene.

Jones is a former undercover federal narcotics agent who works as a liaison between the prosecuting attorney's office and all other law enforcement agencies in the four county area. He is on 24-hour call.

Tom Tatum, the prosecuting attorney, is a strong law-and-order man. He is a true stickler. Everything has to be exactly right. His cases are prepared with meticulous care.

That preparation shows up on his record. In 1983, there were six homicides in Tatum's district.

330

All were solved and all those charged were convicted.

Tatum insists on and practices complete cooperation between all law enforcement agencies in his district. It was apparent that the fire was set to cover murder.

Officers suspected robbery immediately as the motive. The Horns were known by everyone in the community to keep large sums of money in their home. They had formed this dangerous habit when they ran their prosperous little grocery store/service station, because it was so far to the bank.

Joe Jones, and Deputies Maughn and Knight sifted through the still smoldering ashes, searching for clues. The fire had been somewhat contained by the concrete walls, but it still had done its job well. Virtually all clues had been destroyed.

The investigators did find a few valuables— several rolls of coins, about $735 worth, some old coins, jewelry, Mabel's wallet and purse, John's wallet. But they didn't find Jake's wallet, and Jake was the one who always carried upwards of a thousand dollars in cash in his pocket. A .38 caliber pistol was also found. These items of evidence were sent to the Arkansas State Crime Lab.

Sergeant Jim King of the Arkansas State Police joined in the investigation. He took dozens of photographs of the crime scene.

It took all the expertise that the investigators could muster to piece together the logical sequence of events. There were massive amounts of blood found in front of the closet door where Mabel Horn had been found. A recliner in the den where Jake had died was also blood soaked. And the bedroom where John Lewis had died showed signs of a battle so fierce that the commode had been knocked aside. The bathroom walls had been splattered with the old man's blood and brains.

Sheriff Dennis pieced together from his meager clues this possible chain of events. Sometime during the evening, Mabel Horn had opened her door on the west side of the house to someone she knew. As she turned to lead her guest to the living room, that person had struck her on the back of the head over and over with a blunt instrument. Then she had been stabbed viciously and her throat slashed. Her life's blood had soaked deep into the carpet.

Next, the killer had entered the den, probably creeping up behind the unsuspecting Jake as he lay in his recliner, watching television. Jake may have felt only the first of the many blows, and did not know when the knife entered his heart or when his head was almost severed from his body.

Usually only Jake and Mabel were in the immaculate home. But tonight, Jake's brother, John, was visiting. He was in a small bathroom near the back of the house. Perhaps he heard strange noises and started toward the front of the house, sleuths reasoned.

The murderer cornered John, swinging his weapon and beating the old man. But John managed to defend himself somewhat. The autopsy was to show some cloth fibers and skin under his fingernails.

But John had died as his brother and sister-in-law had. Massive head injuries, throat cut and chest stabbed.

As Jones and others sifted ashes and charred remains for clues, Sheriff Dennis and Sgt. King questioned shocked and frightened neighbors.

A couple of nearby neighbors had noted some movements around the Horn home the evening before. But there wasn't anything unusual. There had been some dogs barking between 8:30 and 9:00 p.m. There had been more barking between 11:00 p.m. and 1:00 a.m., but no real outstanding commotions.

The nearest neighbor reported seeing a red vehicle parked at the Horns' home but was uncertain as to the time—maybe 9:00, maybe 10:00. And what kind of vehicle—"a truck I think," or "a different kind of car." But one thing the neighbor was certain of—the vehicle was red in color.

This last bit of information helped investigators a lot. Sheriff Dennis knew his county and his constituents well. He immediately recalled someone he knew who drove a red vehicle, not exactly a truck, not exactly a car. The sheriff had had some problems with this person before.

A pickup order went out and in a few short hours a very shaky young man faced a ring of grim-faced interrogators. The young man admitted being near the Horn home between 11:30 p.m. and midnight. But he swore he didn't stop or enter the house. And he was driving a red vehicle.

But by coincidence, he saw another red vehicle, a pulpwood truck parked at the west side of the Horns' house. When he drove back down the same road about 20 minutes later, the red billet truck was gone.

There can't be very many red billet trucks in all of Arkansas. There was only one in Yell County. And its owner, a newcomer who had moved there only a month ago, lived less than two miles from the homicide scene.

His name was James Theral Metcalf, 42. He was driving a red pulpwood truck when police officers stopped and arrested him.

Sgt. King and Deputy Jim Pickins interrogated the itinerant billet hauler. The time was March 24th, 13 hours after the triple homicides. Metcalf, after refusing to have a lawyer present, made a statement that was taped by King and Pickens.

After the interrogation, James Metcalf was charged with three counts of capital felony murder and ordered held without bail.

Every member of the community was relieved that the Horns' murderer had apparently been captured. They had all felt the killer had been someone just passing through. But the case was to take some strange twists and turns before the trail of justice ended.

Investigators now began backtracking on that trail. Their background check showed no previous criminal record for James Metcalf. He had moved his wife and seven children from place to place all over the state, working briefly here and there, never making more than the barest living.

But Metalf had fallen on even harder times, sleuths found out. The severe Arkansas winter had kept him from making any money at all. He owed everybody in the whole county that he could charge anything to. He had been forced to mortgage his billet truck, the only thing of any value he had.

Then on March 24th, he had started paying his debts. He visited several of his creditors and the lawmen following him accounted for $1100 he spent that day.

James Metcalf also visited a barber shop early

that morning. The hair on the front, back, and sides of his head was singed. He explained to the barber that an aerosol can had exploded in the trash, and he had been standing too close.

Some additional evidence had been confiscated from Metcalf's truck and house. One of these items was a ball peen hammer. The hammer was sent to the crime lab and the report came back. There is no trace of blood, hair or foreign matter of any kind on this instrument. It is unusually clean, dirt and debris free, not like a used work hammer.

Investigators drew their own conclusions as to why the hammer had apparently been scrubbed.

John Horn's fingernails had traces of fiber and flesh under them. Metcalf had a scratch on his stomach. But the fibers didn't match any of the burned fibers found in the ashes of the crime scene.

Dr. Fahmy Malak, state medical examiner, reported that the probable cause of death was multiple head injuries. Each victim had been struck nine or ten times with a blunt instrument, something resembling a hammer. John Horn had been alive but unconscious at the time he was burned.

The approximate time of death was placed between midnight and 3:00 a.m. The effects of the fire hindered exactness.

The trial was set for mid-November. Metcalf was jailed in Dardanelle, many miles from Carter Cove, for his own safety. His court-appointed attorneys worked diligently, preparing his defense. Then Metcalf decided to help himself.

Metcalf wrote a letter to his family on April 17th. He asked a cellmate who was being released to smuggle the letter out. The cellmate agreed.

But after thinking it over, the man decided he was in enough trouble already, so he gave the letter to Sheriff Dennis, who passed it on to Tom Tatum, the prosecuting attorney.

The letter was interpreted by Tatum as being in code. Metcalf was trying to tell his family to establish that the hammer was in the house all night and could not have been in the truck the night of the murders. Also, according to Tatum's version, Metcalf told a relative of a way he thought she could slip messages to him without getting caught.

Jury selection was extremely difficult. Too many people had known the Horns and had already decided on guilt or innocence. Almost 300 people were called before the seven women and five men were seated.

Expert witnesses built the case for the prosecutor. Dr. Malak used a life sized acetate overlay of Mrs. Horn's skull, matching the imprints to the hammer shape of the hammer found in Metcalf's truck. The overlay and prints were identical. Malak testified that the other victim's death blows also matched the hammer's shape.

Linda Taylor, Questioned Documents Examiner, testified that the smuggled letter was written in Metcalf's handwriting.

Then the real fireworks began. Prosecutor Tatum introduced into evidence Metcalf's statement that he had made to authorities 12 hours after the crime.

The defense objected vigorously. One by one, they listed every conceivable reason why the statement should be denied. One by one, Prosecutor Tatum discounted their reasons. Once again, Tatum's meticulous preparations paid off. After long and deliberate consideration, the judge ruled the statement of Metcalf and that of his relative would be allowed.

Copies of the taped statement were given to the jury. Then the taped confession was played in the hushed and crowded courtroom. It began: On March 24, 1983, this taped statement was made by James Theral Metcalf to A.S.P. Investigator Sgt. Jim King, CID Division and Deputy Sheriff Jim Pickens. The gist of the statement was this:

Metcalf parked his red pulpwood truck at the front door of the Horns' residence, the door on the west side.

He knocked on the door, and Mabel answered it. She asked him to come in. Metcalf made no attempt to disguise himself. He was welcomed as a friend.

When Mabel turned around, Metcalf struck her with the hammer. He savagely attacked the old woman, striking her nearly a dozen times with the ball peen hammer.

After that he said he went blank. Some things he could remember and some things he could not. After he struck the woman, he said everything exploded.

After striking the woman near the front door, he went into the house to the kitchen-den area. Jake was sitting in his recliner, watching television. Metcalf struck him several times with the hammer also. The chair was saturated with blood. This victim was caught completely unawares. He literally never knew what hit him.

The third victim was able to fight for his life. Metcalf didn't know Horn's brother, John Lewis, would be there. He came into the room.

The two scuffled around. But the elderly man was no match for the muscular billet hauler. John did manage to scratch his assailant. The fight continued into the bathroom. The commode was knocked over. But the vicious slayer knocked the small man down and struck him 9 or 10 times.

Metcalf then made a trip back through the house. Wielding a newly sharpened knife, he slashed the throats of each of his helpless victims. So vicious were the slashes that their throats were cut clear back to the neck bone, their heads nearly severed from their bodies. There was blood clear up the sides of the wall, up on the ceiling.

Before Metcalf went to visit the Horns, whom he said he considered friends, he sharpened his fish scaling knife. He said he sharpened it because it was broke, and not because he intended to use it when he got to the Horns. He said he didn't know when he decided to rob the Horns, that at first he planned only to talk to them. At the time he made the statement, he told officers he didn't know where the knife was.

After he sharpened the knife, he put it in his pocket. He said he didn't remember cutting anyone's throat. In fact, he almost got sick when the officer told him about it, Metcalf said. Each of the victims was stabbed several times, another part of the crime that Metcalf claimed he could not recall.

Metcalf remembered taking about a thousand dollars, mostly in twenties. But he said he couldn't remember if he took it from Jake's billfold or a dresser drawer.

The fire was an accident, Metcalf told his interrogators. It just sort of exploded. When his hair caught fire, he got really scared. But there was a billfold and partially burned papers found in the small bathroom where the fire "accidentally" started, apparently left there by the killer.

Metcalf said there was no blood on his clothes. But he went straight home after the triple murders, washed up and threw some of his clothes in the fireplace, a shirt, a T-shirt and a towel.

He took his jeans outside and tried to burn them. He then took the laces out of his boots. He didn't remember what he did with them.

Metcalf said he and his wife were having serious problems and had a big fight about money on the night of March 23rd, just before he left the house.

When he left the house, he was severely depressed. He said he couldn't remember when he decided to rob the Horns. He vowed he never planned to kill them. The officers pointed out that Metcalf was well known to the Horns, in fact they were pretty good friends. He could not have robbed without being recognized.

Metcalf said he went to the barber shop the next day and got his singed hair trimmed off. He then made a tour of the town, paying some of his most pressing bills. He was out just riding around in his red billet truck when he was arrested.

The prosecution ended its case with the reading of the statements. They had called 22 witnesses.

The defense called six witnesses in its two hour session. They attempted to prove that Metcalf's mental condition, due to marital problems, made him say and do things that made him look guilty when he wasn't. They pointed out that it was common knowledge that the Horns kept large sums of money in the house.

Metcalf did not testify.

The jury deliberated for nine and one half hours. They returned with a verdict of guilty. Sentence was set at three life terms without parole.

When the sentence was read, Metcalf, who had been impassive throughout the lengthy trial, burst out, "I didn't kill those people. They were already dead when I got there."

A capital felony conviction is automatically appealed.

"MANHUNT FOR THE GREEDY KILLERS IN THE RED CORVETTE!"

by Kathleen Chandler

When Ellen Johnson arrived at the home of Mrs. Franklin in Pell City, Alabama to do the housekeeping, she was puzzled that no one was home. The door was unlocked, so Ellen stepped inside. Lights were on, and she heard the sound of a television coming from the bedroom. But when she cautiously peeked through the bedroom door, the room was empty.

Ellen Johnson became concerned. She had not been told the Franklins were going away somewhere. Judy Franklin's purse was still in the house. Paul Sr.'s wallet lay in plain sight under the bed. As far as Ellen could tell, all the clothes and suitcases were in their usual places, as were two bottles of medicine Mr. Franklin took every day for a liver ailment.

Concern gave way to real worry, and Ellen decided to call police.

In the gathering dusk of a hot July evening, investigators from the St. Clair County Sheriff's Department arrived on the scene.

The lights were still on, and the TV was still playing. The family's two dogs, a big German

Shepherd and a beagle cross breed, still roamed the yard. There was no evidence of burglary, robbery, or a struggle. No missing suitcases. No clothing gone. "Nothing is missing out of the house except them," said St. Clair County Chief Deputy Gene Newman.

Something was missing from the basement garage, however. Paul Franklin Sr.'s bright red 1968 model Corvette was not in its customary parking place. Beyond that, it was as if the Franklin family had vanished into thin air. "Something like this," declared Newman, "is about like what they show on the *Twilight Zone*."

Worried relatives declared emphatically that they would have been notified if the Franklins were planning a trip. Petite, pretty Judy Franklin was an avid gardener. She wouldn't have gone away without asking someone to care for her flowers.

As for Paul Franklin Sr., he had multiple health problems. It was completely out of character for him to simply pick up and go somewhere, leaving behind all his credit cards, his clothes, and even his medications.

Nor had handsome, lively ten-year-old Paul Jr. mentioned a trip to anyone.

"It's like they vanished into thin air," said Gene Newman.

Careful questioning in the area revealed that the Franklins were well liked by all of their neighbors. Judy Franklin was often seen jogging around the neighborhood, offering a smile and a friendly wave as she passed by. She was, according to one resident, "the sweetest woman that ever lived."

Her husband Paul was well known in the community, having made an unsuccessful bid for the office of coroner in the fall of 1982. In a newspaper interview given during the campaign, he described himself as a salesman who had previously worked in the insurance and investment fields. When asked about his qualifications for the coroner's position, Franklin stated: "I've had vast experience in multiple deaths" and spoke of retrieving bodies in Vietnam.

Police learned that on the evening of July sixth, a Wednesday night, Mrs. Franklin had spoken by phone with a neighbor. No one had seen or spoken with any of the Franklins since. Relatives reported trying unsuccessfully to reach the family by phone several times later that night. This seemed to narrow down the time of their disappearance from sometime after about 6:30 on July 6th.

"It's the most baffling thing in our county for a long time, or ever, for that matter," stated St. Clair County coroner Charles Foreman.

Days passed. Careful investigation of the house and grounds by officers from the St. Clair County Sheriff's Department and the Alabama Bureau of Investigation turned up nothing new. The Franklins had not returned home, nor had they contacted anyone.

On Sunday, July 10th, the St. Clair County Sheriff's Department appealed to the public for help. Print and broadcast media were given these descriptions: Paul Franklin Sr., white male, age 34, height 5 feet, 6 inches, weight 160 pounds, brown eyes, brown hair. Judy Franklin, white female, age 34, height 5 feet 2 inches, weight 130 pounds, blue eyes, blonde hair. Paul Griffin Franklin Jr., white male, age 10, height 4 feet, weight 60 pounds, brown eyes, brown hair.

Newspapers and television were provided with a recent studio portrait of the missing family. Anyone with any information was asked to contact the St. Clair County Sheriff's Department.

Meanwhile, a massive search effort had been mobilized. Searching the rolling, wooded terrain from the air were ten National Guard helicopters, a state owned helicopter, and 20 small aircraft flown by volunteers. Investigators scouted the nearby Coosa River and Bald Rock Mountain, a local landmark, extending the search into the dense and somewhat foreboding Talladega National Forest.

"We've been over the county four times," said Chief Deputy Newman on Monday, July 11th. "Every day we get more concerned for the family."

Along with a description of the missing family, law enforcement officials had broadcast a description of the missing car. All available data on the red Corvette had also been fed into the National Crime Information Center's computer.

Six days had passed with no sign of the Franklins or the car. Their Pell City neighbors were uneasy and quite concerned, calling the situation "upsetting, difficult to accept, and just plain weird."

Early Monday morning, the phone rang in the police department of the nearby town of Childersburg. A local druggist had seen some of the publicity regarding the missing Pell City family and their car. A red Corvette, wasn't it? Well, here in his parking lot was a sometimes customer of his, a guy who every once in a while brought by a used car for him to look at. Today he was driving a bright red 'Vette. The customer said he had traded someone for the car, but something didn't feel quite right. The druggist was concerned. Childersburg police fed the car's description and tag number into the NCIC. The druggist's suspicions were justified. It was the Franklins' missing car.

Driving the candy-apple red Corvette was 26-year-old John Peoples. A native of nearby Talladega, Peoples made a living "trading cars," according to Chief Deputy Newman. He had a bill of sale for this one "a very suspicious bill of sale, scrawled on notebook paper," Newman recalled. The bill of sale gave Peoples the car, valued at about $9,000 in return for half interest in a supper club located in a small town near Childersburg.

A quick phone call to the club's owners revealed that Peoples owned no part of the club, although he did have operating rights during some of the summer months. He had done some car trading with the club's co-owner. The trade had involved a 1977 Lincoln Continental. The man had no paperwork on the deal, but he emphatically denied ever selling or trading Peoples any ownership rights in the club.

Peoples was taken in for questioning.

"Investigators questioned him from about 3:00 p.m. until about 1:30 a.m. when he was finally charged with the theft of the vehicle," Newman said. "But as far as finding the family goes, we're no closer." Peoples was characterized by Newman as "not helpful," and Newman said there was "no useful evidence" in the car.

Speaking to the press, Newman announced, "We don't have any evidence that it's foul play or that it's not. We don't know how to treat it."

On Tuesday, July 12, 1983, John Peoples was

formally charged with theft by deception in Talladega Circuit Court. Bond was set at $25,000. Peoples remained in custody at the St. Clair County Jail. There was still no sign of the missing Franklin family.

The flamboyant young man with the red Corvette was a well known figure locally. Mustachioed, six-foot six inch, 275-pound John Peoples was active in the Childersburg P.T.A. The father of two small children, he "almost single-handedly" built a much needed playground for the elementary school. John was currently self-employed, running a small landscape business. He had worked several years for a Pell City construction firm and made a brief foray into grocery store ownership. The grocery store, according to Talladega County Sheriff Jerry Studdard, had been the beginning of financial troubles for John Peoples. He "started with bad checks and could never gather back the money he made." But Peoples had no criminal record. Said Sheriff Studdard, "Most people, you write them a bad check, all they want is their money. John always made good."

Paul Franklin Sr. was part of the reason Peoples could always make good. The two had met when Peoples' landscape company did some work for Franklin at his home, and on some property owned by Franklin in Talladega County. According to Sheriff Studdard, "He and John got to be real good friends."

"I knew Franklin helped Mr. Peoples on different occasions . . . in one way or another," said Peoples' former boss at the construction company.

"He (Franklin) was good to John," Studdard recalled. "He (Peoples) tried to be a big wheel. Always wore a big hat, western boots, had a Lincoln Continental . . ."

As for the red Corvette, Peoples continued to assert that he had traded for it, fair and square. He had remarried recently, and had promised his new bride an antique Corvette for her birthday, knowing that his friend Paul Franklin had one, and hoping that Franklin might be willing to trade for it. And Franklin *had* been willing to trade for half interest in the supper club, claimed Peoples. He had a bill of sale to prove it, didn't he?

Peoples said he had picked up the car on Thursday morning. The battery was dead — he'd had to push the car out of the garage and jump start it, then nurse it along . . . No, he said, he hadn't seen Franklin that day . . .

That bill of sale was fast becoming more of a liability than an asset. It had been established that Peoples did not own half interest in the club he claimed to have traded for the car. Now, a Pell City District Attorney who had done legal work for the Franklins looked at the bill of sale and recognized the writing. It was *Judy* Franklin's. Sheriff Studdard recalled, "He recognized her writing and said, 'Something's not right here . . . Paul never let his wife sign anything. He always signed for himself.' "

On Wednesday, July 13th, Peoples changed his statement. He told investigators, including A.B.I.'s Ed Traylor and Sheriff Studdard, that he had indeed gone to the Franklin house on Wednesday, July 6th, intending to trade for the Corvette. When he arrived, he said a "Mafia connection" was already there, hustling the Franklins out of their house and into a big black limousine driven by another Mafioso.

Concerned for his friend's safety, Peoples said he set out to follow the big black car, driving Paul's restored Corvette. The car gave him trouble, Peoples claimed, "stalling and choking out," making it difficult to follow the fleeing black limo.

Peoples persisted, nursing the sputtering sportscar east along Interstate 20 toward the nearby town of Lincoln. Suddenly, peoples explained, the big black car left the Interstate and proceeded at high speed down a series of side roads off Highway 77. The Corvette continued to give trouble, said Peoples, but he somehow managed to keep the limo's taillights in sight.

Peoples said he had become confused, and was now following the kidnappers down roads he did not recognize. Suddenly, Studdard recalled Peoples as saying, the Mafia car stopped, and he heard the familiar voice of Paul Franklin Sr. calling "John . . . John . . ." Then Peoples said, according to Studdard, "I knew I didn't need to be there." Shaken and fearful, he drove away in the red Corvette. "I didn't call the law because the Mafia was involved," Peoples said, adding, "They'll kill ya."

According to Sheriff Studdard, who had known Peoples a long time, one thing bothered him about that statement. Studdard remarked to Traylor, "He says he 'don't know' where this road is. That's got to be a story. He's been all up and down these roads."

Investigators from several law enforcement agencies questioned John Peoples more closely about the stopping place of the black limousine, and he finally told them that it might have been somewhere along County Road 377 South, coming back from Talladega. Area lawmen, guided by Peoples, began searching the heavily wooded areas off the two-lane blacktop.

At 6:30 p.m. on Wednesday, July 13, 1983, in a pine thicket just a few feet from the road, investigators found the fully clothed bodies of Paul Franklin Sr., Judy Franklin, and Paul Franklin Jr. No apparent effort had been made to conceal the bodies, except for placing them a few feet off the road. It was hot summer, and the bodies were already beginning to decompose badly, but it looked as if they had been killed by blows to the head.

All three bodies were taken to Cooper Green Hospital in the nearby city of Birmingham, where authorities hoped an autopsy would help determine the cause of death. Talladega County Coroner Clarence Haynes placed the time of death at about midnight on Wednesday, July 6, 1983. Besides having been struck on the head with a blunt instrument, Mrs. Franklin appeared to have been shot once in the arm. That wound did not look fatal.

A shocked Pell City mourned its loss. Neighbors were saddened, outraged, frightened and perplexed by turns. What could possess someone to abduct an entire family from its home and brutally murder all the members? "A multiple murder is something that doesn't seem like it would happen around here," one neighbor said.

Another neighbor remarked, "This is the kind of thing you hear about someplace else, not the kind of thing you would expect here in Pell City, right at your back door. It's frightening to think about what has happened."

On Saturday, July 16, 1983, Paul Sr., Judy and Paul Franklin Jr. were buried in Birmingham.

Even a complete autopsy had been inconclusive in determining the cause of Paul Franklin Sr.'s death. His wife and son had died from "blunt force trauma," according to Coroner Haynes. Robbery appeared to have been the motive for the multiple slayings, said Talladega County District Attorney Robert Rumsey. Franklin "reportedly kept large sums of money in his home," he said. He declined to say if any money was missing from the Franklin home.

As to the location of the triple homicide, Talladega County Sheriff Jerry Studdard felt strongly that the killing had occurred in Talladega County. "I think the evidence is going to show it happened there, on County Road 377," said the granite-jawed veteran lawman.

On Thursday, July 14, 1983, another suspect in the Franklin murder case entered the picture. It was learned that this suspect, along with Peoples, had allegedly stolen a dump truck belonging to a relative. The man's name was Timothy Millard Gooden, and he was a third cousin of Peoples. When police questioned Gooden about the stolen dump truck, he casually volunteered the information that he had dropped Peoples off at the Franklin house on the night of July 6th, the date of their disappearance.

Law enforcement officials involved in the Franklin case asked Peoples if he would be willing to be polygraphed. Peoples agreed. Sheriff Studdard was in the car with Peoples on the ride to Gadsden, some hour and a half drive from the St. Clair County Jail where Peoples was being held. Peoples seemed calm and unafraid, chatting casually with the officers about his various brushes with the law and his friendship with the Franklin family. "You ought to have heard what all he told us," recalled Studdard, "I mean, it was . . . wild!"

For the polygraph operator in Gadsden, it was even wilder. Peoples began dictating the exact form questions should take. According to Studdard, Peoples said, "You ask me did I kill all three of them at one time. You ask me that." Informed that the person administering the polygraph would decide on both the form and the content of the questions, Peoples declared, "I'm not gonna take the polygraph."

The ride back to St. Clair County was considerably more subdued than the ride to Gadsden had been. Peoples was quiet and deep in thought. Studdard recalled saying to him, "John, if you've got anything you need to talk to me about, you let me know." Peoples made no response.

Upon his return to the St. Clair County Jail, Peoples began telling other inmates that he had powerful friends who were going to help him. Sheriff Studdard said, "He said he had some people were gonna come break him out." Concerned, St. Clair County lawmen transferred Peoples to Ashville, north of Pell City but still in St. Clair County. Once there, Peoples sent a note to the jailer requesting to speak with Studdard.

The burly lawman drove to Ashville, where Peoples told him, "I want to tell you what I really know . . . I can remember where they left Judy and them by the side of the road. I remember seeing some quilts and things that came from the Franklin house."

Investigators were dispatched to the area Peoples described. They found what appeared to be a twisted piece of a .22 caliber rifle.

A few days later, acting on a "tip," officers found the rest of the rifle in the woods near an abandoned foundry, not far from where the Franklin family's bodies had been found. A Pell City gun dealer identified the Winchester .22 caliber rifle as one Paul Franklin Sr. had purchased to deter pests, specifically free roaming dogs.

On July 19, 1983, John Peoples again requested to talk with Sheriff Studdard. Studdard and St. Clair County Sheriff Lewis Brown made the trip to Ashville. Studdard confronted Peoples, saying "John, we've checked all this out. There's no Mafia involved in this. There's just you and Timmy (Gooden)." Peoples looked thoughtful. Then, according to Studdard, he said, "I'll tell you about it if you promise you won't write anything down."

While Brown and Studdard listened, Peoples made the following statement: Paul Franklin Sr. had invested $45,000 in Mexican gold pieces. Early in the summer, he had called John Peoples to drive him to Birmingham with the gold, which he intended to sell. Peoples and Franklin sold the gold to a rare coin dealer in Birmingham for $50,000 making a profit of $5,000 on the deal. Peoples said he and Franklin were partners on the deal, all $50,000 of it. Franklin, as was his habit, received the money in cash, taking it back to Pell City in two bank bags. While Peoples watched, Franklin pried the grille off an air duct and threw the bags inside. Then he called a relative, who had loaned him the money to invest in the coins, informing that relative of the sale and offering immediate repayment of the loan. Peoples said that he listened very carefully because "Paul promised him some of the money." The relative came and collected the $45,000 loan, leaving Franklin and Peoples with $5,000 profit, which, according to Sheriff Studdard, Peoples felt was half his. During the next week to ten days, Franklin spent about $2,000. Peoples became nervous about his cut, and on the night of July 6, 1983, went to the Franklin home with the "cousin" Timothy Gooden, to collect his share of the money.

When Franklin insisted the money was gone, Peoples began arguing with Franklin and forced him down the basement stairs. He pushed Franklin into the red Corvette, shouting to Timothy Gooden to follow in the truck with the woman and the boy. They drove to the woods near Talladega. At this point Sheriff Studdard recalled, Peoples found himself unable to continue. "He never would say . . . he would always break down and cry when he got down to the point of hitting the woman and hitting the little boy."

Studdard said to Peoples: "John, you need to write a statement. He said 'You write this out: I am guilty of the charge ya'll are investigating.' "

In August of 1983, a grand jury handed down indictments: John Peoples was charged with five counts of capital murder. He was also charged with robbery and kidnapping. His third cousin, Timothy Millard Gooden, was charged with kidnapping and robbery. Gooden and Peoples were to be tried separately on all counts, with Gooden slated to testify for the prosecution in Peoples' murder trial. Both men pleaded innocent to all charges.

Defense Attorney Pete Short filed several motions, one for a change of venue, and several contending that the prosecution evidence was inadmissible due to the fact that it was obtained while his client was being illegally held on a misdated warrant.

On Monday, November 28, 1983, a jury of ten women and four men (12 jurors, two alternates) was impaneled. Talladega County Circuit Judge Jerry Fielding had ruled not to dismiss the indictments or to move the trial to another location. He ruled favorably on a motion allowing Peoples to serve as co-counsel in his own defense, a position which would allow him to address the jury.

In opening arguments Wednesday morning, November 30th, Talladega County District Attorney Robert Rumsey told the jury they would learn that Peoples had forced Mrs. Franklin to sign a bill of sale for the car, and that he beat her and her son when his rifle failed to fire. Probably her last movement," Rumsey told the packed courtroom, "was to grab the leg of the little boy."

In testimony given the same day, a former neighbor of John Peoples testified that she had seen Peoples driving a red Corvette at about 1:30 a.m. on July 7, 1983. "He got out of the car and said, 'How do you like my wife's early birthday present?' " the neighbor testified.

Then Ellen Johnson came to the stand. Sometimes in June, she told the jury, Peoples had come to the Franklin home asking for money. "John came in and spoke: 'Paul, I need some money.' Mr. Franklin said, 'You owe me $1,500. I can't let you have anymore.' " Peoples then said, "I got to have some money somehow."

The most damning testimony against Peoples came from Timothy Gooden. Prosecutor Rumsey explained that Gooden had agreed to be a witness in return for a recommended life sentence instead of facing the electric chair.

In three hours on the stand, the 24-year-old Gooden gave the following testimony: On July 6th, Peoples took Gooden to the Franklin home. He told Gooden to wait in the truck, explaining "They've got a bad dog." Fifteen or twenty minutes later, Gooden testified, Peoples motioned him to come in. Paul Franklin Sr. and his wife were sitting at a table with "a bunch of papers" and a telephone "thrown down on a couch." According to Gooden, Peoples asked Franklin several times to sell him the red Corvette. Each time, Franklin refused, saying the car was for his son when he grew up. "John wanted the car bad," Gooden recalled. Peoples left the room in a moment, returning with a gun. He gagged and blindfolded the woman and the boy, then took Paul Franklin Sr. downstairs.

"I heard some commotion from the basement," Gooden said. Meanwhile, Gooden testified, he permitted Judy Franklin to use the bathroom, then took her and Paul Jr. downstairs. Franklin was lying on the floor. "I couldn't say if he was dead or alive."

Gooden said Peoples put Franklin in the Corvette, covering him with a blanket. Gooden put the woman and the boy in the truck and followed Peoples to a wooded area near Talladega County road 377. Gooden watched while Peoples dragged Franklin into the woods. Then Peoples returned to the truck. "She (Mrs. Franklin) asked him what is he going to do. He said it didn't matter," Gooden said. Then, "He led the woman and the boy into the woods . . . The woman was asking, 'Please don't.' I heard a gunshot and a woman screaming."

Gooden did not claim to have been an eyewitness to the actual act of killing. After that, said Gooden, he drove the truck home. Peoples came by at about 2:00 a.m. and picked up the truck. He told Gooden, " 'I will fix you up later (with money).' I didn't see him no more," Gooden concluded.

In an attempt to discredit Gooden's testimony, Defense Attorney Pete Short revealed that the witness had stated something completely different during an earlier interview with police, that he dropped Peoples off at the Franklin residence and then went home to bed. Gooden, however, stuck to his present statement. "What I have said today is the truth," Gooden revealed.

On Wednesday, December 7, 1983, exactly five months to the day after the Franklin family had been reported missing, the jury declared that John Peoples had murdered them, recommending 11 to 1 in favor of the death penalty.

At the sentencing hearing on Friday, January 27, 1984, Defense Attorney Short argued that John Peoples should be sentenced proportionately with Timothy Gooden, who had admittedly assisted in the Franklins' abduction. "What kind of justice is it when one person walks down the aisle grinning?" Short asked.

Prosecutor Rumsey contended that Peoples "destined his life" when he "brutally murdered" the Franklins. "People like John Peoples lost their right to live," declared the D.A.

Judge Fielding sentenced Peoples to death in the

electric chair, setting the execution date for April 13th. Peoples' face was expressionless.

Alabama state law mandates an automatic appeal.

Asked how he felt about the sentence, Short replied, "I don't have any particular reaction to the sentence. I never criticize judges."

Late in September of 1984, Timothy Millard Gooden pleaded guilty to robbery charges in the Franklin case. He was sentenced by Judge Fielding to life in prison.

EDITOR'S NOTE:

Ellen Johnson is not the real name of the person so named in the foregoing story. A fictitious name has been used because there is no reason for public interest in the identity of this person.

"SEX-HUNGRY FIEND 'HAD A STOMACH' FOR SLAUGHTER!"

by Robert Carlsen

It was a real puzzle for homicide detectives in the city of Bloomington, Illinois. Why would anybody want to slaughter a mother and her three children in the normally tranquil community?

Murders were nothing new to the Bloomington Police Department, but they had never seen anything quite on a scale like the slaughter of the Bible-reading family. It brought back memories of other hideous murders of a similar nature. But those always had occurred elsewhere.

It was the evening of Tuesday, November 8, 1983 when relatives started to worry about Susan Hendricks and her three children. They were supposed to come to dinner but never made an appearance. The relatives knew that if Susan had planned to miss the engagement, she would have telephoned. It was not like the young woman to snug her relations. She and the children were looking forward to the dinner, and the relatives knew something was wrong. She would have called if it was at all possible. Perhaps she'd gotten in an automobile wreck on the way over, they speculated.

And while they were fretting, Susan's husband

had been telephoning his home from Wausau, Wisconsin. He couldn't get hold of anybody, so he telephoned a neighbor twice to ask if she knew where Susan and the children were.

When he contacted relatives and learned that they hadn't been able to locate Susan, all involved decided it was time to get in touch with the police.

The police dispatcher quickly ascertained that the young woman and her children had not been involved in a auto wreck, and then he dispatched a patrol unit to the Hendricks home.

The fashionable, two-story home was located on Carl Drive in a new, upper-middle-class subdivision. When patrol officers arrived, they noticed that the house was dark and appeared to be secure. The officers checked the front, sides and back of the house.

There were no windows busted, and the doors weren't kicked in, although the rear sliding glass door was unlocked and open a little. There was no sign of forced entry.

Susan Hendricks' 1972 Cadillac was in the garage. The policemen received permission from headquarters to enter the house, as relatives were greatly concerned about the family.

Their concern was justified, but came far too late to do the Hendricks family any good. The 30-year-old woman and her three children were found dead 'in their respective bedrooms upstairs. They had been brutally chopped with an ax and sliced with a butcher knife. Both weapons were found on a bed.

Officer Michael Hibbens checked the other room in the house to make sure the killer still wasn't there while his partner radioed the information to headquarters. Homicide detectives and crime scene technicians were soon on their way to the death house.

Bloomington is a city of 40,000 persons and is located about 129 miles southwest of Chicago. It is almost in the center of the state. It is a city where some folks still feel it's safe to leave their doors unlocked at night. Apparently Susan Hendricks made that mistake and paid a heavy price.

Mrs. Hendricks was found in the master bedroom. The three children were in another bedroom. The two younger children were dead in one bed, the older child dead in another. All the victims were in their pajamas and had suffered severe head and/or neck wounds, crime scene technicians could see from the outset. Whoever killed them entered the house quietly and crept from room to room to commit the atrocious murders.

"All the victims apparently were hacked and stabbed to death," the coroner told detectives. For an exact cause of death in each case, the detectives would have to wait until the autopsies were completed and the results revealed.

Detective Sergeant Gene Irvin was assigned to spearhead the task force which eventually would increase to twelve and involve lawmen from the Bloomington Police Department, the nearby Normal Police Department, the McClean County Sheriff's Department, the coroner's office, the Illinois Division of Criminal Investigation, and the Department of Law Enforcement.

Although it appeared on the surface that the Hendricks family may have been slaughtered during the course of a burglary, Sergeant Irvin and other detectives weren't convinced of that.

Drawers in the downstairs portion of the home were open and contents strewn about. But in other drawers, the contents appeared intact. Also, if there was a burglar, he overlooked many valuables, including a microwave oven and other electrical appliances, an expensive 35 millimeter camera, a television and other items.

And that was just half the story. Tommy Martin, the crime scene supervisor, told Detective Irvin that the drawers in the children's bedroom were pulled out. There was blood on the outside of the drawers, but not on the contents inside, Martin told Irvin.

"In my opinion, a burglary was staged to throw us off the track," Martin told the sergeant. "The burglars apparently didn't even look behind the china cabinet," Martin said.

It is not unusual for persons to hide wall safes behind cabinets, mirrors or pictures. But the burglar or burglars apparently weren't even interested in checking on that.

"Who would want to murder them and then stage a burglary?" Sergeant Irvin asked his men.

Was it possible that Susan had let the killer into her house? That seemed like a possibility, since there was no sign of forced entry. But if she let her killer in, that meant only one thing—she knew the person who slaughtered the family.

Chief Deputy Coroner Dan Brady supervised the bagging of the victims' hands and removal of the bodies.

"No defensive wounds," Brady told Detective Irvin.

"It just doesn't make any sense," Sergeant Irvin

told his men. "There's just no apparent motive here. All we know is that whoever did it felt it necessary to stage a burglary."

"Maybe somebody had it in for the family, or perhaps the husband," one of the detectives speculated. "Maybe he was the target and the killer missed. It's been known to happen."

But if that was the case, why wasn't there some evidence of a struggle? Why wasn't there evidence of forced entry? Detectives were hoping those questions would be at least partially answered when they found David Hendricks, the husband and father of the family.

Crime scene technicians went through the house with a fine-tooth comb. They even went through sewers in a two-block radius. There was no evidence that the killer or killers washed up in the bathroom after the murders.

There wasn't so much as a soiled towel in the upstairs hamper. The only speck of blood that technicians found was on a vanity, and that speck was too old to even be able to type it or tell when it got there.

As the house was carefully searched and the bodies methodically removed, news hounds gathered at the scene and were hungry for a morsel or two of information. Police Chief Lewis DeVault arrived and asked detectives for the names and ages of the victims.

"Susan Hendricks is 30. She's the mother," Sergeant Irvin told the chief. "The other three found in the house were her children; Rebekah, nine, Grace, seven, and Benjamin, five."

Sergeant Irvin told the chief about the apparently staged burglary. They decided the best course of action was not to reveal everything they knew. That, of course, is standard procedure in any department. Certain details of the crime are kept out of the press because only the killer would know exactly what the interior of the house was like when he left.

Chief DeVault would not say whether there was any sign of robbery or burglary or whether the police knew of any motive for the killings. At that point in time, they actually didn't have a motive, but the chief wasn't about to reveal that. The less the killer knew about progress of the police investigation, the happier the detectives would be. Chief DeVault told reporters the condition in which the patrol officers had found the exterior of the house, and he revealed that some type of weapon had been found in one of the back bedrooms, but he declined to go into detail on that matter.

As close as detectives could figure, the killings probably took place late Monday night or early Tuesday morning. They drew that conclusion because all the victims were in their bedclothes.

They also believed that information the husband could supply concerning the time of his departure from the home would be of vital importance in helping them crack the case, if it was to be solved at all.

But until the husband returned home from his business trip, detectives questioned relatives and neighbors.

The subdivision in which the Hendrickses lived was one of the newer developments on Bloomington's far east side, and consequently it wasn't as thickly populated as some other portions of the city. There were homes under construction and vacant lots in the surrounding area. But there was still enough persons in the area to make it worthwhile for detectives to fan out and start asking questions.

Although the hour was late, the doorbells started to chime and several tired residents were startled to see uniformed policemen and detectives standing at their doors wanting to ask a bunch of questions about the Hendricks clan.

Some of the neighbors knew little or nothing about the family and couldn't be of any help to the sleuths. But others were more helpful.

"My five-year-old son played with the Hendricks children Monday night," a woman told detectives when they asked if she'd seen them at all. She said the children were playing in front of the two-story home until Mrs. Hendricks called her own children in for dinner. That was important information. Now the detectives knew that the victims were alive around dinnertime Monday.

Another neighbor recalled that on Tuesday morning she noticed the Hendricks children were not with the group of kids waiting for the school bus. Every morning the Hendricks children and others would wait at the corner for the bus, which would take them to Adlai Stevenson School. Detectives made a note of that. They would contact the school the next day to confirm the information.

That wasn't the only odd thing the neighbor noticed on Tuesday. "I noticed that the shades were drawn, and thought the children might be sick," the neighbor told police. "My son went over there about eleven o'clock and knocked at the door, but there was no answer."

That information seemed to confirm the detec-

364

tives' original theory that the four were murdered sometime Monday night or early Tuesday morning.

Relatives also were questioned and their answers seemed to fit in well with the scenario that was taking shape. One relative said that on Monday evening, Susan Hendricks attended a baby shower while her husband stayed with the Hendricks children until she came back. Apparently he went on his business trip after that. She knew this because she had talked to him by telephone on Tuesday, and when nobody could get a hold of Susan, he had asked her to contact the police. David Hendricks had gone to Wisconsin on business, but the last thing the relative knew, he was coming back home because he was worried about his family.

David Hendricks was true to his word. As the investigation was still being conducted at the murder scene, he drove into the neighborhood and stopped his car. He was too late to help his family. The worst had happened and there was nothing he could do about it.

Upon emerging from his car, Hendricks said, "There's something wrong. What's wrong?"

He was told by a detective that his family was dead. Chief Deputy Coroner Dan Brady came up to Hendricks and introduced himself. He extended his hand, but Hendricks said he was shaking too badly to shake anybody's hand.

"Can I go inside the house?" Hendricks asked detectives. They told him he couldn't. Then he turned to Brady.

"Is everybody dead?"

"Yes," Brady responded.

"Oh my God," the father said. Again he asked, "Even Benjy?"

Brady nodded.

"They're with God, now," said Hendricks, a devoutly religious man.

Sergeant Irvin told one of his detectives to get in contact with a church elder who could comfort Hendricks. Det. Charles Crowe took Hendricks to a neighbor's house and talked with the man for nearly an hour.

Crowe, with 17 years of experience as a detective, was considered to be somewhat of an expert at interrogation. Although Hendricks was not considered a suspect at that point in time, neither could he be eliminated. Detective Crowe watched Hendricks closely as they talked. He watched for certain reactions to specific questions.

Although Crowe couldn't pinpoint why he felt as he did, he believed Hendricks could be involved in the grisly murders, and he expressed that to another detective after he was done with the conversation.

On the morning of November 9th, Detective Crowe asked Hendricks to come to the police station to answer more questions. As he had done the night before, Detective Crowe made sure Hendricks understood his rights before questioning began.

"I left Monday night for a sales trip to Wisconsin," Hendricks, who sold a back brace which he'd patented, told Detective Crowe. "On Tuesday, I made several phone calls to home, none of which were answered, which began to bother me," he told the detectives.

His wife was supposed to have eaten dinner at a relative's home on Tuesday night. David Hendricks told detectives he learned by telephone that she didn't keep the appointment, and he began to get very concerned.

Hendricks said that when he left his home at midnight, he kissed his wife and children goodbye. Earlier in the evening he'd taken his children out for pizza.

Hendricks related the same story which he had told Detective Crowe the night earlier. Still, Crowe believed that the evidence pointed to Hendricks. If Hendricks had wanted to murder his family, he would have wanted it to look like somebody else did it, hence, the staged burglary, Crowe speculated.

At the conclusion of the Tuesday morning conversation, Detective Crowe looked at Hendricks and said, "We'll get you sooner or later."

Up to that point in the case it was just a gut feeling on Detective Crowe's part. He couldn't prove Hendricks had killed his family. But then David Hendricks made his first crucial error in the case. He held a press conference and revealed information which the detectives believed only they and the killer could have known about.

His eyes were red and puffy from weeping. He spoke softly as he answered reporters' questions. He told the press the same story he'd given to the police. But he also revealed that some things in the house appeared to have been stolen. How could he have known that? He hadn't been allowed in the house the previous evening.

"I just want to let everybody know that I think the people who are gone now, the four that I loved so much, are the greatest people that ever lived on this earth. Susie was a truly beautiful person, beautiful much more than skin-deep beauty.

"I'm very religious. I believe the Bible to be God's word. We read the Bible every day together."

To the television cameras, he said, "I know Susie and my three children are much better off and I'd wish them back for me as a selfish thing, but I know that they're with the Lord Jesus in heaven and I'm satisfied knowing that."

Hendricks was asked by a reporter what should become of the person responsible for the killings, if he should receive the death penalty.

"I'd like to see him get saved. It would be worth it if one person made it to heaven — don't you think so?"

It was a touching statement that moved many to tears. But Detective Crowe was not so moved by it. His sympathies were with the victims. He had his doubts about the husband, especially when Hendricks mentioned the possible burglary.

Detectives wore out shoe leather that day in their effort to find some tangible clue they could sink their teeth into. While they were doing that, pathologist Dr. Antonie Romyn was busy conducting the autopsies.

Mrs. Hendricks, 30, sustained a gaping cut on the left side of her head. Rebekah, 9, suffered a fractured skull below her left temple. Mrs. Hendricks and Rebekah had been found sleeping alone. The two younger children, who had been sleeping in one bed, also suffered severe wounds.

Grace, 7, had a deep, gaping cut along the neck. It severed her windpipe. The cut could have been caused by a knife.

Benjamin, 5, had a fractured skull and his windpipe was slashed. All the wounds were consistent with ax or knife wounds, Dr. Romyn said.

Detectives believed the children might have been murdered before the mother. A knife hole in a blanket indicated that Mrs. Hendricks' head had been covered when she was murdered.

The contents of the children's stomachs were sent to Dr. John Dwyer, a forensic botanist of St. Louis University.

Dr. Dwyer could peel layers off the onions from the vegetarian pizza found in the stomachs. It was his opinion that only about two hours of digestion had occurred before the children were murdered. The contents of the mother's stomach indicated that she hadn't eaten very much the evening she was murdered, and tests on her were inconclusive.

But when detectives got the report, they knew their case hinged on the digestion. In two interviews, Hendricks had told police he left home around midnight. In his interview to the press he'd said 11:00 p.m.

He'd told detectives he took the kids to dinner around 7:00 p.m. The children were murdered within two hours of eating, according to digestion analysis. That meant David Hendricks had been home when his family was slaughtered.

But the detective work was far from over. Detectives still had no motive. Why did David Hendricks, a pillar of his community and member of a conservative church, murder his family?

Detectives went to the pizza restaurant in the nearby community of Normal where Hendricks had taken his children on the night of the murder. A check of the cash register records revealed the only one vegetarian pizza had been ordered that evening around 6:30 p.m. It took about 20 minutes to prepare the pizza. Detectives could prove that the children consumed the pizza around 7:00 p.m.

Their investigation also revealed that the businessmen called upon by David Hendricks on November 8th were not expecting any visits. Although the businessmen were used to salesmen dropping in unexpectedly, Hendricks hadn't made any appointments that day and, during his visits, he appeared to be in a hurry.

While that was going on, other detectives questioned the school bus driver to learn if he had noticed anything unusual or suspicious on Tuesday morning. Although they felt David Hendricks was their best suspect, they couldn't ignore other possibilities. Perhaps the bus driver had seen a suspicious car parked in the Hendricks driveway or prowling about the neighborhood. Anything at all was possible investigators knew.

But the school bus driver couldn't tell detectives anything that they didn't already know. The Hendricks kids simply didn't get on the bus that morning.

The principal at the school said he was not alarmed by their absence on Tuesday. "I'd assumed they'd taken the day to travel or something," the principal said.

Also, what puzzled detectives was the fact that the Hendricks home and the suspect's car were free of any traces of bloody clothing. And the only blood of significance was found in the rooms where the victims had been murdered.

Detectives checked with the sanitation department and learned that on Tuesday morning the garbage along the subdivision's route had been picked up. A team of sleuths and sanitation workers went to the local dump to begin the arduous task of looking for clothing among the tons of garbage. Their efforts would prove fruitless, however.

Another policeman checked at David Hendricks' airplane hangar, but also came up with nothing. If Hendricks had killed his family, as police believed, he did a meticulous job of eliminating any clues which might connect him to the slaying scene.

The days turned into weeks, and detectives kept at their task. Finally, they turned up what they believe could have been a motive for the murders.

As a part of his business, Hendricks occasionally hired professional models to wear his back brace. But these models weren't hired to pose for pictures for brochures. Instead, they were hired for private sittings and Hendricks would ask them to disrobe.

When detectives learned of this, they did a complete background check on the suspect's professional dealings with models.

Detectives learned that Hendricks had contacts with ten models between 1980 and 1983. They ranged in age from 16 to 23.

The modeling was done at Hendricks' business, at his home, at the home of one model, and other locations.

Detectives learned that Hendricks' early contacts with models were of a professional nature, but that his later contacts with different models became blatantly sexual.

Detectives talked to one model who said she appeared for a 1981 session in leotards, but that Hendricks asked her to strip to her brassiere and underpants so he could get a closer fitting.

The detectives' search for models went beyond the town of Bloomington. They located a model in Phoenix, Arizona who said she'd modeled for Hendricks about two weeks prior to the murders.

She told detectives that Hendricks had said he was a doctor when he asked her to strip for a closer fitting for the back brace.

The model claimed Hendricks admitted he had doubts about his marriage, and then, after they spoke for awhile, he asked her to take him sightseeing.

When they got to an isolated spot, she claimed he tried to kiss her, but she shunned his advances.

She said Hendricks admitted having affairs. "He said, 'I've had several affairs, and I don't think anything is wrong with it,'" the model quoted Hendricks as saying. Hendricks later would deny the statement.

Detectives presented their findings to McLean County State's Attorney Ronald Dozier. It appeared to the lawmen that Hendricks' patented back brace had brought in an income which enabled the suspect to become more adventurous in his dealings with women. They believe his contacts with the various models indicated he desired more sexual experiences and that he was tiring of his wife.

Some of the models said Hendricks marked on their naked bodies with pens, felt their breasts, massaged them and complimented them on their bodies. All of these separate incidents by themselves might not have meant much, but considering Hendricks' fundamental church background, such behavior was frowned upon by church elders. Hendricks was ashamed of such behavior, the lawmen believed. He desired the models, but felt trapped in his marriage because of his church beliefs, lawmen believed. And therein lay the motive. Their theory would be put to the test in court.

On December 5, 1983, David Hendricks, 29, was arrested at his business office. Relatives and some friends were shocked.

The key to the entire case was the undigested food in the children's stomachs.

"It looks to have been well planned," Attorney Dozier said of the murder. Hendricks had not left a single incriminating clue. Although the murder weapons were found, there wasn't a print on them.

Coroner Anderson told reporters that the victims died of ". . . massive cerebral and various internal injuries."

But the significant clue, the coroner explained, was something the apparently level-headed killer overlooked. The food.

"The testing was a long, time-consuming and extremely difficult process," Coroner Anderson said. Anderson stressed that it wasn't just his opinion he was relying on. He had wisely consulted other experts on the matter as well. "The experts agree the deaths took place prior to the time Mr. David Hendricks said he left his house to make a business trip to Wisconsin," Coroner Anderson said.

"He was questioned initially," State's Attorney Dozier said of Hendricks. "Later he was interrogated a little more forcefully. Since that time he has refused to answer any more questions."

Dozier said that during the course of the investigation, there were other suspects, but police investigation gradually ruled them out. None of them looked as good as the spouse, and the food in the kids' stomachs was the clincher.

In October of 1984, Hendricks went to trial. There were 110 state's exhibits and 70 witnesses. As expected, the pivotal issue was the undigested food.

On Thursday, November 29th, a jury found David Hendricks guilty of murdering his family after deliberating for 6½ hours over a two-day period.

Hendricks, then 30, showed no emotion as Woodford County Circuit Judge Richard Baner read at 2:15 p.m. the guilty verdicts to a hushed and packed courtroom.

Only a little over a month later, on January 12, 1985, Judge Baner sentenced Hendricks to life in prison without the possibility of parole.

"BOMBS AND BULLETS BLEW AWAY FIVE!"

by Joseph Koenig

With his 85-year-old mother having problems with her heart, Robert W. Newsom, Jr., was dividing his time between his home in Greensboro and the brick house on Valley Road in Old Town, North Carolina, where Hattie Carter Newsom had lived for more than 40 years. Far from being a chore, the 60-mile round trip and protracted stays among the friends of a lifetime were the happiest part of his week.

"Bob, Sr., that's Hattie's husband, had passed on in 1980," a family friend would recall, "and Hattie'd been all alone ever since. At 85, that's hardly what you'd call fun and so she just lived for her boy's visits. And Bob and Flo, Flo's his wife, they liked Old Town so well they'd agreed to move into the main part of the house while Hattie moved to a white, wood frame apartment she was havin' built for herself in the rear."

In the third weekend of May, 1985, as they had so often during that warm, delicious spring Bob and Florence Sharp Newsom made the familiar drive to the brick house on the 3200 block of Valley Road in Old Town just outside the Winston-

Salem City limits. At the age of 65, Bob was a well-to-do consulting engineer who formerly had worked for the giant R.J. Reynolds Tobacco Company in Winston-Salem. His wife, one year older, had retired from teaching school less than six months earlier.

Around 10:30 on Sunday evening, May 19th, a friend of the Newsoms received a troubling call from a relative of Bob and Flo in Greensboro. The caller explained that he was worried because he was unable to reach anyone in the brick house on Valley Road. The family friend, who was also Hattie's doctor, said he'd run out right away and phone back as quickly as he could.

Along with his wife, the doctor raced out to Valley Road. Finding the big house strangely silent and uninviting, the couple went around back to investigate.

"Oh, what we saw," the doctor's wife would say later. "We went to the back window and we saw Mrs. Newsom on the couch and her daughter-in-law on the floor."

At first glance, the scene was a peaceful one. Hattie Carter Newsom lay covered with an afghan and the television set was on. But the blood which marred the alabaster whiteness of the elderly woman's throat was too obvious to be ignored and the couple quickly contacted the Winston-Salem police. Because the house was located just outside the city limits, Forsyth County Sheriff E. Preston Oldham's deputies were also summoned.

Inside the house, the lawmen quickly confirmed that the two women were dead, evidently the victims of shotgun blasts. In a narrow foyer just outside the living room was a third body, that of

65-year-old Robert W. Newsom, Jr.

"What it looks like to me, Mr. Newsom was slain first," one investigator said. "The killer cut him down in the hallway, maybe after he let him in, and then went into the living room where he shot the women. The older woman almost certainly was asleep when all this was happening."

"Any sign of forced entry?" another investigator asked.

"The rear storm door's been kicked out and there's glass all over the yard. Thing is, that's a sign of forced exit, not entry. It's still too soon to say the killer got inside."

Because the house appeared to have been ransacked, detectives ascribed the obvious motive of robbery. However, because they were uncertain as to what, if anything, was taken, they kept an open mind about the matter.

Sheriff Oldham, cornered by newsmen, said that he would not theorize as to the time the slayings took place, or the precise nature of the crime.

"I won't speculate," he said. "It has the makings of a very difficult case. The investigation is continuing and I am not going to say anything until we know for certain."

Oldham did say that he had asked for and received the help of the State Bureau of Investigation and District Attorney Donald K. Tisdale. No fewer than 14 investigators eventually would be assigned to the case on a full-time basis, visiting the crime scene over and over again as they awaited the results of autopsies on the three victims.

"None of the victims' personal items appear to have been taken," one investigator said. "We found their rings and wallets and purses, although they'd

377

been scattered all over the place. The other puzzling thing we found is that whoever killed them also seems to have attempted to build a fire near the bodies, probably to destroy evidence. There were a great number of items gathered into a circle between the living room and the foyer about three feet from where Mr. Newsom's body had been found. But there was no accelerant used."

The autopsies, which were completed later in the week, indicated that all three victims had been shot at least twice and Florence Sharp Newsom's throat had been sliced open. No weapon was found.

News of the gruesome slayings had a predictably dismaying effect on the tight-knit Old Town community.

"It's an absolute nightmare," said a close neighbor of Hattie Newsom. "Of all the places in the world, I would not expect something had to happen here. Hattie was such a sweet old lady. She was a member of the Bethabara Moravian Church since 1943 and about the hardest worker they had. Last year, when she retired from some of her church activities, the church held Hattie Newsom Day to honor her. But she never really did slow down. She still worked on the church committee and made her famous chicken pies and candles that the church sold to raise money."

"She was a tiny woman," another neighbor recalled, "maybe five-foot-two and old, but she didn't need much caring. I'd see her going around her yard with a wheelbarrow all the time and then she'd come by to give away some of her nice fresh vegetables, or maybe some of the ones she'd canned."

Of Robert W. Newsom, Jr., a former employee

would say, "He was a terribly nice man, the kind who wouldn't even have a gun in the house. In 1968, I think it was, he was elected president of the Twin City Kiwanis Club and he'd also been president of the Goodwill Rehabilitation Center."

"I couldn't say enough nice things about Florence and Bob," said a former principal of Old Town High School where Florence Newsom had begun teaching business in 1952.

A Reidsville native who had studied at the University of North Carolina at Greensboro when it was still a woman's college, she had retired from the Jefferson Academy in Greensboro in December, 1984.

On Tuesday, May 21st, as investigators were hunting for fresh leads in the baffling case, State Bureau of Investigation agents were contacted by an Albuquerque, New Mexico man, who had some information he thought they might be interested in. The caller, who identified himself as the former husband of Susan Lynch, the 39-year-old daughter of Robert and Florence Newsom, pointed out that less than a year earlier his mother and sister were slain in a manner remarkably similar to the bloodbath in Old Town.

It was July 24, 1984, when 68-year-old Delores Rodgers Lynch and her daughter, Dr. Jane Lynch, 39, were found shot to death at their home in Prospect, Kentucky, on the outskirts of Louisville. Each of the women had been shot twice and, as in the Old Town case, the crime scene—a large and secluded house—appeared to have been ransacked.

And, like the triple slaying in North Carolina, the Prospect double murder remained unsolved.

On Wednesday, May 22nd, Lieutenant Dan

Davidson of the Kentucky State Police told reporters that "We plan to send two officers to North Carolina next week to review the situation there with the officers there . . . We just want to make sure there is no connection. There is a lot of similarity there."

That same day, Sheriff Oldham told newsmen that a key had been found in the back door of the Newsom home, but "We have not determined yet if the attackers were let in or let themselves in."

Thursday, investigators revealed that they still had not determined whose key was found in the door or if, in fact, the killer had used it to gain entrance. That same day, all three Newsom victims were laid to rest in Forsyth Memorial Park some three miles from the scene of their deaths.

Five days later, on Tuesday, May 28th, the homicide probers finally satisfied themselves that the key had belonged to one of the victims. It had been found, said Sheriff's Captain Ron Barker, on a ring of keys which probably was the property of Robert W. Newsom, Jr.

"We don't think whoever did this had a key," Barker said. "At first it obviously looked that way, with the glass door broken and the key still in the knob."

Now it seemed more likely that Robert Newsom had left his keys in the door accidentally or was stopped by someone as he was entering the house.

"Those are about the only two (reasonable ideas)," Barker said. "All those possibilities cause different scenarios to be created in your mind and every scenario carries with it different suspects and leads."

Barker went on to say that the keys and everything else found at the scene had been processed for fingerprints by the State Bureau of Investigation Crime Lab and that the results of those tests were expected soon.

"We still think robbery may be a motive," another prober said. "We just learned that a cocktail ring belonging to Hattie Newsom and a necklace belonging to her daughter-in-law are missing."

That same day, Hattie Newsom's estate, placed at more than $900,000, was certified in the office of the clerk of the Forsyth County Superior Court.

On Friday, Captain Barker said that investigators believed the same weapon had been used on all three victims and that the angle of the deadly wounds indicated that it had been fired inside the living room.

"The deaths had to be almost simultaneous because of the way they were all found together," he said. "They weren't scattered all over the house like they had been running or anything."

Barker went on to say that along with other Forsyth County investigators he had been meeting with Kentucky State Police homicide probers who had come to exchange information about the Lynch case. The Kentuckians, Barker said, "are here looking more for help from us than we are from them. They have exhausted all their leads, so you can see then that members of the same family, even though the relation is just by marriage, is something that may be a new lead for them."

Barker revealed that police had spoken with witnesses who had been guests of the Newsoms on the night of the killings and who said that everything was all right inside the Valley Road home when they left around 9:30. Probers believed the victims were watching television when the killer entered the house.

"We're just about sure the shooting took place between 9:30 and midnight," one detective said, "because the victims were not wearing pajamas."

On Thursday, May 30th, Detective Lynn Nobles of the Oldham County, Kentucky Sheriff's Department, told newsmen that the weapons used to kill the Newsoms had not figured in the slayings of the Lynches.

"We were looking for leads that could help our case and unfortunately there is nothing that we can go back to Kentucky and work on immediately.

"You have some circumstances that are similar, but whether or not they are just a coincidence, or the same shooter, we are not at all certain."

"They had very little physical evidence we could compare," said Captain Barker. "And because they don't have any concrete leads or suspects, we are not helped that much. We can't establish any strong ties between the two cases other than the family connection."

What the Kentuckians were able to provide, however, were the facts of the deaths of Delores Rodgers Lynch and her daughter. It was about 8:00 on the steamy Sunday morning of July 22, 1984, as the 68-year-old woman was getting out of her car in the driveway of her home on the 1000 block of Covered Bridge Road that she was shot twice with a small-caliber firearm. Her daughter, Dr. Jane Lynch, a former teacher and speech pathologist and a recent dental school graduate, was shot twice inside the house near an upstairs bedroom. When the bodies were discovered two days later, the place appeared to have been ransacked although nothing was taken.

With no better lead to work with, investigators both in Kentucky and North Carolina turned their attention to the link between the cases—39-year-old Susie Sharp Lynch, whose former mother-in-law and sister-in-law had died in Prospect and whose parents and grandmother had been slain in Old Town. A handsome, dark-haired woman and the mother of two sons, ten-year-old John Wesley and Thomas Lynch, who was nine, Susie had gone back to live in North Carolina after her divorce. At the time her parents were slain she was making her home in Greensboro with the boys and with 32-year-old Frederick R. "Fritz" Klenner Jr., a first cousin.

Susie, the investigators learned, had been an exceptionally bright youngster and an honors graduate of North Carolina's Wake Forest University where she majored in history. Two years after her 1968 graduation, around the time her father was leaving his job as an industrial engineer with R.J. Reynolds Foods in Winston-Salem for a new position with the Lorillard Corporation in Greensboro, she married a young dental student with whom she subsequently moved to Lexington, Kentucky, and from there to Beaufort, South Carolina, and then Albuquerque, New Mexico.

Susie, family friends would remember, did not get along well with her mother-in-law. But there appeared to be few problems with her marriage prior to the move out west in July 1976. In New Mexico, apparently uncomfortable with the informal life style, she grew sullen and in 1979 the marriage broke up and she brought her infant boys back to North Carolina.

383

After a quick layover in the Tarheel state Susie and the boys moved again, this time to Taiwan. Prior to her departure, she retained an attorney to handle the details of her upcoming divorce. When she returned to North Carolina several months later, Susie had changed noticeably. She seemed fearful now, especially of somehow losing custody of the boys. With no place else to go, she moved back to her parents' place in Greensboro. It was around this time, acquaintances say, that she began growing attached to her cousin, Fritz Klenner, also a recent divorcé and a loner with few close friends.

In the early 1980s, Susie Lynch left Greensboro again to return to Wake Forest as an anthropology student. In 1982, she enrolled as a business student at the University of North Carolina at Greensboro.

"She seemed obsessed with the idea that her ex-husband was somehow going to take the boys away from her," a family friend remembers. "And she became moody and withdrawn and estranged from her parents. About the only person she could relate to was her cousin Fritz and it was about this time she moved in with him."

"We felt at that time she had a problem, yes," a relative would say later. "Specifically, that she was becoming isolated, uncommunicative and too protective of her children. And that process continued."

Susie's fears for the boys grew so pronounced that she began accompanying them to the bus stop when they left for school each morning. But the boys did not appear to be thriving under her over-protection. In Albuquerque, a relative of Susie's ex-husband remembers:

"John always just looked like he was emaciated. Their arms were black and blue from vitamin shots that Fritz was giving . . . and they were full of penicillin shots. They'd come out with sacks of vitamins, antihistamines, eardrops."

The boys, she went on, were reluctant to speak about their home lives, but eventually opened up enough to say that they often slept on the floor and frequently accompanied their "Uncle Fritz" to gun shows. When they spoke of such matters, "They would say, 'Mother is going to kill us.' . . . She was very strict with them. Oh, and their teeth, their teeth were terribly dirty."

Fritz Klenner, the homicide probers learned, was also an enigmatic figure, a personable, good-looking young man whose great obsession was the accumulation of as many handguns and high-powered firearms as he could afford to buy. From 1979 until the spring of 1985, he was issued more than 50 permits for pistols alone.

In November of 1984, a relative would recall, Susie Lynch paid a visit to him at his office. The woman was carrying a pistol which she claimed she needed for protection. Fritz Klenner, she went on to say, was spying on her husband, something he was well-trained to do because he worked for the CIA.

"I reached (Susie's) parents by telephone," her relative would recall, "and told them of the substance of my conversation, that I felt she was suffering from delusions and I thought they needed to know that . . . They were concerned, they were wondering if her stress and anxiety over the possibility of losing her children was really causing her to think or act irrationally."

On May 17, 1985, detectives learned, one day before his death, Robert W. Newsom, Jr., had phoned his daughter to say that he was going to testify in her former husband's behalf in a Rockingham County, North Carolina, court hearing concerning extended visitation rights for the boys.

On Thursday, May 30th and again on Friday, May 31st, the murder probers learned, Fritz Klenner had visited a number of friends in the Winston-Salem area to say that the police believed he was a suspect in the Old Town killings. What he did not know, however, was that Kentucky lawmen also wanted him for questioning about the murders of the Lynches a year before.

About 2:00 on the bright Monday afternoon of June 3rd, the homicide probers watched Fritz Klenner, Susie Lynch and the boys drive up to their apartment on Hunt Club Road near the Guilford College campus in Greensboro. Barely half an hour later, the foursome began loading Klenner's 1980 Chevrolet Blazer with a large quantity of weapons and camping equipment. Fearful that Klenner was preparing to flee the area, the officers sought—and received—permission to arrest him for the Newsom slayings even though no warrant had been drawn up.

Not long after, the lawmen curbed the Blazer at the intersection of Guilford College Road and Friendly Avenue. It was an ironic choice of locale. For as Greensboro police, Forsyth sheriff's deputies and SBI agents moved in on the four-wheel drive vehicle from the rear, Fritz Klenner leaned out the passenger's window with an automatic weapon and shot Greensboro Police Officer T. H. Dennis once in the shoulder and once in the abdomen. The officer, clad in a flak jacket, was only slightly injured.

"It sounded like a line of firecrackers," a witness would tell newsmen. "Whoever was shooting had to have two hands to hold it. It looked like a fire with silver sparks coming out of it."

As the lawmen scurried for cover, the driver of the yellow Blazer tore across the center line and headed the wrong way on Friendly to Guilford College Road, then turned north. With a long line of police cars in its wake, the vehicle headed along New Garden Road to US 220 into Summerfield, then turned right onto North Carolina Highway 150, stopping from time to time to allow Klenner to squeeze off some more shots at his pursuers.

A number of civilian cars were hit by gunfire and Kentucky State Police Detective Sherman Childers was hit by flying glass. Oldham County Detective Nobles suffered minor injuries when a bullet struck his revolver, spreading shrapnel from the weapon into his shoulder. The men followed Officer Dennis to Moses Cone Hospital in Greensboro, where all three were treated for their injuries and released.

Meanwhile, as the Blazer approached the intersection of NC 150 and Bronco Lane, about 15 miles from the start of the chase, a tremendous explosion tore it apart and all four occupants were killed. The police were stunned.

"Speculation is that they were trying to rig some explosive device when the vehicle blew up," Greensboro Police Spokesman Joanna Kilodin told the first newsmen to learn of the tragedy." It was just full of explosives."

Fearful that more explosive might remain in the

wreckage, Greensboro police set up a 100 square yard cordon around the Blazer, then moved in cautiously for a look. Ropes were used to lift the bodies of all four victims from the twisted metal.

Other investigators rushed to the apartment on Hunt Club Road where Fritz Klenner had lived with Susie Lynch and routed all the other occupants of the building outside on the chance that additional explosives might be stored there. At the same time, officers called for an explosives expert and the Greensboro Bomb Disposal truck. At 8:30 p.m., the Bomb Squad used its own explosives to blast open a second Blazer found outside the apartment. At 8:55, they blew open the front door of the Klenner unit.

"We thought the second Blazer and the apartment might be booby trapped," one lawman explained. "You can understand why we weren't taking any chances."

Outside the apartment house newsmen spoke with some of the neighbors, who were not allowed to return to their homes until 11:15 p.m.

"You'd never see Klenner when he wasn't wearing his camouflage fatigues and carrying some guns to his car," one said. "We always thought he was one of those survivalists. We thought he was maybe doing some of those war games.

"It all makes sense now. I saw him on a couple of occasions walking out of the apartment with a rifle in his hand and I thought it was an M-16."

"Yes," another neighbor agreed. "He was always wearing camouflage. And the kids were, too.

"The truck, he was always working on it at strange hours of the night. It's funny, because we were saying to ourselves all year that we were going to find out what he did with the truck."

At a Tuesday, June 4th press conference, Sheriff Oldham announced that investigators believed Fritz Klenner had hitched a ride with a friend from Greensboro to Old Town on the evening of May 18th, and, after Robert Newsom, Jr. let him inside the brick house, he shot his aunt, great aunt and uncle with a shotgun, ransacked the place to make it look like a robbery and then fled in Hattie Carter Newsom's gold Plymouth Volare. Not long after, because he was driving so slowly that he appeared to be having car trouble, he was stopped by a Winston-Salem police officer on University Parkway and then allowed to go on his way.

"An exact, hard-core motive will never be known," Oldham said. "It could have been revenge, it could have been greed, it could have been personal problems. It could have been child custody. It could have been anything. Now we'll never know."

"The case is closed. Based on our district attorney's opinion, the physical evidence and Klenner's own statements that link everything together . . . the Newsom case is resolved . . .

Out of all the deaths, the two most tragic are those two innocent kids who got caught up in it . . . "Whether the bomb was accidental, or intended, we'll never now."

In Kentucky, Sergeant Dennis Clark of the Oldham Sheriff's Department said the investigation into the Lynch murders was also closed.

"Our detectives have said that they were absolutely sure that he had committed the murders here."

In Greensboro, Police Captain C.F. Allen said that the damage to Susie Lynch's body indicated

389

that she was holding the bomb in her lap when it went off. Whether or not she intentionally detonated it, or it blew up accidentally as she was trying to throw it out the window, he said, was not known.

On Wednesday, a medical examiner reported that while Fritz Klenner and Susie Lynch had died in the explosion, ten-year-old John Lynch and his brother, James, 9, were shot in the head at close range moments before the bomb went off. Ed Hunt, a district supervisor for the State Bureau of Investigation, said autopsies indicated the presence of arsenic in the stomach of each boy.

Ballistics tests on the bullet found in John's head, Hunt pointed out, indicated it was fired from a pistol discovered near the wreckage of the Blazer.

"In our opinion," Hunt said, the gun "came from that vehicle. It was found cocked and loaded lying beside a telephone pole to the left of where the explosion took place."

The wound in James' head showed stippling around it, "which indicates that the child was shot at very close range."

Speaking with newsmen, District Attorney Tisdale said that an informant had told his investigators that Klenner might attempt suicide if authorities tried to arrest him.

"We had an insight into him, that he wouldn't be taken alive," Tisdale said. "They were trying to handle him with kid gloves, but this man couldn't be handled with kid gloves.

"To be quite honest with you, if they weren't going to have the children, nobody was.

"It was obviously family matters."

Other sources close to the probe revealed that authorities had found five pistols, two shotguns, an automatic rifle and a semi-automatic in the wreckage of the Blazer. Four more pistols, four semi-automatic rifles and two shotguns were found at the Hunt Club Road apartment, as was a large quantity of survivalist literature, loaded shoulder packs and tinned and packaged foods.

On Thursday, June 6th, Robert Pence of the FBI told newsmen that Fritz Klenner's apparent association with North Carolina right wing hate groups had aroused the Bureau's interest, but that no active investigation was underway.

A friend of Klenner said that although the dead man was "strongly anti-communist and very patriotic," he had not spoken of his membership in any right wing organizations. Klenner, he said, was interested in collecting guns, coins and stamps, anything, in fact, "that was collectible."

"He said he was a member of the Delta Group U.S. Special Forces Reserve. He knew about the mobilization of the reserves earlier this year. He also predicted the Russians' recent move on the Afghan front . . . His information seemed pretty good."

Fritz and Susie Lynch, he went on, were living together before he got to know them.

"He said that they lived together without . . . any intimate relationships. He said that they just shared an apartment and he had taken up with the kids."

From other sources came rumors that Fritz Klenner had bolted the bomb which killed him into his Chevy Blazer making it a permanent fixture of his rolling fortress.

An acquaintance told investigators that not only had Klenner convinced Susie Lynch that he was a CIA agent, but had her believing that she, too, worked for the spy organization. Susie reportedly told a family member that she carried a gun because she was with the CIA.

On Friday, June 21st, District Attorney Tisdale revealed that investigators had spoken with a friend of Fritz Klenner who was believed to have driven Klenner to Old Town on May 18th because he thought Klenner was a CIA agent on a mission to kill criminals involved in Latin American drug or arms traffic.

"It's hard to accept that somebody would buy that," Tisdale told reporters, "but I think that after hearing all of the evidence, you would be fully convinced."

In Kentucky, Lieutenant Davidson said that he intended to keep probing Fritz Klenner's possible involvement in the Lynch slayings.

"As far as me closing the file on this, it is going to be a long time coming. I want to make sure that there are no accomplices involved here, or anyone who aided."

"THE HUNTER'S QUARRY WAS A FAMILY OF FIVE!"

by Ed Barcelo

The death clock was set and running a countdown for slaughter.

The place? Not a likely setting for wholesale massacre, more of a place for hunting and trapping, an outdoorsman's paradise known as Brockway Township, Michigan, about 80 miles north of Detroit, and some 20 miles west of a point where Lake Huron flowed into the St. Clair River. Beautiful, rugged country, but the fierce winters were legendary and not for the faint-hearted. Remote country, too, for the nearest town of any size was a place called Yale, a two-mile rocky-road drive to the east.

At 4:00 a.m., April 7, 1982, a bathroom light went on in a brick one-story ranch home on Carson Road. The man-of-the-house was readying himself for another grueling 60-mile drive to work. And what a hell-raising ride it was going to be, the man might have thought. A freak, post-winter snowstorm was belting the countryside, and the weather bureau had issued a traveler's alert, a warning of hazardous driving conditions throughout the state. Serious enough to warrant area school closings.

But treacherous as the drive might be, some 30 minutes later the man backed his car out of the snow-covered driveway and headed for his job in Warren, Michigan. The time: 4:30 a.m.

Horror lay four hours away, shortly after daybreak.

But dawn crawled in. And a bleak morning it was in the Michigan outback, with night's darkness desperately hanging on, compromising, finally admitting a cold, grayish light to the east as bleak as death's pallor.

Approximate time: 6:00 a.m., and the man who had made the long drive to Warren, Michigan was now at work. In the man's home, 60 miles away, Mrs. Bette Giuliani and her four children, unaware that the schools were closed, squeezed out the last hour of sleep. Soon, they would stir. Soon, the mother would rise, robe herself and awaken the children.

But on this bleak, cold April morning, the out-of-bed-and-off-to-school routine was a preparation for death.

At 7:40 a.m., 100 minutes later, Ellie Burns, a Brockway Township housewife, phoned her neighbor, Bette Giuliani. The two women were members of a four-woman bowling team, and each Wednesday morning, after the children were off to school, the women made the several-mile drive to a Port Huron bowling alley. Following the league play, Ellie and Bette would coffee-klatch in a nearby restaurant. Today's routine would be no different, except for the closing of the schools.

As usual, Bette Giuliani was in good spirits, though neither of the two women thought favorably of the inclement April weather. But Ellie hadn't phoned to talk about the weather, she wondered if her bowling partner would mind if she brought her pre-schooler to the bowling alley.

Mrs. Giuliani doted on the youngster and said it would be fine.

That was the end of the conversation. Except that Ellie told Mrs. Giuliani that she'd be there to pick her up at about 8:30 a.m.

Less than 45 minutes later—promptly at 8:30— Ellie Burns parked her car in the Giuliani driveway. With her in the car was her 13-year-old daughter, Carol Ann, and a younger daughter, four-year-old Patricia. While the mothers bowled, Carol Ann would visit Mrs. Giuliani's daughter, Cindy Jo, (Cynthia) also 13.

Caught in a brisk wind, hair flying over her shoulders, Carol Ann ran to the Giuliani side door. She pounded on the door and shouted her friend's name.

Shivering and getting no response, the teenager rapped again, harder. But still no answer. Now she tried the doorbell. And no answer.

Puzzled, shrugging her shoulders, the 13-year-old returned to her mother's car. "There's nobody home," she said.

Mrs. Burns frowned. "That's impossible. I just spoke to her on the phone 30 minutes ago and told her I was coming over."

The teenager slid back into the car. "Well, nobody answered."

Resolutely, Ellie Burns climbed out of her car and went to the side door. Her daughter trailed after her. Mrs. Burns rapped once, then tried the knob. The door was unlocked.

"Bette?"

Silence. Only the howl of the wind.

Above that howl, Mrs. Burns exchanged puzzled

395

glances with her daughter. The lights were on. Where were they? She repeated her friend's name, then tentatively crossed the living room. Her daughter followed.

Reaching the hallway, which neatly bisected the ranch-style home and led to the kitchen, bedrooms and bathrooms, Ellie Burns couldn't immediately comprehend what she saw.

Three of the Giulianis, Bette among them, were stretched out on the floor. In that instant, a thought flashed through Ellie Burns' mind: "What are they doing sleeping in the hallway?"

And then she saw the blood, the shot-up faces, the empty shell casings, and she screamed, "Oh my God!"

Instinctively, she turned away and herded her daughter into the Giulianis' kitchen. Seconds later, she lifted the wall phone and called the sheriff. As she spoke, her eyes fell on a kitchen clock. The time was 8:36 a.m., she would later remember. A time for tears.

Then, with the call completed, Ellie Burns lost control of her emotions. Sobbing quietly, held protectively by her daughter, she sank to her knees and prayed.

For St. Clair County Sheriff Deputy Barry Lang and Detective Bruce E. Lindke, who arrived at 9:00 a.m., the moment was akin to walking in on a massacre. The place was a slaughterhouse, a sight that churned the investigators' stomachs.

Bodies and blood and shell casings were everywhere. Nearly every wall in the house was bloodspattered and much of the carpeting was stained in crimson. In all, the lawmen counted five bodies: Mrs. Bette Giuliani and her four children, two boys and two girls. All had been shot to death. All had been struck by one or more bullets. All had been shot in the head.

A small Blood City, the Giuliani home. A study in scarlet.

Minutes later, Detective Robert V. Quain, a 19-year veteran arrived. No less shocked than his two fellow investigators, Quain discovered the lifeless body of nine-year-old Dean Giuliani, dressed except for his shoes, in a bathroom shower stall. The little boy had been shot twice in the face at close range.

Tears crowded Quain's eyes. The kid had been trying to hide from the killer—that was his later impression. A kid without a face.

Gingerly stepping over the fallen bodies, the investigators inventoried the scene.

The body of 50-year-old Bette Giuliani lay sprawled on the hallway floor near the kitchen. Also in the hallway, a few feet away, was the body of a daughter, 17-year-old Kathleen Giuliani. Eric Giuliani, 19, had been slain in his bedroom. The youngest girl, Cynthia, who was 13, was found dead in a second bathroom, next to her parents' bedroom.

The late Giuliani family. Five human beings shot to pieces and turned into inanimate matter. More grisly than the veteran lawmen could stand. Incredible horror without meaning. And the apparent instrument of that horror—a .22-caliber rifle—lay on the hallway floor near the bloodied, bullet-riddled bodies.

Speechless, chilled by a gruesome scene they would never forget, the officers tried to unglue themselves from their personal emotions. In years to come, the men would be unable to recount the exact words they exchanged. Nor would they want to remember. But on April 7, 1982, after senses were collected, the lawmen did the things they must: Phone their office, then contact the St. Clair County Coroner's Office.

Almost as dazed as the two witnesses who had unwittingly walked in on the multiple-slaying scene, the detectives questioned Mrs. Burns and her daughter.

Questions and answers came with difficulty. Mrs. Burns, ashen-faced, blank-eyed with shock, was in no emotional state to answer questions. Nevertheless, she provided lawmen with the names and ages of the Giulianis. She also recounted the earlier phone conversation with her late friend, Bette Giuliani.

When the officers asked her who Bette's husband was, Mrs. Burns explained that he was at work. A General Motors plant in Warren, Michigan, she said, and because it was so far away, he left before daybreak.

The lawmen exchanged glances.

Then, they wanted to know how Bette Giuliani had sounded on the phone that morning. Was there any indication that something was wrong? Did she sound nervous?

Pausing to wipe her tears and speaking in a voice that threatened to crumble, Mrs. Burns said Bette sounded fine. She gave no impression that anything was out of the ordinary.

This told the lawmen something about the time element. If Mrs. Burns' recollection was correct, it could then be assumed that the faceless killer or killers arrived at the Giuliani home sometime between 7:40 and 8:30 a.m.

Was the family having troubles?

None, she said quickly. Nothing out of the ordinary. The family got along just fine.

Mrs. Burns said she'd known the Giuliani family for nine years, ever since the latter had moved here from Capac, Michigan. They were an active, pleasant family, popular in the rural community, churchgoers, hard workers. The children helped their father toil the family's 40-acre farm, which produced much of their food.

In the face of Mrs. Burns continuing praise for the Giulianis, the lawmen found the slayings all the more baffling. For if the family had no known enemies, why this senseless multiple horror?

The answer, if one existed, was knotted in its own paradox; that is, the assumption that the Giulianis had no enemies. Clearly, they had one enemy. A very deadly enemy.

In the minutes that followed, the yard filled with police vehicles of every description. St. Clair Sheriff David J. Doktor and more deputies arrived. Detectives and police officers from nearby Yale, Michigan were on hand to assist and lending the gruesome scene its forensic officialdom, was Yale assistant medical examiner, Dr. Benjamin C. Clyne.

In later court testimony, Dr. Clyne would say, "I didn't touch the bodies, but I could see evidence of bleeding from the head, mostly.

"The oldest boy was on the floor in a bedroom, the mother and a girl were in the hallway, and the other girl was on the floor in the bathroom. The youngest boy had got into the shower.

"The rifle wasn't real close to anybody. It was near the bedroom where the oldest boy was found, about three or four feet from the girl and her mother in the hallway.

"The mother was dressed and the little boy was dressed except for his shoes—some were in night clothes. I don't really remember."

And while the coroner's people would need autopsies to accurately determine how many times each victim had been shot, it was obvious that four of the slain victims had multiple gun shot wounds in the head, and one of them had been blasted three times.

In all, the investigators counted 14 empty shell casings, and it appeared that each bullet had struck its mark. But something peculiar was noted by the lawmen. The Giulianis apparently hadn't offered any resistance to the killer's attack. There was no sign of a struggle, no evidence of forced entry.

This seemed to say that the killer or killers was someone known to the Giulianis. The facts also hinted that the slaughter happened too fast for any resistance. The assailant had entered the home, destroyed an entire family — maybe all in less than two to three minutes.

But again, why? While the lawmen exchanged conjectures, other law enforcement agents tramped to neighboring farmhouses to ask questions.

In the blood-spattered Giuliani murder home, police technicians photographed the slaughtered victims, while other specialists dusted the home, inside and out, for fingerprints. The carpeting was studied for trace evidence: dried mud, weeds and any other foreign particles. Most important, the apparent murder weapon, the .22-caliber rifle and empty shell casings were bagged for the ballistics experts.

But none of this would come quickly. In fact, the specialists would spend the entire morning and afternoon in the Giuliani home, searching for clues that might lead to the identity of the killer. Thirty minutes later, at 1:00 p.m., with the victims' bodies still exactly where they'd fallen, state police lab technicians from Madison Heights arrived at the Giuliani home to search for clues.

While this was taking place, Detective Lindke and a Giuliani neighbor drove to the General Motors plant in Warren, Michigan, and confronted Mr. Giuliani with tragic news.

Later, the neighbor said, "We took him to a friend's home. He's better off down there. He wanted to come back home, but he stayed down there. He's in shock. He doesn't believe it's happened. Now they're wiped out. Why? It's so unreal. It just scares you so."

But the mind-reeling family massacre was equally traumatic for the investigators, each of whom was now emotionally committed to finding the killer. To that end, seeking a motive, the detectives had to know more about the Giulianis.

Friends described 17-year-old Kathy Giuliani as an extraordinarily talented singer. "Music was her life," said her high school music teacher. "Out of all the kids that I have seen at Yale in the last ten years, if anyone could make it professionally in music, she could have."

But there was nothing in the blonde high school senior's background to suggest a murder motive. With music as her all-consuming passion, Kathy did not attend parties or hang around in local teenage haunts. She simply preferred to stay home and practice her music.

However, her older brother, Eric Giuliani, 19, was more outgoing, according to friends. "Everybody knew Rick (nickname). He was a nice guy, very athletic," said one acquaintance.

A 16-year-old girl who occasionally dated the handsome murder victim said, "He liked going to movies and parties. But I don't know who would do a thing like this."

Said the high school athletic director, "He was a real nice kid—well-mannered."

Others characterized Eric as a person who loved to

401

hunt and trap animals. He also loved cars and motorcycles, several friends said. "I saw him at a lot of parties," another friend recalled. "Everywhere there was a party, he'd be there."

But Eric Giuliani was also interested in his future. Following high school graduation, he had worked in an auto factory. But he soon decided he was not cut out for factory work and enrolled at a local town college. He didn't drink much, his friends said, and one friend had seen him as recently as the night before.

"He was playing pinball in the arcade," the friend said. "But there was nothing suspicious looking."

But where was the motive? investigators asked themselves.

Of 13-year-old Cynthia, the youngest Giuliani daughter, the road was equally blind. Nicknamed Cindy Jo, the dark-haired junior high schooler had many friends, did well in school and was popular with both boys and girls. One youth boasted that he had gone with pretty Cindy Jo when they were in the sixth grade, a romance that lasted two days.

"She had a lot of boyfriends," an eighth-grade classmate said. "She was real nice and real easygoing."

But less was known of nine-year-old Dean, affectionately called Dino. A teacher described him as "likeable — just a neat little fourth-grade fellow."

Mrs. Bette Giuliani? Extremely liked and respected by school officials for her many volunteer efforts. Active in community affairs, a teacher of religious education classes in their parish church — a fine person.

So there were no known skeletons in the family closet, and their church pastor of six years said, "The Giulianis were a close family. They came to church every Sunday, and they'd come together as a family."

But who had killed them, and why?

Yale police and St. Clair County sheriff investigators worked feverishly throughout the early afternoon seeking the answers. But residents had become shocked, afraid and confused by the slayings. The helplessness and insecurity that gripped these people was mirrored by everything they said.

At the same time, authorities commented that this was Michigan's third multiple killing of a family in the last six weeks.

Seven members of the George Post family of Farwell were found shot to death at their home, February 16, 1982. Robert Lee Haggart, 31, had been charged with murder in those deaths. He was soon to have been divorced from his wife, Garnetta, one of the victims.

On March 13, 1982, five members of the Robert Paulsen family, of Allendale, Michigan, died, also in their home. The Paulsens were shot to death, and a fire was set.

Now, April 7th, and another one . . . and the killer still at large.

But in Brockway Township, things were suddenly happening. In their Carson Road house-to-house questioning of Giuliani neighbors, detectives turned up two witnesses who might have seen the killer that morning. The witnesses described a youth riding past their homes on a ten-speed bicycle, a rifle on the handlebars. One of the witnesses recognized the youth as 16-year-old James Porter.

With controlled interest, the lawmen asked more questions. Porter, a 5-foot-8, 145-pound Yale High School junior, lived only a mile from the Giuliani home, according to the witnesses. More than that, the high school youth reportedly was a long-time friend of the Giulianis; in fact, one witness said Porter and Eric Giuliani had been bosom pals until a few months ago, when a disagreement ended that friendship.

What kind of disagreement? the lawmen wanted to know.

An acquaintance said, "Rick (Eric) and Jim (Porter) were in business together, trapping muskrats and selling the pelts to a dealer. But in November, Rick accused Jim of sneaking into the family's basement and stealing pelts. Jim Porter felt the pelts were his, and it made Rick mad."

The acquaintance said that things weren't the same after that, and the relationship cooled.

"Supposedly they had been in a fight this past week—at a party is what I heard—but I don't know."

Collectively, the information might be meaningful and Porter a hot suspect, the detectives thought. But tips were often worthless and much of this might be readily explained away. For instance, teenage boys frequently had a falling-out with each other, so Porter's differences with the older Giuliani boy could perhaps be nothing. As for Porter being seen carrying a rifle, nothing so unusual about that, not in this part of the country where teenage boys regularly hunted.

Still, routine demanded the detectives pick up the youth and ask him a few questions. Just to clear the record.

Only, Porter was not at home, and by mid-afternoon his whereabouts were still unknown. Which called for a choice. The lawmen could let time slide, wait for the boy to return home. Or they could act now. Following a hasty conference, the investigators decided not to wait and an APB was issued for 16-year-old James Porter.

Meanwhile, in the gloom of late afternoon, with a bitter wind sweeping across Carson Road, saddened neighbors stood in front of the Giuliani home and watched the eerie procession of blanketed stretchers being carried to waiting ambulances.

In the neighborhood and in nearby Yale, investigators probed for more information on Porter. The words they heard were not praiseworthy.

The Yale High School principal said James had been disciplined for fighting in school. "The fact of the matter is, he was known as a fighter," the principal said.

Students who knew Porter described him as a rowdy who liked to flirt, drink and play the macho man.

"Let's put it this way," said a mother whose daughter befriended Kathy Giuliani, one of the murder victims. "There have been problems with the boy . . ."

Several residents in the area reported recent petty thefts in their yards. There were suspicions but no investigation or charges.

The pelt dealer, who had had many transactions with Eric Giuliani and James Porter, remembered an incident during a hunting trip up north in which Porter and Eric got into a shoving match in a store. The dealer described Porter as "pretty—light blond hair, blue eyes. He looks like the all-American boy, really. He was all right until he opened his mouth."

But while friends and casual acquaintances were generally in agreement that Porter was a cocky bully who liked to fight and intimidate people—a young kid with a mean streak toward people and animals who would try to justify his misdeeds, none could conceptualize the 16-year-old turning the Giuliani home into a slaughterhouse. He was bad, it was said. But not that bad.

Then, at about 6:00 p.m., April 7th, Yale Police Chief Randall Packard cruising on Main Street, spotted a red late-model Chevrolet with two youths in the front seat. Thinking one of them might be Porter, Packard turned on his flasher lights, gave chase and pulled the car over to the curb. Perfunctorily, he radioed for a back-up. In a matter of seconds, a St. Clair County Sheriff Department patrol car sped down the street from the opposite direction and squealed to a stop. Deputy Ray Gleason jumped from the car and drew his service revolver.

Gleason ordered both occupants of the car to freeze, then told the passenger, a young man with blond hair, to get out and put his hands on the car roof. Then Gleason placed a pair of handcuffs on the youth and put him in the rear of his patrol car.

An unmarked police car arrived, followed by two Sanilac County Sheriff Department patrol cars, driven by Sergeants Daniel Dundas and David Hall.

Chief Packard ordered the driver of the Chevrolet out of the car and put him in his patrol car.

The passenger was blond-haired James Porter, and his driver-companion was 18-year-old Henry Willis, of Yale.

Willis was later released, but Porter, a juvenile, was taken to the Yale Library. With a family member present, detectives questioned Porter for four hours. The youth denied any knowledge of the Giuliani shootings and insisted he'd been home all morning except for a short time when he went to check on some of his animal traps. Later he'd joined with his friend Henry Willis, he said, and the pair had driven to Port Huron. But authorities, uncertain of the youth's alibi, lodged him in the Port Huron Detention Center, pending further investigation.

Meanwhile, one of Porter's arresting officers commented on the youth's arrest.

"Jimmy wasn't scared. Anyone stopped by a police officer, even if it's for a traffic violation, gets a little nervous. Not Jimmy, he wasn't nervous—he was real cool. His buddy was petrified, but Jimmy showed no signs of any emotion.

"It just wasn't . . . normal . . . ," the officer said. "He was calm, unusually calm. When I was patting him down for a weapon, he asked, 'Are you going to tell me what this is all about?' I told him, 'no, that in a minute detectives would talk to him.' A short time later he asked the same question—just before we took him over to the library where he was questioned."

To bolster their suspicions, the authorities now focused their attention on the apparent murder weapon used in the mass murders—the .22-caliber rifle found in the hallway near the bodies. But the Michigan State Police Crime Laboratory in Michigan Heights quickly determined that this was not the murder weapon. The tracings on the ejected shell casings did not match test firings of the rifle found in the Giuliani home.

Subsequent questioning of Giuliani acquaintances revealed that Eric Giuliani did own such a gun. But teenager James Porter also owned a .22-caliber rifle, and a family member searched the house, found the gun in a rear-bedroom closet, and turned it over to the detectives for ballistics and fingerprint studies.

Michigan State Police Crime Laboratory specialists Detective Sergeant J. Bullock and Lieutenant Robert White quickly went to work. Provided with a bullet taken from the body of 17-year-old Kathleen

Giuliani and 14 empty shell casings found in the murder home, the crime experts determined that the fatal bullets had been fired by Porter's .22-caliber rifle. The sleuths further determined that a left thumb print found on the rifle matched that of the juvenile suspect.

While detectives searched for more evidence and tried to tie in a motive, authorities charged the 16-year-old youth with five counts of aggravated murder and five counts of possession of a firearm during the commission of a felony. Appearing in court, Porter calmly pleaded innocent to all charges.

Meanwhile, St. Clair County Prosecutor Robert H. Cleland petitioned Probate Judge Robert R. Spillard to designate jurisdiction in the case: Would Juvenile Court retain jurisdiction or would James Porter be tried as an adult?

Ultimately, Judge Spillard ruled that Porter would be tried as an adult, which elated the investigators. Tried as an adult and convicted on the charges, Porter would face a mandatory sentence of life in prison without parole. But if Judge Spillard had ruled that Probate Court would retain jurisdiction, Michigan law mandated that Porter, if found guilty, would have to be released from custody at age 19.

Despite their satisfaction with the ruling, the detectives and prosecutor knew the investigation was far from complete. Their case, such as it was, was based solely on ownership of the murder weapon and the statements of two witnesses who on that fatal morning had seen the Porter boy, armed with a rife, riding his bicycle past their houses. More was needed—a motive; information from other witnesses; facts to lend credibility to police charges against the high school junior. And without this additional information—a St. Clair County Grand Jury indictment notwithstanding—the case would be weak.

In the quest for more damning evidence, detectives requestioned the witnesses who had seen Porter on his bicycle that morning. One, a housewife, said:

"He was out here on his bike in front of our house—my daughter saw him. He was riding on his bicycle toward his house. He wasn't going fast. He was just riding home—he didn't appear to be in any hurry.

"It was about 8:15 in the morning. We know that for sure, because my daughter had gone next to her grandmother's and woke her up. My mother-in-law looked at the clock, and it was 8:14.

"My daughter didn't see any gun, but our neighbor did. He said he saw Jimmy on the bicycle with the gun when he rode by his house. His dogs were barking and when he went to check on them he saw Jimmy."

The neighbor, also requestioned, reaffirmed his earlier statement. He told detectives he'd seen Porter riding his bicycle west on Yale Road, and some time later he'd seen the youth riding east on Yale Road, back toward his home. The witness said he was certain Porter was carrying a rifle.

Meanwhile, sources close to Porter said the youth now claimed he remembered little of what happened before 9:00 a.m., April 7th, the morning of the murders. The sources said Porter did not remember being there, going to the Giuliani home. Porter also told a source that he had been plagued with blackouts before April 7th, including once when he awakened to find himself in a field near his home, with his .22-caliber rifle in his hands. He said he didn't remember how he had gotten to the field.

Skeptical of these reports, detectives continued their investigation. Again, the authorities fielded statements of Porter neighbors. One neighbor said, "I know Jimmy Porter killed our dog—but I don't know what he did with the Giuliani family."

The neighbor told police that Porter was seen firing a gun on her property. The next day she found her 9-year-old dog shot to death at the rear of her home. "I didn't see him shoot the dog, but I know he did it. And last summer he pointed a gun at one of my six children—we reported that to the police."

Others, noting that Porter was always hunting with his rifle, reported they'd frequently complained to police about shot-up signs and buildings in their yards. The residents thought Porter was the culprit, but they couldn't prove it.

Still searching for a motive, detectives quizzed a Giuliani relative. "Jimmy never had to knock to come in the Giuliani house," the relative said.

But the relative noted that Eric Giuliani suspected Porter of stealing money from their home on several occasions, which ultimately led to a fight between the two teenagers in the family driveway—this on March 21st, less than three weeks before the mass murders.

Digging for facts of a possible burglary angle, detectives requestioned Porter's friend, Henry Willis, who had been driving the car on the evening that Porter was arrested.

Following intense questioning, Willis cracked. He confessed that Porter had taken Eric Giuliani's bank book in March—a month before the murders—forged Eric's signature and withdrawn $300 to $400 from Eric's account. Willis also stated that Porter again had Eric's bankbook on April 7th, the day of the murders. This time, Porter withdrew $1000.

Willis, at the time unaware of the Giuliani murders, stated he picked up Porter at the Porter home about 1:30 p.m. that day. Then they drove to the bank.

"Jim was filling out the withdrawal slip. He wrote Eric's name and the amount . . . $1000. Jim went into the bank to get the money. We were going to split it."

"Did you reach this agreement together?" Willis was asked.

"Yes," Willis answered. Then he said Porter came out of the bank and handed him $500. "I didn't have to ask him for the money, he handed it to me and I put it in my pocket — tens, twenties, fifties — maybe fifteen bills."

Wilis said that he and Porter then drove to Port Huron and went on a spending spree. On their way home, Porter tossed Eric's bankbook in a creek, Willis said.

So police now had a motive for the horrible murders — a cheap robbery that had left people dead. And the prosecutor was now ready to do battle.

As expected, James Porter, who had now turned 17, pleaded innocent to the crimes, and innocent by reason of insanity. To that end, Porter's lawyer, Dennis Smith, solicited the services of Dr. Emanual Tanay, a psychiatrist renowned for his frequent testimony in court proceedings.

Following his examination of the defendant, Dr. Tanay testified, "He described to me what happened. He got up that morning between 7:30 and 8:00, went outside and saw a pheasant. He had a gun in a case, and he told me rode a relative's bicycle. He said he had a strange feeling. He knew he was moving. He saw people. He saw a neighbor plowing snow.

411

"He said he was in a trance. He came to the Giuliani residence. He used a side door. He just simply kicked in the door.

"He said he saw Kathleen. He fired right away at her. Then he saw Mrs. Giuliani come out of the bathroom; he shot her. Then Cindy; he shot her. He made a few steps forward to a bedroom where Eric was in his underwear and shot him. He walked into the utility room and heard some sound. It was nine-year-old Dean and he shot him. He said he got on his bicycle and rode home.

"He fixed himself two pieces of toast, and he said everything was like nothing had happened. He has a clear memory as to what happened, but he was in a depersonalized state. He was there, but he wasn't there. He was there in a dreamlike state. He said, 'The whole thing took maybe sixty seconds.'"

Tanay said he asked Porter why the Giulianis didn't resist. Porter told him, "Because it was all so quick. There wasn't any movement."

But the Circuit Court jury was unaffected by Tanay's "dreamlike, depersonalized" description of the defendant. The jury had heard psychiatrists, a psychologist and three people from the St. Clair County Juvenile Detention Center testify that Porter admitted killing the Giuianis. They also had listened to the testimony of several crime lab experts—33 prosecution witnesses in all. In summation, that jury was convinced of James Porter's guilt.

Unanimously agreed that the youthful defendant was mentally competent when he planned the robbery and cold-bloodedly executed the five Giulianis, the jury found James Porter guilty of five counts of aggravated murder and five counts of possession of a firearm during the commission of a felony.

Subsequently, St. Clair County Circuit Judge

James T. Corden sentenced the convicted blond killer to life in prison, with no provision for parole.

But while observers note that justice has been served, those same observers are mindful that the Giulianis are forever dead.

EDITOR'S NOTE:

The names Ellie Burns, Patricia Burns, Carol Burns and Henry Willis are fictitious and were used because there is no need for public interest in their true identities.

"NEW YEAR'S EVE
SLAUGHTER IN SKAMANIA!"

by Gary C. King

The soft gentle snow that began falling shortly before 8:00 p.m. on December 31, 1986, significantly slowed the traffic that runs through Skamania, Washington, on State Road (SR) 14, near Beacon Rock State Park.

As the evening wore on and the snow continued falling in this tranquil community of only a few hundred residents, an occasional car, truck, or motorcycle inched by the Skamania General Store at a turtle's pace, the drivers on their way to an evening of revelry at their homes or at the homes of friends.

Occasionally, drivers slid their vehicles into the store's parking lot so they could go inside and buy beer, wine, and party treats, knowing that the store closed at midnight. Others simply stopped by for gas, oil, and a little conversation. There were no clues to the clerk on duty or to the customers that came in that night that, within the next few hours, three people would die violently inside a house at the foot of Woodard Creek Road, just around the corner from the store and barely visible from SR 14.

Early the next morning was the first day of 1987 and consequently, the first day on the job for newly elected Skamania County Sheriff Raymond Blaisdell. It was a day he'd eagerly been awaiting. Shortly after dawn he received a call at home from one of the deputies, the first such phone call in an official capacity, to say the least. The call was far more serious than he'd bargained for.

There had been a shooting, he was told. A triple homicide in nearby Skamania. It was the first homicide in years in this usually peaceful, unincorporated community, located about 50 miles east of Vancouver and about 10 miles west of Stevenson along the Columbia River Gorge in the southern part of the state. Bleary-eyed and barely able to believe what he was hearing, Blaisdell took down the information and said he'd be at the scene as soon as possible.

It had warmed up during the night and there was no snow on the roads as Blaisdell raced to the home of James P. Butler, 48. As he climbed up the 21 steps that led to the entrance of the neat, well-kept brown home with white trim, the sheriff was met by one of his deputies. Three people had been shot to death inside, he was told, including Butler, his wife Margaret, 35, and his stepdaughter, Amy Stevenson, 18.

As he conferred with Deputies Mike Grossie and Christopher Ford, among the first to arrive at the residence, Blaisdell noticed the tell-tale crimson stains on the swivel rocking chair in the living room, itself red in color but considerably lighter in contrast to the massive bloodstains. Blaisdell observed more bloodstains, smears actually, on the floor that led through the living room, down a hallway, and into the master bedroom. Following along the bloody pathway, he observed two bodies when he entered the bedroom, a male and a female. Both were lying on the bed, and

415

they were identified as James and Margaret Butler.

As he examined the bodies, Blaisdell wondered which of the victims had been dragged from the living room to the bedroom. Closer examination of James Butler's clothes answered his question. Judging from the distribution of the bloodstains and smears, it appeared that he'd likely been the one dragged to the bedroom. Likewise, closer examination of Margaret Butler indicated that she had been killed as she lay sleeping. Both, noted Blaisdell, had been shot in the head.

Amy Stevenson's body, naked from the waist down, was found lying on her bed in the basement bedroom of the home. It appeared that she had been shot at least twice, once in the right temple and once in the cheek. A .22-caliber single-shot bolt-action rifle was found on a pile of clothes near the entrance to her bedroom, and an expended cartridge was in the weapon. It appeared to the sheriff that Amy had been sexually assaulted at some point. She was also pregnant, he was told.

News of the slayings raced quickly through the community.

"It was horrible," Sheriff Blaisdell said of the triple murder. "Very violent. Terrifically violent . . . the community is upset over it. They can hardly believe it could happen here. I think it's hard for people in a small community to realize we're not much different than people in other parts of the world."

State criminalists Ken McDermott and Roger Ely arrived at the Butler residence later that morning. In processing the house for clues, the two criminalists, along with county detectives, found a dozen rifles and two old pistols inside the house, all of which would undergo firearms examinations to determine if they had been fired recently. They also found a bag of marijuana with an identifiable fingerprint on it, the value or significance of which, if any, was not known at this point. Also found was a collection of Indian artifacts, which they soon learned belonged to Mrs. Butler. She, along with her son, Sean, collected them as a hobby.

The criminalists determined that James Butler had been sitting in the red rocking chair in the living room when he was shot in the head. They wondered why the killer deemed it necessary to drag the body into the master bedroom. He must have had a significant reason. But what was it?

Because Amy's body was naked from the waist down, the criminalists concurred with the sheriff that she had been sexually assaulted. But because the location of Amy's body, relative to bloodstains found in her bedroom, indicated that it had been moved, criminalist Ely surmised that the sexual assault occurred after death. "(That) suggested to me, upon visual observation, that sexual intercourse was after death," said Ely. Because of the suspicions of sexual assault, Ely combed Amy's pubic hair in an attempt to collect foreign hair.

The extreme violence, the bag of marijuana, and the numerous firearms found inside the Butler home, caused investigators to consider the possibility that the killings and the sexual assault were drug-related.

Additional searching by the probers resulted in the discovery of halogen lights and cultivated marijuana plants inside a spacious garage behind the house, indicating that Butler may have had a commercial growing operation set up there.

Further probing revealed that Butler was having severe financial difficulties, and had talked of suicide on a couple of occasions. There had been other problems that involved the Children's Services Division concerning Amy, and the family was known to have had other turbulent problems, among them heavy drinking by James and Margaret. Was it possible that Butler had killed Amy and his wife, then turned the gun on himself? Was murder-suicide a plausible theory in this case? If it was, then what about Sean Stevenson, 16, and an older relative of Margaret's, both residents in the house? How did they figure into the scenario? And why hadn't they been killed as well? The aroused public, as well as the law enforcement officials, had many questions they wanted answered.

Those questions were partially answered when authorities revealed later that day that Sean Stevenson had been arrested in Long Beach, Washington, some 150 miles west of Skamania, early that morning. Although details were sketchy at first, investigators said Stevenson stopped and asked a woman on the street where the Long Beach station was located at approximately 6:30 a.m. on January 1st. Long Beach Patrolman Steve Graves was just going off duty when he noticed the youth walking in front of the stationhouse and asked him if he needed any help.

"I think you're going to want to talk to me after the terrible thing I did," Graves quoted Stevenson as saying. Graves then asked Stevenson if he wanted to talk about it.

"He said he had just killed his stepdad, mother, and sister in Skamania," said Graves. He then put his arms out in front of him to be handcuffed without even being asked, said the patrolman. Authorities said Stevenson told Graves that he and James Butler had had an argument over Stevenson's desire to go to a New Year's Eve party and that Butler had grounded him, and "one thing led to another." When asked why he killed his mother and sister, Stevenson replied, "You'd have to be there to understand."

Did the cops have their killer? Maybe. Did they understand the motive at this point? Not really, they admitted. As the case unfolded it took on historical, personal, and legal twists that inspired several rumors

418

and split the opinions of many of those involved in the case, including area residents.

In the hours that followed, another Long Beach patrolman, John Dodge, questioned Stevenson about the three murders in Skamania. When asked what had happened, Stevenson responded, "I'll tell you the same thing I told the other officer. I killed my stepfather, my mother, and my sister."

A short time later, Stevenson was taken to an Ilwaco, Washington hospital where facial and body swabs were taken from the suspect as well as scrapings from under his fingerprints. As the nurse was about to take the fingernail scrapings, Officer Dodge warned Stevenson not to try anything when he removed the handcuffs. Stevenson responded, "I don't want to die just because I shot those people in Skamania." Following the fingernail scrapings, Stevenson was asked to disrobe so that the body swabs could be taken, and when he did so it was noted that he was not wearing underclothes.

"I asked him why he wasn't wearing any underpants," said Dodge. "And he responded that he didn't have time to put any on, that he had to get out of there fast."

Christopher Ford, a Skamania County deputy sheriff, was among those who traveled to Long Beach to pick up Stevenson to return him to the Skamania County Jail. When he arrived he found the 1977 Ford pickup, registered to James and Margaret Butler, that Stevenson had driven there, parked at the police station parking lot. Inside the pickup he found a scope-equipped .30-caliber Marlin rifle behind the seat. He also found three pistols, one shotgun, and another rifle inside the truck, as well as two suitcases, a gallon of milk, and several other items. All but one of the firearms were loaded, said Ford and several pieces of broken pottery similar to that found in the master bedroom of the victims' home was found inside the pickup. In describing the suspect, Ford said that Stevenson appeared tired and calm, and exhibited "no emotional behavior. He wouldn't talk unless spoken to. He did not seem concerned about anything."

As the investigators began to gather background information on the victims and the suspect, they soon learned that Stevenson's mother, Margaret, was divorced from his father in 1979 and married James Butler, a short time later. The grandson of a pioneer store and saloon operator, Butler was a native of nearby Camas. He workers in construction and at one time operated a garbage-transfer station. But because of the depressed local economy, Butler's recent work record was sporadic at least, prompting rumors of a murder-suicide spree due to financial stress.

There was also the fact that Butler and his stepson had a rough relationship, and Sean's dislike of his stepfather was no secret to the community.

"They didn't do many things together," said one area resident who knew the family. "There was always a rivalry, always friction. I heard that from Sean and from his stepdad. But there were never any threats I heard about. Neither had ever said one was going to do bodily harm to the other." The investigators were also told that Amy, a senior at nearby Stevenson High School and member of the school's volleyball team, was on the honor roll and was active in student government. However, she had become pregnant by an Air Force airman, which caused friction between her and her mother. Investigators were told that Amy's mother wanted her to get an abortion, but Amy had made plans to marry the airman as soon as she graduated.

Stevenson, a descendant of a family for whom the town of Stevenson was named, was attending ninth grade at Stevenson High School. He was described "as a real quiet boy" who never caused any problems. A relative described Sean as a hard worker who was "always proud of being a sportsman and a fisherman." A large boy at 6-feet 4-inches, and 200 pounds, Sean was actively recruited for football and basketball. However, he was more of a loner than a joiner, and neither sport seemed to interest him. His relationship with his sister was described as good, and those familiar with his family life said he knew Amy was pregnant and was protective of her. He had no prior criminal record.

"They always behaved very well together," said a high school official regarding Sean and Amy. "I've known those kids since grade school, and I can't bring myself to believe that he would do that to Amy." Others, however, had different feelings.

"Some are adamant that he did it, and others think he is completely innocent," said one Skamania resident.

"I'd say it is a toss-up," said another. "Some people think he's guilty, some think he isn't. Amy was such a sweet girl. I didn't know the boy. I think people are just waiting now to see what happens in court. We don't know the details."

"People are still grief-stricken and in shock," said still another resident. "But the closer you are to people who know Sean, the more you don't accept that (he's guilty). He is a real special young man. (He told me about his) verbally abusive relationship with his stepfather. He understood what a serious condition he was in. I respected his ability to cope with it. He showed tremendous maturity."

Meanwhile, Sean Stevenson was charged with aggravated first-degree murder in the death of his sister, Amy, with rape being the aggravating factor, and two counts of first-degree murder in the deaths of his mother and stepfather, charges which, if convicted, could bring the death penalty or life in prison without possibility of parole. Skamania County Prosecuting

Attorney Robert K. Leick moved to have Stevenson remanded to adult court to face the charges.

"We're dealing with a mature 16-year-old, both physically and mentally," said Leick, who added that Juvenile Court jurisdiction would end when Stevenson reached age 21 if he were convicted as a juvenile. "That's sufficient . . . reason, given the nature of these allegations, to bind it over to adult court." Fearing that Stevenson might not get a fair trial in Skamania County due to the amount of publicity the case received, the case was moved to nearby Clark County.

After hearing more than two hours of arguments on the remand subject, Clark County Superior Judge Thomas Lodge agreed with the prosecutor and ruled that Stevenson be tried as an adult. "These persons were shot in separate rooms by a person with some time to reflect on what he was doing . . . To kill someone with a high-caliber rifle by shooting them in the head is the most aggressive manner of crime known to man . . . I don't think the public would tolerate anyone who has committed three aggravated murders being on the streets in 45 months," he said.

Stevenson was assigned local attorney John Thomas Day, for his defense. He was also appointed L. Eugene Hanson, of Goldendale. Stevenson eventually pleaded not guilty to the charges against him, and his attorneys said they were exploring the possibility of an insanity plea. But several days later, after doing some investigating of their own, the attorneys said they were planning an alibi defense. Day said witnesses would testify that Stevenson was not at the scene when the crime occurred.

Why, then had Sean made all those confessions? Of course, no one could say for certain. But his attorneys insisted that when he came home at approximately 1:30 that morning and found the bloody carnage inside his home, he suffered "traumatic amnesia," a psychological ailment sometimes suffered by wartime soldiers, and felt responsible for the killings only because he witnessed the horrible aftermath. The condition may have caused him, said his lawyers, to "disassociate from reality and fabricate facts."

"We now have three psychiatrists or psychologists," said Day, "who say there simply could not have been a real confession based on facts. He can't remember a thing. There's no one asking this boy anything further because the questions only implant fresh error in his mind." Day further suggested that Sean dragged the body of his father from the living room to the bedroom before leaving in order to spare an elderly relative, a stroke victim who lived with them, from finding the body. The relative, it should be noted, is partially paralyzed and unable to speak.

Day went one step further by saying that he believes financial stress may have been a motive for a murder-suicide spree by James Butler himself. He also suggested that because of the evidence of a gun battle inside the home and the fact that marijuana and growing equipment was found on the property, another person may have committed the crimes to cover a robbery of the indoor marijuana-growing operation.

As the case continued to unfold, Day and his investigation turned up still another mystery to be solved in an already difficult case. According to the investigation, neighbors reported a dark maroon pickup with one or perhaps two unidentified passengers visit the Butler residence on the afternoon before the killings (December 31st). This, coupled with the mysterious fingerprint found on the marijuana bag, raised the possibility that one or more of the passengers from the truck had committed the homicides.

In opening statements at his trial, Sean Stevenson was described by Prosecutor Leick as a lust-driven killer who "threatened to blow his mother away" three weeks before the killings. Leick told the jury that as Stevenson fled Skamania County early New Year's day he was "peculiarly dressed," carrying a cartridge belt with live ammunition while he made "terrible dangerous" remarks to a store attendant while trading marijuana for gasoline at 2:30 a.m. Leick also said investigators found a sexually explicit magazine near the bed in his room, opened to a page with a fold-out photo of a naked woman.

On the other hand, defense attorney Day described Sean as an unaggressive, "lovable person, a very fine young man, who's never been in trouble." Day described life at the Butler home as being "fraught with great terror and problems," including financial difficulties and alcohol abuse. Day said the Butler home was filled with guns and ammunition, "ripe for an explosion," and described James Butler as an alcoholic who was conducting "a commercial-sized narcotics operation." He said that Sean's mother, who was almost "constantly intoxicated," was "near death" on the day she was killed from alcohol and marijuana poisoning.

Day hinted at an incestuous relationship in the family, saying, while remaining vague, that "something was horribly wrong in Amy's life" that "caused her to get protection. (The problem required) special counseling for Sean, even though he had nothing to do with it." In describing the alibi defense, Day said Sean was visiting friends at a nearby residence early January 1st when he and the others heard noises that sounded like firecrackers or gunshots at approximately 12:30 a.m. Ten minutes later, said Day, Sean became worried and went home. He subsequently went into shock after discovering the bodies at his home, and had been unable to remember anything from that moment until he was arrested.

The murder-suicide theory was quickly ruled out

when Dr. Larry Lewman, a Portland pathologist who performed autopsies on the victims' bodies, testified that the shot that killed James Butler was fired at least 30 inches from his head. "I can't conceive of a scenario where any of these wounds was self-inflicted," said Lewman. Lewman added that the .30-caliber slug that killed Margaret Butler, fired from a distance of approximately six inches, "virtually destroyed the right side of her brain." Lewman said that Amy Stevenson was killed with a .22-caliber bullet fired into her right temple, and a .30-caliber bullet was fired into one of her cheeks. Both guns were less than three inches away when fired, he said, and the .22-caliber gun appeared to have been fired first.

When questioned by defense attorney Hanson about other health problems the victims may have had, Lewman became visibly irritated and said, "These people had violent, unsurvivable wounds. I wasn't running around looking for leprosy."

Lewman's testimony and conclusions were supported by criminalist Roger Ely from the Washington State Patrol Crime Laboratory, who testified that no weapon was found near the rocking chair where James Butler was killed, even though investigators removed a .30-caliber bullet, which apparently passed through Butler's head, from the chair.

Ely testified that even though a dozen rifles and two very old pistols were found inside the house, none of the weapons could have fired the large .30-caliber bullets without having first been modified or posing a hazard to the shooter. The bullets, he said, were found in or near the three victims. Ely, in concurrence with Dr. Lewman's testimony, said the evidence also indicated that Amy had been shot first with the .22-caliber weapon, sexually assaulted, then shot again with the .30-caliber weapon.

Additional testimony revealed that spermatozoa

were present in Amy's body, apparently the result of the sexual assault, and that she was carrying a child when she died. Toxicologists also testified that blood and urine tests of the Butlers indicated they had consumed alcohol and marijuana prior to death, but tests of samples from Amy revealed no drugs.

Michael J. Grubb, a state firearms expert and criminalist, testified on the third day of the trial that of all the guns found inside the 1977 pickup that Sean Stevenson was driving on the day of his arrest, only one could have fired the bullets that killed the victims. Grubb explained to the jury that the rifling, grooves that improve a bullet's trajectory, on the inside of the Marlin's barrel are unique to that rifle and produce identifiable marks on the bullet as it passes through the barrel. Which is also true with any firearm, he said.

As a result, said Grubb, the murder weapon has to be the Marlin found inside the pickup or one just like it. Likewise, he said, a .22 bullet taken from Amy's head was consistent with those found on the pile of clothes in her bedroom. Grubb agreed with other witnesses regarding the unlikelihood that the crimes were a murder-suicide.

"I can't see any way that a person could hold this rifle more than two feet away and kill himself," said Grubb, referring to the Marlin and the fact that James Butler had been shot from a distance of at least 30-inches. Grubb also testified that combings of Amy's pubic hair in search of hair from another person proved negative. Grubb said that foreign hair is obtained in only approximately 10 percent of all combings.

A state fingerprint examiner also testified that neither the Marlin nor the .22-caliber rifle, the suspected murder weapons, bore any fingerprints. He did say, however, that a bloodstained $100 bill found inside

Sean's wallet had a fingerprint in blood, but it was not identifiable.

Criminalist Kenneth McDermott testified that he found human blood on an athletic shoe worn by Sean Stevenson when he was arrested. He also said the two pairs of blue jeans found in Stevenson's possession on January 1st contained small amounts of human blood. McDermott said the stain on one pair could have come from Stevenson or 90 percent of the population. However, he said a stain on the second pair contained evidence of blood that could not entirely have been Stevenson's own. McDermott said that the blood on the shoe was consistent with the blood type of James Butler and that blood found on the $100 bill was consistent with the blood type of Margaret Butler. But, he said, there was no way to determine exactly where the blood came from or how old the stains were.

McDermott also said that tests of body fluids from Amy Stevenson, Sean Stevenson, and James Butler did not rule out either the defendant or Butler as the young woman's sexual assailant. However, a Vancouver doctor testified that James Butler had had a vasectomy several years earlier, and that it was extremely unlikely that he had been the source of the spermatozoa found inside Amy's vagina.

In other testimony, Tom Malone, 19, an acquaintance of Stevenson's, said the defendant made the remark that he had killed his stepfather and that he expected to go to jail for it. Malone said he ran into Stevenson about 2:40 a.m. on January 1st at the home of a mutual friend.

"First he said he though he had killed his stepfather, and then before I could say anything he said he did it," said Malone, who had unrelated criminal charges pending at the time. "He didn't say he shot him or anything, just killed him. He said, 'I guess I'll be sharing a cell with you.'" Malone said Stevenson told him he was going to Canada, after which Malone jokingly suggested that he go to Mexico instead. "I think he figured out that I didn't believe him." Malone said Stevenson then got into a pickup and left.

Another witness, Tina Lindstrom, recalled a conversation she heard the preceding fall during a visit to the Butler residence. Lindstrom said that she, Margaret Butler, and Sean Stevenson were talking when Sean showed her a pistol. Lindstrom said she told him it appeared to be an excellent weapon for a woman, after which Margaret said Sean had given it to her. However, recalled Lindstrom, Sean said, that he hadn't given it to his mother just as James Butler walked into the room. Having overheard the statement, James Butler said, "see how two-faced he is? One moment he gives you something, and the next he takes it away," said Lindstrom, quoting Butler. While he was still holding the weapon, said the witness, Stevenson said, "I'm going to put it under my pillow and when you come downstairs one morning to wake me up and I don't want to go to school, then I'm going to take it out and blow you away."

Larry Green, a clerk who lives in an apartment over the Skamania General Store, testified that Stevenson knocked at his door at 1:50 a.m., wanting gasoline for his parents' 1977 Ford pickup. Green said Stevenson was wearing a bandolier with ammunition in it. After putting gas in the truck, Green said he watched Stevenson leave, driving eastbound toward his home, located only a few hundred feet east of the store. A short time later, at approximately 2:30 a.m., Green said he heard the same truck driving west in front of the store at a high speed.

"I heard a rig zoom down the highway," said Green. "I saw the truck screaming down the road heading west." Green, however, said he was unable to see who was driving the truck.

Jody Coates, 15, a resident of Long Beach, had befriended Stevenson the previous summer. She testified that she was awakened early New Year's morning by a phone call from Stevenson who asked her to go to Mexico with him. During the conversation, she testified that Stevenson said, "I just shot my family" and "I thought he was just joking."

Two witnesses for the defense, Jake Adams, 23, and David Miller, 31, testified that Stevenson was standing on a porch with them early on January 1st when they heard the sounds of shots or firearms coming from the vicinity of the Butler home. Miller said he heard four shots over a period of several minutes, and both men said they finally concluded that the noises were gunshots, because they were louder than firecrackers.

"But we didn't think anything about it," said Miller. "Out there in Skamania you hear gunshots all the time." The two men said they heard the shots between midnight and 12:30 a.m., and Miller said Stevenson left his home about 1:30 a.m., stating that he wanted to go home and go to bed. Miller told the jury that a neighbor woke him up at 7:00 a.m. and said, "I guess the Butlers had a hell of a party last night. I asked him what happened and he said, 'They're all dead.'"

In other testimony, a forensic scientist hired by the state told the jury that he fired test shots from the two suspected murder weapons inside the Butler residence to determine if the shots could be heard at Miller's home nearby. The scientists said that a defense investigator at the Miller house could clearly hear the shots.

At one point in the trial, jurors were shown a videotaped interview of the elderly, speech-impaired relative who resided in the Butler residence at the time of the killings. The relative, now living in Minnesota, was asked by Prosecutor Leick how many shots he heard the night of the murders. The elderly relative held up three of his fingers.

"Did James Butler rape Amy?" asked Leick.

No, responded the relative by shaking his head from side to side.

"Did Sean rape Amy?"

No.

"Do you know who raped Amy?"

No.

"Did Sean kill Amy?"

Yes, he responded, shaking his head up and down.

The videotaped interview was supported by testimony from Deputy Mike Grossie, who told the court that he met the elderly relative at the Skamania General Store around 8:00 a.m. on January 1st. The relative was in the back on an ambulance at the time Grossie questioned him.

Grossie said that when he asked the elderly relative if the killer was James Butler, he responded no. When asked if the killer was Sean Stevenson, he responded yes. The relative then pulled a photo of Sean from his wallet and showed it to Grossie.

Toward the end of the trial two men showed up after reading newspaper accounts of the maroon pickup seen by neighbors leaving the Butler home the afternoon prior to the killings. The men testified that they stopped by the Butlers to view the collection of Indian artifacts, nothing more. There was no evidence to suggest any other reason for their visit.

In one of the more dramatic moments of the trial, the defense brought in fingerprint expert William Zeller, a retired police officer from Sale, Oregon. Zeller was asked to identify a fingerprint found on a small plastic bag of marijuana recovered from James Butler's bedroom. Zeller testified that the print did not belong to Butler or to Stevenson, at which point the defense attorney suggested that another person could have been inside the Butler house on the day of the killings.

Then, in a scene right out of a Perry Mason drama, Prosecutor Leick brought Zeller another set of fingerprints to examine. After comparing the print taken from the bag with the prints provided to him by the prosecutor with a small magnifying glass, Zeller promptly announced that the print taken from the bag belonged to the person whose prints were handed to him by the prosecutor. When asked to read the name from the fingerprints card, Zeller announced that the print belonged to Ray Blaisdell, unaware that Blaisdell is the Skamania County sheriff. The prosecutor's move had worked, evidenced by the gasps from the jury box and spectator section. He'd successfully blown the defense theory of another person right out of the courtroom.

At another point in the trial, the prosecutor brought in a surprise witness, another relative of the defendant's. The relative testified that Stevenson had called him at his home in Minnesota a few days after his arrest. The relative said that Stevenson told him, "I shouldn't have done this, but sometimes I get so angry I don't know what I'm doing."

A Portland psychiatrist testifying for the defense said Stevenson suffered from "psychogenic amnesia," and he said he has seen hundreds of amnesia cases like Stevenson's. The psychiatrist said that descriptions from witnesses who said the defendant looked dazed the day of his arrest were "very consistent" with memory loss following a traumatic experience. The psychiatrist said he had been fooled before, but in this case he said he was "99 and 44/100 percent sure" of his diagnosis.

On the other hand, a Seattle psychiatrist testifying for the state said it was not possible to conclude whether Stevenson did or did not suffer from amnesia. "There are all kinds of conscious and unconscious reasons a person might want to hold back such information," he said, particularly if that person faced serious criminal charges. "The data are equivocal," he said. "I am not going to give a diagnosis of amnesia. There are too many alternatives to that diagnosis." The psychiatrist said it was difficult for psychologists or psychiatrists to distinguish between amnesia and someone who feigns an "inability to remember."

The Seattle psychiatrist said jurors should rely on the other evidence in the case instead of on the opinion of mental health experts.

Near the end of the trial, Stevenson was put on the witness stand in his own defense. His testimony was consistent with that of two other witnesses, Jake Adams and David Miller, who said they were all together at Miller's house, not far from the Butler residence. He said it was about 12:30 a.m. when they all heard the sounds of gunshots that appeared to come from the Butler home.

"I didn't pay any attention to it," said Stevenson. "I just walked back into the house and got another beer." An hour or so later, he said, he walked home and entered the house through the back door.

"I smelled something I can't really describe," he said, telling how he'd just entered the kitchen. "It smelled pretty disgusting. Then I turned the corner to the living room and I saw James Butler in the red chair. His face looked long and out of proportion. His nose was sagging. His face didn't look the way it was supposed to. He was dead."

"What was the next thing you remember?" asked Day.

"I remember that I was on the highway, just about ready to miss the Longview industrial area turnoff (to Long Beach)." When asked questions about his sister and the elderly relative that lived with him, Stevenson broke into tears. Stevenson denied killing any of the victims.

432

"If you don't remember, how can you say that?" asked Deputy Prosecutor Grant Hansen.

"I already told you, I wouldn't do that," said Stevenson.

In closing arguments, the two prosecutors told the six-man, six-woman jury that rage, caused by being grounded by his stepfather and the ongoing friction between them, prompted Stevenson to kill his relatives.

"Rage is the only reason anyone would rape Amy Stevenson with her head half off," said Prosecutor Leick. "Rage is the only reason someone would shoot their mother." Leick also cited the numerous confessions Stevenson made to police, friends, and relatives, including statements in which he gave exact locations where the victims' bodies were found.

The defense continued to contend that Stevenson suffered from traumatic amnesia and that his mind was left blank, susceptible to suggestion, and added "things along the way to make it more convincing." Defense attorney Hansen said that details given to the police by the defendant were "cold, factual statements that turned out to be accurate."

The jury was out for more than 20 hours over three days. However, on Friday, May 8, 1987, they returned with their verdicts. They found Stevenson guilty of one count of aggravated murder in the death of Amy Stevenson and two counts of first-degree murder in the deaths of his mother and stepfather. The jury concluded that Amy was murdered to conceal a rape. Stevenson bowed his head slightly as Judge Robert Harris read the verdicts, and tears filled his eyes.

The same jury that convicted Sean Stevenson spared him his life by sentencing him to life in prison without possibility of parole for the murder and rape of his sister, and 320 months were added for the murders of his mother and stepfather, primarily so the murders couldn't be perceived by the public as "free murders." Stevenson is serving his sentence at the Washington State Prison in Shelton while his lawyers are preparing his appeal.

EDITOR'S NOTE:

Tom Malone, Tina Lindstrom, Larry Green, Jody Coates, Jake Adams and David Miller are not the real names of the persons so named in the foregoing story. Fictitious names have been used because there is no reason for public interest in the identities of these persons.

APPENDIX

"Michigan's Mystery of the 'Graduate Family' Slaughter"
Master Detective, December, 1987
"Family Massacre on the Michigan Reservation!"
Master Detective, November, 1989
"Enraged Lover Massacred a Family of Five!"
Inside Detective, February, 1985
"A Whole Family Was Massacred for Revenge!"
Official Detective, June, 1987
"17-Year Track of the Family Slayer!"
Master Detective, February, 1990
"They Mowed Down the Whole Family!"
Front Page Detective, April, 1983
"Riddle of the 'Gentle' Man's Rampage of Death!"
Inside Detective, September, 1983
"Grisly Slaying of a Family of Four!"
Front Page Detective, December, 1985
"One Whole Family Was Massacred!"
Official Detective, July, 1989
"The Inferno Shrouded a Triple Murder!"
Front Page Detective, July, 1989
"Manhunt for the Greedy Killers in the Red Corvette!"
Inside Detective, May, 1985
"Sex-Hungry Fiend 'Had a Stomach' for Slaughter!"
Front Page Detective, June, 1985
"Bombs and Bullets Blew Away Five!"
Front Page Detective, December, 1985
"The Hunter's Quarry Was a Family of Five!"
Inside Detective, August, 1983
"New Year's Eve Slaughter in Skamania!"
Official Detective, January, 1988

ORDINARY LIVES DESTROYED BY EXTRAORDINARY HORROR.
FACTS MORE DANGEROUS THAN FICTION.
CAPTURE A PINNACLE TRUE CRIME . . . IF YOU DARE.

GOOD VERSUS EVIL. HEROES TRAPPING MONSTERS.
THIS ISN'T FANTASY. IT'S LIFE.
CAPTURE A PINNACLE TRUE CRIME TODAY.

JEFFREY DAHMER (661, $4.99)
By Dr. Joel Norris
Everyone knows Dahmer's name, but how many of us know the man behind the headlines? Renowned psychologist Dr. Joel Norris sheds light on the dark forces that compelled Dahmer to butcher and consume the men he loved. Based on unpublished facts about the killer's lifestyle and background, it features extensive interviews with his friends and ex-lovers. Readers may never fully understand Dahmer's behavior or find him sympathetic, but Norris's book outlines how a seemingly normal man can degenerate and lash out while silently passing among us.

ARTHUR SHAWCROSS: THE GENESEE RIVER KILLER (578, $4.99)
By Dr. Joel Norris
Despite his parole officer's warnings, child killer Arthur Shawcross was released from prison early. He headed to Rochester, New York, to begin his next chapter. Shawcross's second chance at life spelled death for eleven women. He conducted a horrible slaying spree, reminiscent of Jack The Ripper, that targeted prostitutes and denizens of Rochester's red light district. Strangling them in remote wooded areas, his insane bloodlust drove him to butcher their naked bodies and to devour parts of their flesh before disposing of them. Ironically, police arrested him by luck when he was observed casually eating his lunch while the nude corpse of his latest victim floated past him in the Genesee River.

CHOP SHOP (693, $4.99)
By Kathy Braidhill
Generations of mourners brought their "loved ones" to Lamb Funeral Home. They trusted the sincere staff, appreciated the sympathetic directors, and knew without question that their relations were in capable hands. They were wrong. Grotesque mutilations and sadistic practices flourished at Lamb's. Like a ghoulish twist on a vampire novel, here the living merrily preyed upon the dead. Fingers were severed to claim expensive rings; teeth were forcefully pulled out for the ounces of gold filling; and organs were fiercely removed to be sold to research labs. The crematorium fires blazed fiendishly around the clock as multiple bodies were stuffed into the chambers for mass burnings. It was a scenario worthy of the Holocaust. *Chop Shop* recounts how unspeakable acts of horror were perpetrated against the ultimate victims: dead men who can tell no tales. Thankfully, Kathy Braidhill broke this case and gave a voice to these victims.

SEX, MONEY AND MURDER IN DAYTONA BEACH (555, $4.99)
By Lee Butcher
Florida's society set always makes a splash in the papers: debutante balls, charity auctions, MURDER. Beautiful heiress Lisa Paspalakis surprised her wealthy family by marrying for love. She wed Kosta Fotopoulos, a waiter, after a whirlwind courtship. This fairytale union was ripe with villains and greed. Fotopoulos and his mistress had already laid plans for Lisa's cold-blooded demise. This is an explosive indictment of greed, decadence, and amorality.

Available wherever paperbacks are sold, or order direct from the Publisher. Send cover price plus 50¢ per copy for mailing and handling to Pinnacle Books, Dept. 711, 475 Park Avenue South, New York, N.Y. 10016. Residents of New York and Tennessee must include sales tax. DO NOT SEND CASH. For a free Zebra/Pinnacle catalog please write to the above address.